ERIC T. PENGELLEY
Department of Biology, University of California, Riverside, California

Sex
and
Human
Life

SECOND EDITION

ADDISON-WESLEY PUBLISHING COMPANY
Reading, Massachusetts
Menlo Park, California
London • Amsterdam • Don Mills, Ontario • Sydney

This book is in the
ADDISON-WESLEY SERIES IN LIFE SCIENCES

Consulting Editor
Johns Hopkins III

Copyright© 1978, 1974 by Addison-Wesley
Publishing Company, Inc. Philippines copyright
1978, 1974 by Addison-Wesley Publishing
Company, Inc.

ISBN 0-201-05770-0
ABCDEFGHIJ-AL-7987

To Daphne

Thou, nature, art my goddess: to thy law
My services are bound!

William Shakespeare
King Lear
Act I, Sc. ii, Lines 1-2

Foreword

Most of the people who read this book will have been born quite a few years after the close of the Second World War. This fact, coupled with the fragility of a feeling for history, means that few readers will realize at the outset how recent has been the change in public sentiment that makes possible such frankness about sex as is to be found between these covers.

Of course everyone knows that 'way back in colonial times the Puritans had great sexual inhibitions. The point can be illustrated by the true story of one Captain Kimble who was thrown into the stocks because, when newly arrived from a three years' sea-voyage, he was so "lewd" as to kiss his wife in public on a Sunday.

Everyone knows also that the Victorian era, the 19th century, still suffered from crippling sexual "hang-ups." But this world did not entirely end with that century. As late as 1938, when a popular pictorial magazine called *Life* printed three dozen small black-and-white photographs of childbirth, there was a great uproar. The magazine was banned in Boston and more than thirty other cities in the United States and Canada. The publisher of the magazine was arrested (but was later acquitted in court).

A Gallup poll taken at the time showed that 76 percent of the populace was against banning *Life*. This story illustrates an important point. Though the majority generally rules in our society, when it comes to highly emotional issues that are in a process of changing, a minority often wields disproportionate power. The reasons are simple. The elderly are more likely than the young to be wedded to disappearing ideals; and, because they have long been on the scene, they are likely to be in positions of power and hence capable of enforcing (for awhile) their wishes against the majority. (Q.E.D.) There is no easy solution to this problem; we will be wise to keep it always in mind.

The natural connection of sexual matters with human physiology might lead one to suppose that medical men would have been the leaders in the movement away from Victorianism. Some few were, but the vast majority were no more enlightened than the people they dealt with. In the judgment of George Corner, himself a physician, men of letters played a more important role than physicians and scientists in overthrowing the prudery of the last century. Corner cites the works of the poet Walt Whitman, the novelist Thomas Hardy, and the adventurer Richard Burton (who translated the *Arabian Nights* into English). Toward the end of the century two medical men entered the scene, the Englishman Havelock Ellis and the Austrian Sigmund Freud. It is significant, however, that both men, in their mature years, scarcely thought of themselves primarily as physicians, and seldom practiced as such (outside the realm of psychological advising). Both men took literature and the art of persuasive writing very seriously. It was their literary power more than their scientific precision that enabled them to move the world.

Ellis and Freud both died in 1939, the year the second World War began. Two years before their death a new and more scientific approach to the study of sex was begun by the American zoologist, Alfred Kinsey. He was, of course, vigorously attacked for entering the holy of holies with new tools, but he won the day. A host of others now carry on Kinsey's tradition, notable among whom are Mrs. Virginia E. Johnson and the physician Dr. William H. Masters, whose findings form an important part of this book.

We are over the hump now. It is now possible to write a clear, frank, decent, and helpful account of the physical aspects of love ("sex") and their ramifications into the more diffuse and even more important areas of life we call "sexuality." Such a book Professor Pengelley has written. His expositions have been amply tested on the firing line, as it were—that is, in the classroom and in individual consultations. Even as late as a mere decade ago such a book for college students could not have been published. Let us be thankful that it can now—and that it has been. Only in the clear light of the truths of sex and sexuality can we hope to reach an understanding of the necessary conditions for intimacy and trust, without which there will be little peace in the world.

Garrett Hardin
Professor of Human Ecology
University of California, Santa Barbara

Preface to the Second Edition

In this second edition of *Sex and Human Life*, there has been considerable updating and clarification, but in addition a new chapter on various psychological and social aspects of sex has been added. It is of course impossible to please all readers, but I have tried to strike a balance between the biological, psychological, and social. Finally I thank all those who have made criticisms and suggestions.

University of California   E. T. P.
Riverside, California
October 1977

Preface to the First Edition

In the fall of 1969 I was asked by the Dean of my College, Mack Dugger, if I would visit the University of California at Davis to observe the teaching there of a course concerned with human sexuality. It was clearly in the back of his mind that he would like me to undertake the teaching of the same subject on my own campus.

I visited Davis with some misgivings, partly because I was not at all sure that such a subject was appropriate for a University, partly because I was not sure that I was suitable to teach it—or indeed that it was in any way necessary. Furthermore, the political climate was hostile, and I was at a stage in my academic career where outside interference or pressure might have done me severe personal damage which I could ill afford. After three days at Davis watching my friend and colleague Professor Milton Hildebrand teaching this delicate subject, and after extensive conversations with his 1,200 students, I came away convinced that the subject in question was a vital one, and that it could and should be taught in a University situation.

Because of the encouragement and backing of my Dean and also my Departmental Chairman, Dr. Eric Edney, I was made to feel secure enough to ride out any potential political or social storm, but both I and my departmental colleagues were concerned about my qualifications to teach the subject, as well as about other possible ramifications. I rationalized my qualifications by saying that I had a Ph.D. in biology and felt that I was a well-trained zoologist (otherwise why had they hired me in the first place?). Furthermore as part of my graduate training I had taken a full year of medical physiology at the Banting and Best Institute at the University of Toronto. I felt sure I could read and discriminate, and in addition I had had some 25 years practical experience and hoped to have a good many more! The department voted unanimously to give my course their blessing and the green light.

I have now taught human sexuality over a period of three years to literally thousands of university students, public and high school teachers, health and social workers, nurses, and even medical doctors, many of whom are the first to admit that they know little about the subject. This book is the outcome of that teaching experience, including many profound discussions with my students, as well as the vast amount of reading I have done.

From the outset I was determined that the subject should be taught on a sound biological basis, and I felt that any "mickey-mouse" boy-meets-girl approach would be a disaster. I think my attitude has been vindicated, and that it has been reflected in the contents of this book. It is my experience that most young students of today want to learn good solid biological information on which they can build their lives and help others. As I have pointed out in the book, sexual education is only partly concerned with making the individual a more effective sexual partner. It has the much wider function of helping the student to understand the vast biological, psychological, social, and political aspects of human sexuality. It is my hope that these pages will help in this enormously important task, and that the reader will in turn be better equipped to discuss and teach the subject. This is a book not so much on "how to do it" as on "how to think about it."

Finally I must point out that I make no claim to any ultimate knowledge on such a complex topic with so many ramifications. I have, of course, tried to be accurate and up to date, but no doubt many with more knowledge than I will find errors, and certainly disagreement with some of my interpretations. I hope that there will be a second edition of this work, and I accordingly invite the criticisms and suggestions of students and teachers alike.

Acknowledgments

As I grow older and, I hope, continue to learn, I become more conscious of the ever-increasing number of people to whom I am indebted. Throughout this book my major direct sources of information have been acknowledged, but I have no illusions that I have acknowledged them all. Such knowledge as I have accumulated over 54 years has come from a vast number of sources, some of which I am no doubt unaware of, and I apologize for any oversights. Nevertheless I wish to express my gratitude to a few special sources for information, insight, and help.

I am eternally grateful to both my mother and father that they brought me up in such a way that I have been able to study and teach human sexuality without any terrible inhibitions or moral overtones, and I am indebted also to my former professors in the Department of Zoology, University of Toronto, who taught me the basic biological concepts which have so largely formulated my ideas.

At a more intimate level my wife, Daphne, has contributed in a great number of ways upon which there is no need to elaborate, except to say that without her encouragement, understanding, and patience this book would never have been written. Both my children have also contributed. My son, David (the younger generation!), read the manuscript, and be- sides being my severest critic, made many helpful suggestions which were duly incorporated. My daughter, Alison, has also helped by teaching me much about the problems of a young girl growing up in this difficult age.

I am also eternally grateful to my long-time research associate, Sally Asmundson, who made many helpful suggestions, but above all—and more than any other person I know—has helped me to understand the day-to-day insults, discriminations, and humiliations heaped on the female sex in this male-dominated world. In this connection also Dr. Loda Mae Davis, a former Dean of Women and an astute observer of the social scene, has taught me much. My thanks are also due to Dr. Mack Dugger, the

Dean of my college, who has been a constant encouragement to me over many years.

I am greatly indebted to Janet Arnold and William Watson who posed so naturally for the photographs involving sexual intercourse. And I wish to express my sincere appreciation to Joshua Clark, who did most of the anatomical drawings, for his excellent work.

I also thank Mrs. Kaylyn Gary, Mrs. Janice Levi, and Mrs. Mary Hickey who typed the manuscript, and I am grateful to Mrs. Cecil Woodham-Smith for locating the source of the letter written by Queen Victoria which appears at the head of Chapter 10.

                                                                    E.T.P.

Contents

CHAPTER ONE
Introduction

Sex education is not "training for promiscuity" either for the present or for the future; its aim should be to increase the individual's understanding of the biological and social condition of human beings.

Carl Ivor Sandstrom
The Psychology of Childhood and Adolescence
(New York, Pelican, 1968).

In his autobiography, written when he was over 90, the British philosopher Bertrand Russell (1872-1970) remarked, "Women need men, and men need women..." He spoke from long experience and deep conviction, and although the idea may seem too obvious even to reiterate, it is something which many human beings rather easily tend to ignore or forget, usually with disastrous consequences. There is no aspect of all the many and complex interactions between human beings which has more importance in their day-to-day lives than that of sexual relations, and it is with these that this book is concerned.

As with virtually all aspects of human behavior there are elaborate laws and codes of morality, both written and unwritten, which govern sexual relations. It is most unfortunate that many of these are based on taboos and superstitions, and above all on ignorance. No one has expressed this more forcefully than the great obstetrician Robert Latou Dickinson (1861-1950), who wrote:

> Full courage faces actuality. The great blockade behind and beneath opposition is really fear. It is panic lest sex become safe, free from risk of pregnancy, disease and disgrace. The church and the law, the parent and the teacher dare not confront tolerance and immunity. They dare not depend on character, on education, on religion, on training in self control, on common or uncommon sense, on anything but the Three Terrors held over youth and adult—conception, infection, detection. Let marriage be long deferred; let limits on reasonable motherhood live under the shadow of apprehension, month by month, for twenty years of conjugal life; let passionate love be penalized and marital maladjustments multiply and divorce and abortion spread, and prostitution debauch and feeblemindedness breed—let all this carry on so long as sex taboos and ignorances are kept intact. Can we call this true morality? Can we uphold it as sense, wisdom, kindness?*

Dr. Dickinson's words were written in 1950, and although they are in large measure still true today, a major step in unlocking the door of ignorance had already been taken by the zoologist Alfred Charles Kinsey (1894—1956), who with his associates wrote the now classic work *Sexual Behavior in the Human Male* (1948), which was followed in 1953 by *Sexual Behavior in the Human Female.* Despite the vicious outcries of those who would stifle new knowledge and who demand a morality based

---

*Dr. R.L. Dickinson, *Techniques of Conception Control*, Baltimore, Williams and Wilkins Co, Copyright 1950 by The Planned Parenthood Federation of America, reprinted with permission of Dr. Dickinson and The Federation.

Alfred Charles Kinsey (Photograph by
Dellenback, reproduced by courtesy of
the Institute for Sex Research.)

on the status quo, Kinsey's works were widely read, and in retrospect it seems not at all unreasonable to assert that in time—unfortunately a period much too long—they led to the laboratory experiments of William H. Masters and Virginia E. Johnson. With the publication of their works *Human Sexual Response* (1966) and *Human Sexual Inadequacy* (1970), Masters and Johnson took the final step of placing the study of human sexual behavior and physiology on a firm experimental scientific basis, rather than on a hodgepodge of myths, half truths, and vague pseudo-psychological theories. Their achievements have been great, though much remains to be done. However, now it can at least be said that human sexuality, like other aspects of human behavior, is subject to scientific study and interpretation. The same may be said to be true for the teaching of this subject, and it is hoped that this book will fill a need for those men and women who would learn to understand and appreciate one of the most basic of all human needs—sexual well-being.

Although the basic need for sexual well-being is reason enough for the understanding of sexual behavior and physiology, today there is yet a greater reason for its study. Sexual relations, in which virtually every man and woman will engage at some time in their lives, all too commonly lead to the reproduction of their kind, and it is no secret to any educated person today that the rate of increase in human numbers is one of our most pressing problems. Unless humans voluntarily reduce this rate in the near future, famine, plague, pestilence, and war will reduce it for them. It was long ago pointed out by Sigmund Freud (1856-1939) that the sexual urge and the procreative urge are quite different. It is simply a biological fact that men and women do not desire to procreate every time they have sexual intercourse. Yet at the same time procreation is normally impossible without sexual intercourse. It is of great importance, therefore, that all human beings should study and understand how sexual well-being can be achieved without simultaneously turning the earth into an overpopulated slum—which will in due course inevitably lead to even greater disaster, if not outright extinction.

To achieve sexual well-being with all that this implies in the cultural, social, economic, and political spheres, men and women in the modern world will have to discard time-worn prejudices, dogmas, and superstitions concerning not only the purely behavioral and physiological aspects of sex, but also the traditional stereotyped roles of males and females. Fortunately there are signs that such processes are already well underway, mostly among the young. All indications point to the fact that when human beings were evolving their survival was by no means certain, and thus a very high reproductive rate was a great advantage. There can be little question that, in order to achieve such a high reproductive rate, the role of the female as simply a reproductive machine was most essential, since of the two sexes only she can bear offspring. It seems probable that many of the elaborate cultural and social patterns which have evolved between the sexes are a result of that original basic biological need to reproduce as much as possible. When John Stuart Mill (1806-1873) visited the United States in 1848 he observed "the whole of one sex is devoted to dollar hunting, and the whole of the other to breeding dollar hunters."

It is now obvious that this traditional role of the female as a reproductive machine, and all that it implies for her, can no longer survive. Humans are no longer in danger of under-reproducing themselves, but rather of over-reproducing. Consequently the role of the female has changed, and it will continue to change more rapidly in the years ahead. It is already obvious that the young women of today have other ideals, and rightly so, than just those of wife, mother, and homemaker. Many women's organizations, under the general title of "women's liberation" are devoted to bringing about just such long overdue changes, and these will inevitably alter the whole economic and political structure of society. Despite all this, men and women, by the very nature of their biology, will need sexual relations as much as ever, and new mores will inevitably evolve to meet these needs. Sexual behavior and physiology must be taught and discussed freely and openly, and it is the aim of this book to help in this process.

It should be understood at the outset that, unless otherwise and specifically stated, the discussions of sexual behavior that comprise much of this book refer to that occurring in the more affluent societies of the western world and the United States in particular.

STUDY TOPICS

1. Describe some of the more important events in the recent history of sexual knowledge and education.

2. Discuss the interaction between sexual attitudes and reproduction.

3. "Women need men, and men need women . . . . " True?

FOR FURTHER READING

Breasted, Mary, *Oh! Sex Education!* New York: Praeger Publishers, 1970.

Brecher, Edward M., *The Sex Researchers*. Boston: Little, Brown, 1969.

Broderick, Carlfred B., and Jessie Bernard (Editors), *The Individual, Sex and Society*. Baltimore: The Johns Hopkins Press, 1969.

Harrison, Richard J., and William Montagna, *Man*. New York: Appleton-Century-Crofts, 1969.

Kinsey, Alfred C., Wardell B. Pomeroy and Clyde E. Martin, *Sexual Behavior in the Human Male*. Philadelphia: W.B. Saunders, 1948, 1953.

Kinsey, Alfred C., *et al., Sexual Behavior in the Human Female*. The Staff of the Institute for Sex Research, Indiana University. Philadelphia: W.B. Saunders, 1953.

Lieberman, Bernhardt (Editor), *Human Sexual Behavior—A Book of Readings*. New York: John Wiley & Sons, 1971.

CHAPTER TWO

Sexual Comparisons of the Human Male and Female

*She hugg'd th'offender, and forgave
th'offence . Sex to the last!*

John Dryden (1631-1700)
Cymon and Iphigenia (l. 367).

The genetic sex of an individual human is determined at the time the egg is fertilized and becomes a zygote. So far as sex is concerned, all unfertilized human eggs are the same, but human sperm are of two kinds; and the kind that fertilizes the egg determines whether the zygote will be potentially male or female. Of course, many other factors, both physiological and environmental, enter into the development of the sexually mature male or female, but the basic genetic pattern is set at the time of fertilization.

Sexually mature males and females are anatomically and physiologically differentiated in a variety of ways. While we can describe the differences in terms of averages or modes, these are merely statistical abstractions of convenience; only the individuals are real. As with all things biological, human individuals vary not only anatomically and physiologically but behaviorally as well, and this should never be forgotten. All we can do here is to describe and discuss the average, or the common situation, keeping in mind that there is no norm except that arbitrarily imposed by humans themselves.

ANATOMICAL DIFFERENCES

The sexually mature male (Fig. 2.1) and the sexually mature female (Fig. 2.2) are distinguished by two rather obvious anatomical features. These are the penis of the male and the breasts of the female. The penis is referred to as a *primary* sexual organ, and the breasts as *secondary* sexual organs. In reference to sexual organs and characteristics, the terms "primary" and "secondary" were introduced by the English anatomist and surgeon John Hunter (1728-1793), who performed remarkable pioneer research in human sexual anatomy and physiology.

In the male the primary sexual organs consist of the *testes,* the *epididymis,* the *vas deferens,* the *seminal vesicles,* the *prostate gland, Cowper's glands, the urethra* and the *penis.* In the female the primary sexual organs are the *ovaries,* the *uterine* or *Fallopian tubes,* the *uterus,* the *vagina* and the *clitoris.* In general terms the primary sexual organs consist of the reproductive glands as well as the accessory organs of those glands, which together constitute the genital apparatus. The primary sex organs of each sex will be dealt with in more detail in later chapters.

The secondary sexual characteristics are those extragenital differences which are commonly associated with masculinity or femininity, but may in part be culturally imposed rather than biologically determined. Nevertheless, there are some obvious secondary sexual differences which are genetically determined—the breasts of the female, for example. The breasts are mammary glands, or mammae, serving the function of supplying milk for the newly born young, and their possession puts humans in the same class with other mammals. In some cultures (including our own) they also serve another function, that of sexually attracting the male. It is interesting that males also have mammary glands, with apparently no function at all. They do not produce milk and they appear to have no special sexual attraction for the female. Mark Twain (1835-1910) described the male mammae as functionally useless, and as an ornament—a mistake!

John Hunter (Reproduced by permission of the President and Council of the Royal College of Surgeons of England.)

In the human species, like so many other mammals, the sexes are dimorphic; i.e., occurring in two distinct forms. Of course, since human genetic variability is enormous, and both our physical and cultural environments play a large part in the development of every individual, there is much overlapping of various physical characteristics between the sexes. Nevertheless, there are certain aspects which are clearly the result of sexual dimorphism. In anterior and posterior comparisons of the male and female (Figs. 2.3 and 2.4), it can be seen that in the male the shoulder

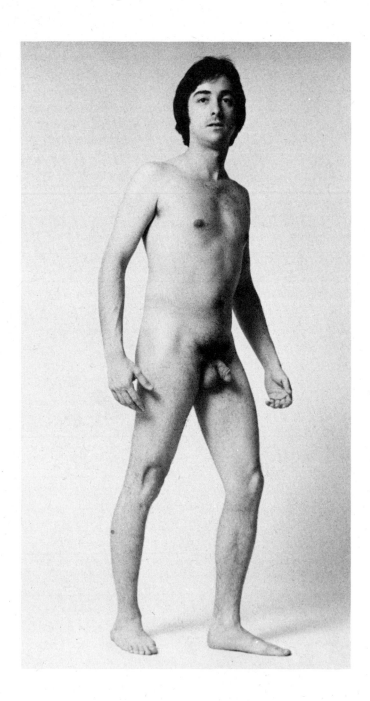

Fig. 2.1. Frontal view of sexually mature male. (Photograph by Wilbur Gregg.)

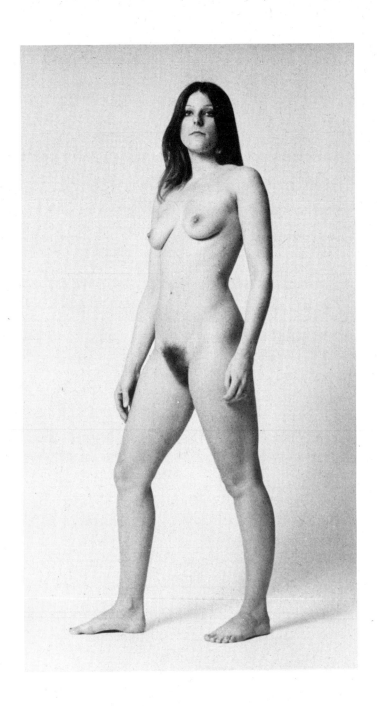

Fig. 2.2. Frontal view of sexually mature
female. (Photograph by Wilbur Gregg.)

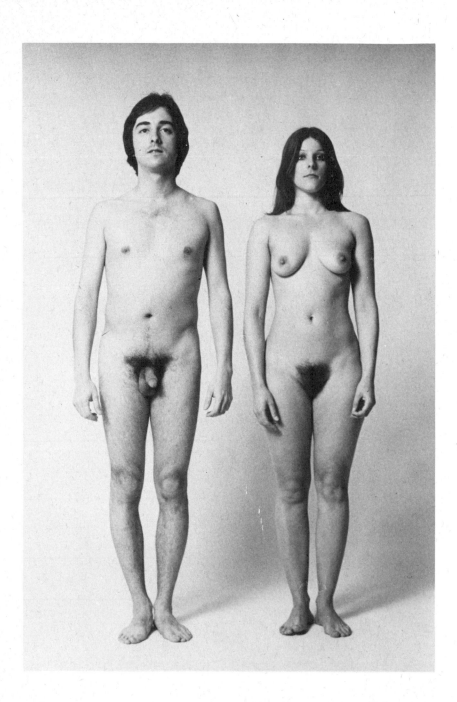

Fig. 2.3. Anterior comparison of sexually mature male and female.

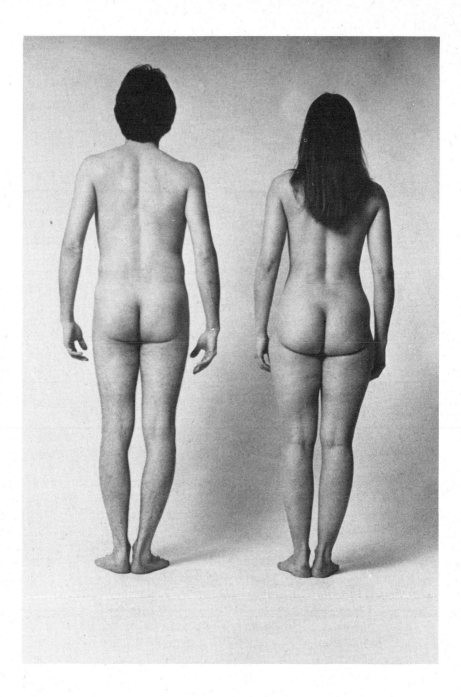

Fig. 2.4. Posterior comparison of sexually mature
male and female. (Photograph by Wilbur Gregg.)

girdle is proportionately wider than the pelvic girdle, while in the female the pelvic girdle is proportionately wider than the shoulder girdle. In other words, men have large shoulders and women large hips. The relatively large hips of the female are associated with and functional in the process of childbirth, but as a result of the large pelvic girdle the thigh bones converge rather sharply toward the knees. This tends to make the female "knock-kneed" and gives her a characteristic gait. In the male, on the other hand, the thigh bones do not converge as sharply, and he tends to be "bow-legged" with just as characteristic a gait.

Another marked anatomical difference between men and women lies in the fact that the superficial curvature of their bodies is not the same (Figs. 2.1 through 2.4). This is mainly due to the different distribution of fat tissue in the male and female. In the female there are distinct subcutaneous fat pads (Fig. 2.5). These fat pads are typically located behind the breasts, in the lower part of the abdomen, over the hips, and over the thighs. It is also chacracteristic of the sexes that, if and when the individuals put on excess fat, men tend to add it from the waist up while women tend to add it from the waist down. This, together with the relatively large pelvic girdle of the female, tends to give women a lower center of gravity than men. Another major anatomical sexual difference is that males are usually more muscular and larger than females. It should not be inferred from this that women are necessarily weaker than men; on the contrary, women can generally withstand more physical stress than men.

Another clearly discernible secondary sexual distinction is the distribution of hair. The possession of hair is a purely mammalian characteristic, and the human species, like most other mammals, does in fact have it distributed over the bulk of the body. However, its degree of development and specialized distribution differ between the sexes. Generally, males possess more profuse body hair than females (Figs. 2.3 and 2.4). This is particularly obvious on the male face in the form of a beard, but it also applies to the eyebrows and the hairs within the ears and the nostrils of the nose. It is usually obvious also on the male chest in comparison to that of the female. The distribution of pubic hair is also different. In the adult male this hair extends upward toward the navel and downward toward the perineum. In the female it terminates above in a horizontal line and does not extend so far downward as in the male. The distribution in the adolescent boy is about the same as in the adult female. In young adults the profuse growth of hair on the head is not noticeably different in the sexes. However, with increasing age, men tend to become bald far more rapidly than women, and this is certainly a secondary sexual characteristic—albeit of dubious distinction.

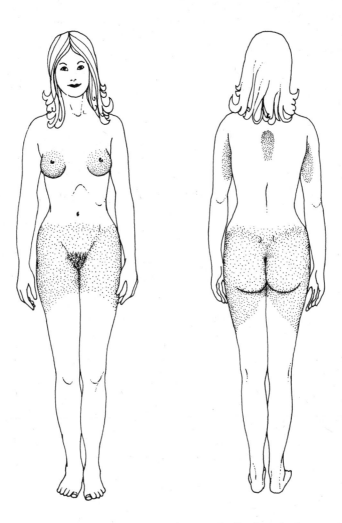

**Fig. 2.5. Distribution of subcutaneous fat
pads in the sexually mature female.**

Another difference between the sexes is in the relative size of the
larynx, or Adam's apple. In the female this remains relatively small
throughout development and into adult life, while in the male it remains
small until puberty, but then undergoes a rather rapid growth and
differentiation which causes the voice to deepen in comparison to that of
the female.

There are other minor anatomical differences, such as the supra
orbital processes of the male, which sometimes prove useful in forensic

medicine (i.e., medicine in relation to law). But there is much overlapping of these and great care must be taken when they are used to determine sex. By and large, however, those anatomical features already mentioned comprise the major dimorphic differences between the sexes.

BEHAVIORAL AND PSYCHOLOGICAL DIFFERENCES

While males and females are differentiated anatomically and physiologically, it is very difficult to determine whether apparent behavioral and psychological differences are of genetic origin or have been conditioned by the particular culture. This is part of the ever-present problem of trying to distinguish between nature and nurture, and in so complex an animal as the human this is a difficult problem indeed. Almost throughout recorded history, and in virtually all cultures, women have been relegated in one way or another to a secondary role beside the male. This phenomenon is of course closely related to the female's reproductive function, but unfortunately the idea is still widespread that this, and all that it entails, is the only, or at least primary, thing for which women are suitable. Thus it is argued that the overwhelming factor in a woman's life is her urge to maternity, and that all her behavior, psychology, and emotions are particularly adapted to that end, whereas the male is supposed to be adapted primarily as breadwinner and defender of wife, children, and home. Women are said to possess greater sensitivity than men and to depend more on their emotions than on their reason and intellect in reaching decisions, an assertion that is sometimes supported by the observation that women are supposed to cry easily, which is an emotional outlet. Love, tenderness, compassion, and kindness are said to be more prevalent in women, and more important to them, than in men. It is even asserted by some medical doctors (all too commonly males!) that "women are never happier than when they are pregnant," and that women are unsuited to positions of responsibility, because they might have to make an important decision at some time during their menstrual cycle when they were not feeling quite up to par. And it is sometimes even inferred from all this sort of "reasoning" that women are less intelligent than men!

Cultural Influences

Any or all of the characteristics associated with male and female may in reality be true for a particular cultural situation. For example, in predominantly Anglo-Saxon societies men certainly cry less than women, but this is not the case in predominantly Latin societies where men cry freely, without social disapproval, when the emotional situation warrants it. Indeed, while proof is difficult, it seems highly probable that much of the stereotyped idealistic behavior of males and females is the result of nurture rather than nature. Research done by the famous anthropologist Dr. Margaret Mead has supplied rather strong evidence in support of nurture as the predominant factor in male and female behavior. In her studies of certain tribes in New Guinea, she found that three of these tribes possessed remarkably different ideals and standards. In one, both males and females behaved in a manner which she described as maternal in its parental aspects and feminine in its sexual aspects. The men were unaggressive and responsive to the needs of others and sexuality was not a powerful driving force between the sexes. In a second tribe both men and women were aggressive sexually and had little of the characteristics associated with maternity. In both these tribes, however, there appeared to be little difference in behavior between the sexes. In a third tribe women were the dominant of the two sexes, despite the fact that the tribe was organized in a patrilineal manner. The behavior of the two sexes was quite different, the men tending to be more emotionally dependent and the women more socially aggressive. Dr. Mead concluded from these studies that the behavior and attitudes commonly ascribed to males and females can in fact be reversed, or considerably modified by both sexes so that males and females have behavioral patterns much more similar than is commonly the case. If this is true, it seems obvious that the behavioral patterns commonly believed to be determined by sex are in fact culturally determined, and that the major differences are between individuals and not between sexes. However we should not overlook the evidence in favor of behavioral differences, due to biological origin. These come principally from two sources. First, the experiments of Dr. H. F. Harlow and his associates (see also Chapter 13) on young monkeys clearly indicate that males and females from a very early age behave quite differently. This can be summed up by saying that males tend to exhibit more motor activity than females, and all that that implies, including more "rough and tumble." In addition both young and adult female monkeys show much more interest in the young than do males. Second, we cannot overlook the influence on behavior of the male hormone testosterone. All studies of testosterone clearly indicate that it has profound behavioral consequences. Of course we cannot make direct interpretations of human behavior from studies on monkeys, but observations of very young male and female children also indicate similar behavioral differences which are probably of biological origin, and it is likely that the hormone testosterone also plays a biological role in behavioral differences between the sexes. Despite such biological differences as there may be, there is no excuse for putting wholly false interpretations on the potential abilities

We do not perhaps realize how completely male-dominated most societies are, and how well both sexes are conditioned to playing what is considered their appropriate role. The French author Simone de Beauvoir, in her book *The Second Sex* (1949), has accurately and dramatically pointed out the ruthless conditioning inflicted on young girls in virtually all western societies. They are conditioned not only in how to behave, dress, and decorate themselves, but also in what they should and should not do in contrast to the male—and still more important, in how to think. De Beauvoir points out that, as a result of this deplorable conditioning, as girls grow into adults they are for all practical purposes incapable of behaving or thinking in any way other than society has deemed appropriate, which is usually that of being mother and homemaker. The very word "housewife" has a double meaning; there are no "house-husbands," at least in the United States. Of course young boys undergo a similar ruthless conditioning in how to behave and think, but it is of quite a different nature from the conditioning young girls receive.

To sum up this discussion of human behavioral and psychological sexual characteristics, it is obviously very difficult to determine which patterns are of genetic origin and which are the result of cultural conditioning. However, with the possible exception of the male tendency to be more assertive in direct sexual behavior (as a result of the physiological effect of the hormone testosterone, to be discussed in more detail later) it would seem on close examination that many of the behavioral and psychological characteristics commonly associated with masculinity and feminity are in fact the result of cultural conditioning. There can be no doubt that the human male and female are anatomically and physiologically dimorphic, but given the inevitable variability of all things biological, any genetic differences ascribed to sex in intellectual ability or psychological and behavioral attitudes are insignificant—if they exist at all.

STUDY TOPICS

1. List the primary sexual organs of the human male.

2. List the primary sexual organs of the human female.

3. What is dimorphism? Are humans dimorphic?

4. Compare the physical secondary sexual characteristics of the human male and female.

5. Compare the behavioral and psychological characteristics of human males and females (see also Chapters 3, 5 and 13). To what extent

are these of biological origin? Do some outside reading on this problem, and discuss it with your friends, parents, and teachers.

6. What do you think are the behavioral and/or psychological differences between the sexes, which are basically biological? On what do you base your ideas?

FOR FURTHER READING

De Beauvoir, Simone, *The Second Sex.* London: New English Library, 1949, 1969.

Dobson, Jessie, *John Hunter.* Edinburgh and London: E.&S. Livingstone, Ltd., 1969.

Friedan, Betty, *The Feminine Mystique.* New York: Dell, 1963.

Harlow, H.F., J.L. Gaugh, and R.F. Thompson, *Psychology.* San Francisco: Albion, 1971.

Harrison, R.J., *Reproduction and Man.* New York: W.W. Norton, 1967, 1971.

Harrison, Richard J., and William Montagna, *Man.* New York: Appleton-Century-Crofts, 1969.

Hutt, Corinne, Sex Differences in Human Development. *Human Development* 15: 153-170, 1972.

Mead, Margaret, *Male and Female, a Study of the Sexes in a Changing World.* New York: Mentor Books, 1957.

CHAPTER THREE

Male Sexual Anatomy and Physiology

Before Man made us citizens, great
Nature made us men.

James Russell Lowell (1819-1891)
On the Capture of Fugitive Slaves.

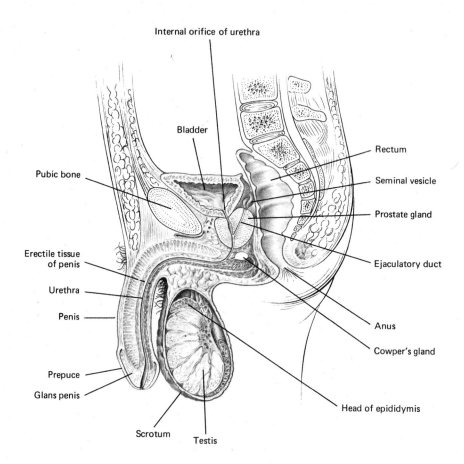

Fig. 3.1. Internal structure of the male sexual organs.

MALE SEXUAL ANATOMY

The general anatomical relationships of the human male's sexual organs are shown in sectional view in Fig. 3.1. The paired *testes* are the primary sex glands of the male and have two known functions, the production of *sperm* and the production of the male hormones called *androgens,* (the prefix "andro" means male). The testes are somewhat ovoid in shape and are suspended from the pelvis in a thin-walled muscular sac called the *scrotum.* In the embryonic state the testes are found within the abdominal cavity, but usually just prior to birth they descend into the scrotum. The interior of each testis is divided into a series of *lobules,* each of which consists of highly coiled *seminiferous tubules* (Fig. 3.2), within which the sperm are produced. In between the seminiferous tubules there lie multiple groups of secretory cells called the *interstitial cells* of Leydig, (Franz Leydig, 1821-1908). It is within these cells that the two principal male hormones, *testosterone* and *androsterone,* are produced and released directly into the blood stream. At the triangular apex of the lobules the seminiferous tubules from other lobules combine together and empty into a group of larger collecting tubules which in turn join the canal of the *epididymis,* which is about 6 meters long and much coiled. In due course the epididymus empties into the *vas deferens.* Figure 3.3 shows in diagramatic form the arrangement of the pathway from seminiferous tubules to vas deferens. When sperm are produced within the tubules, fluid is also produced which helps to sweep them along toward the epididymis; however, the ducts of the intervening pathway absorb much of this fluid, otherwise the epididymis would become greatly extended, since it is in the epididymis that the sperm are stored.

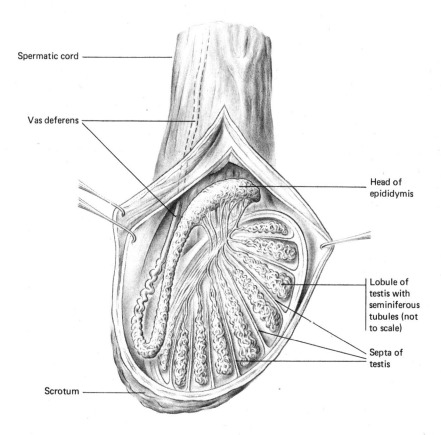

Spermatic cord

Vas deferens

Head of epididymis

Lobule of testis with seminiferous tubules (not to scale)

Septa of testis

Scrotum

Fig. 3.2. Internal structure of a testis.

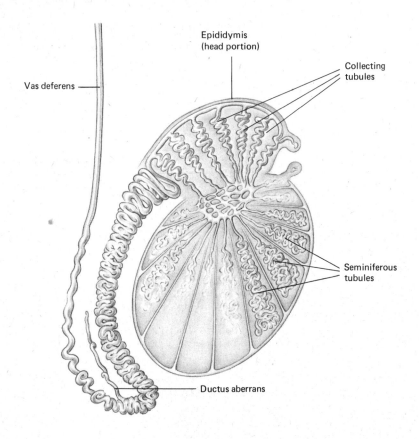

Vas deferens

Epididymis
(head portion)

Collecting
tubules

Seminiferous
tubules

Ductus aberrans

Fig. 3.3. Cross section of testis, showing relationship of seminiferous
tubules, epididymis, and vas deferens.

The vas deferens leads from the epididymis, on the upper end of the testis, into the *spermatic cord*. This cord, which is really tubular, also contains the arteries, veins, lymphatic ducts and nerves which supply the testis. In passing, it is worthy of note that the testes are profusely supplied with sensory nerves, which makes them one of the most sensitive of all the male organs. The spermatic cord passes out of the *scrotum* through the *inguinal canal* (Fig. 3.4) and into the abdomen, thus the vas deferens finds its way into the abdomen and thence over the top of the bladder and behind the *ureter* to the base of the bladder. This rather tortuous pathway which the vas deferens takes is in fact the reverse of the pathway taken by the testis as it descended before birth. In the embryo the testis initially lies toward the back wall of the abdomen, but as it descends it crosses to the inguinal canal and thence into the scrotum. As it does so it takes its vascular supply, nerves, and ducts with it, which accounts for the pathway of the vas deferens in the adult. On reaching the base of the bladder the vas deferens is joined by its opposite number, and at this point also the bilobed *seminal vesicle* glands drain into the common *ejaculatory duct* which then passes through the substance of the *prostate gland*. Within the prostate gland the ejaculatory duct is joined by the duct which empties the bladder, and upon emerging from the prostate into the *penile urethra*, it is also joined by the paired ducts of *Cowper's glands*, (William Cowper 1666-1709). The penile urethra thus serves both a sexual and urinary function. The complete relationship of these ducts and accessory glands is shown in lateral view in Fig. 3.4, and in posterior view in Fig. 3.5.

The *penis*, besides serving the function of conducting urine to the exterior via the urethra, is also functional as the male copulatory organ by which semen is introduced into the female and which makes possible internal fertilization. The penis (Fig. 3.1) is a long cylindrical organ. The skin covering the external surface of this organ terminates in a hood-like,

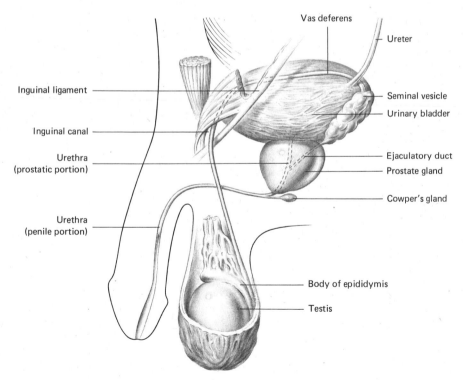

Fig. 3.4. Relationship of the internal and external male sexual organs.

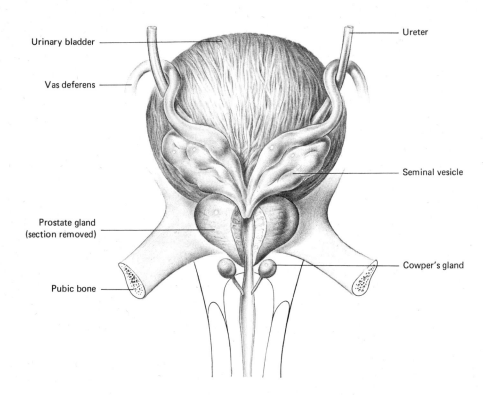

Urinary bladder

Vas deferens

Prostate gland
(section removed)

Pubic bone

Ureter

Seminal vesicle

Cowper's gland

Fig. 3.5. Relationship (in posterior view) of bladder, accessory sex glands, and ducts.

rectractable extension called the *prepuce*, which surrounds the *glans penis*, or tip of the organ. In many societies it is common practice to remove the prepuce from the penis surgically in an operation called circumcision. The size of the penis is not apparently directly related to the size of the individual. In the flaccid state it varies in length from about 6 to 12 centimeters, with a diameter of about 2.8 centimeters. The internal anatomy of the penis (Figs. 3.6 and 3.7) consists mainly of three distinct tracts of sponge-like erectile tissue—two rather large *corpora cavernosa* and a single *corpus spongiosum* which surrounds the urethra and terminates in the glans penis. In the flaccid state the arterial flow of blood into the penis is equal to the venous outflow, but when erection takes place the arteries dilate, increasing the inflow of blood. This causes engorgement of the erectile corpora tissue which in turn squeezes the penile veins so that the flow of blood back to the body is reduced. (There is probably nervous control as well.) Thus the flow of blood into the penis greatly exceeds the outflow and the organ becomes large, stiff, and erect,

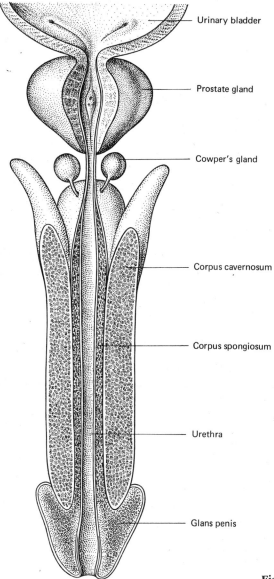

— Urinary bladder

— Prostate gland

— Cowper's gland

— Corpus cavernosum

— Corpus spongiosum

— Urethra

— Glans penis

Fig. 3.6. Longitudinal section of penis.

or tumescent. The length of the erect penis varies from about 12 to 21 centimeters with a diameter of about 4 centimeters. There is no direct correlation between the size of the flaccid and erect penis. In fact a man with a relatively small penis may have a relatively large erection and a man with a relatively large penis may have a relatively small erection.

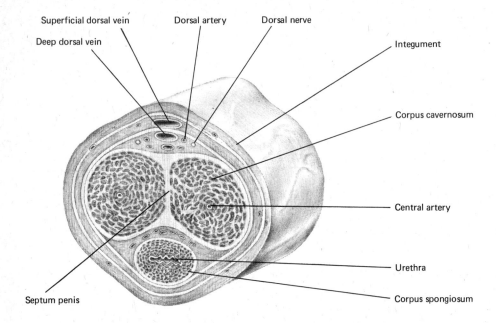

Superficial dorsal vein

Dorsal artery

Dorsal nerve

Deep dorsal vein

Integument

Corpus cavernosum

Central artery

Urethra

Septum penis

Corpus spongiosum

Fig. 3.7. Cross section of penis.

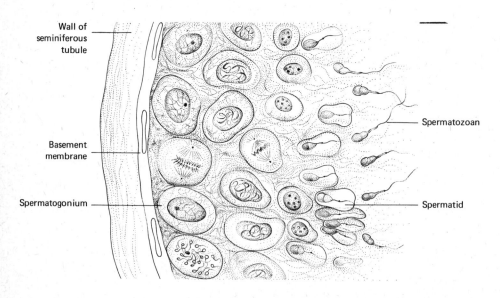

Wall of
seminiferous
tubule

Spermatozoan

Basement
membrane

Spermatogonium

Spermatid

Fig. 3.8. Spermatogenesis taking place in
seminiferous tubules and vas deferens.

FUNCTIONING OF THE GENITAL SYSTEM

Now that we know the general anatomy of the male genital system, it is necessary to consider how it functions. At birth, the basal layer of the seminiferous tubules contains cells called *spermatogonia* (Fig. 3.8), which apparently remain inactive until puberty. As puberty is approached, these cells start to divide, a process which eventually terminates in the production of sperm, though sperm themselves are not usually produced until just after puberty. Once sperm production is established, however, it normally continues into old age. The sequence of events that produces functional sperm cells is referred to as *spermatogenesis* (Fig. 3.9), and comprises a complex series of cell divisions. The spermatogonia divide into somewhat smaller daughter cells called *primary spermatocytes,* which have a rather rapid rate of growth. All divisions to this point have been *mitotic*, by which the total number of chromosomes (46 in the human species) remains the same. However, in the next two divisions — referred to as the *meiotic* or *reduction* divisions — the number of chromosomes in each cell will be reduced to 23, and in addition the cells will be of two types, one with a so-called X chromosome, which is potentially a female determining sperm, and the other with a so-called Y chromosome, which is potentially a male determining sperm. These two divisions are from the primary spermatocyte into the secondary spermatocyte, and from this into *spermatids*. The spermatids thus have 23 chromosomes each, and are either X or Y. Without further division, but by complex morphological changes, each spermatid evolves into a motile *spermatozoan* or mature sperm cell. The final maturation of spermatozoa takes place in the epididymis and vas deferens (sperm withdrawn directly from the testis are infertile). Once in the epidymis the sperm are transported towards the ejaculatory duct by cilia lining the epididymis and vas deferens.

Human sperm cells (Fig. 3.10) are comprised of three parts, a head, a body, and a tail. They are about 55 microns (thousandths of a mm.) in length, too small to be seen with the naked eye, but easily seen under the ordinary light microscope. A great deal is known about human sperm since they are easy to collect by masturbation, and are easily stored and studied. The sperm head contains all the chromosomes (which in turn contain the hereditary DNA material) and it also contains certain enzymes which function in the actual process of fertilization. The body is the active metabolic part of the cell and supplies it with energy, while the whip-like tail functions as a motile organ. Healthy sperm swim in tadpole-like fashion at about 1 to 4 millimeters per minute (3 to 7 inches per hour), and they usually swim against mucous currents and against gravitational pull.

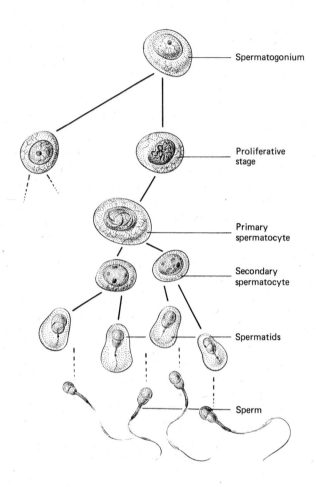

Spermatogonium

Proliferative
stage

Primary
spermatocyte

Secondary
spermatocyte

Spermatids

Sperm

**Fig. 3.9. Diagrammatic representation of the
sequence of events in spermatogenesis.**

Spermatogenesis is a process peculiarly sensitive to temperature.
Strangely enough, sperm cannot survive very long at the normal human
body temperature of $98.6°F$, and they certainly cannot be produced at
this temperature. It is interesting, however, that they can withstand much
lower temperatures, and can even be stored for long periods of time and
still retain all their fertile powers. The temperature of the scrotal sac is
normally 3 to 4 degrees below body temperature, which appears to be the
optimal temperature for sperm production. The scrotal sac has a rather
remarkable mechanism by which it regulates its temperature at this
optimal point for sperm production. The sac is suspended by a thin layer

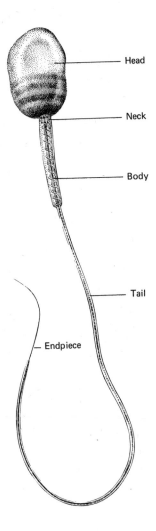

Fig. 3.10. Drawing of a human sperm.

of smooth muscle. If the external temperature drops, the muscles contract, pulling the sac and its testicular contents tight up against the body, thus raising their temperature. If the external temperature rises, the muscles relax and the sac falls away from the heat of the body, allowing the testes to become cooler. This phenomenon is easily demonstrated simply by taking a cold or hot bath. *Cryptorchism* (i.e., hidden testes) is a deformity in which the testes fail to descend into the scrotum. In such cases no viable sperm are produced, simply because the testicular temperature is too high, but in all other respects the individual is sexually normal. It has been suggested, and with good reason, that some forms of modern clothing may cause temporary male sterility or perhaps an increased mutation rate in the sperm. For example, tight-fitting undershorts press the testes close up against the body and raise their temperature considerably. Occupations which expose men to very high temperatures for long periods of time may cause temporary sterility due to inhibition of spermatogenesis.

Sperm Production

In human males, from puberty to old age, sperm are produced continuously and in enormous numbers. Exact figures are difficult to obtain and they may vary depending on conditions, but a figure of 500,000,000 plus per day is a reasonable estimate. If not ejaculated, most soon lose their potency, degenerate, and are absorbed. They do not normally become motile until suspended in seminal fluid, but once this occurs they become extremely active. Sperm are gradually and continuously passed along the epididymis and vasa diferentia by ciliary action and also by peristalsis.

Sexual Excitement

The mechanisms and processes involved in sexual excitement culminating in ejaculation are complex and little understood. (The causes of sexual excitement, often equally complex, are somewhat better understood.) Nevertheless, some form of reasonable description can be attempted. As already described, any form of effective sexual stimulus may cause erection of the penis by increased blood flow. The stimulus may be entirely psychic and may occur in the waking or sleeping state. It may be tactile or due to stimuli through other senses, or, as is more commonly the case, it may be due to a variety of stimuli. In any event, the process initiates a series of nervous reflexes, resulting in erection and eventual ejaculation. As the sperm reach the ejaculatory duct they become suspended in the secretion from the seminal vesicles, the prostate gland, and eventually by secretions from Cowper's glands. The secretion from these glands is a complex, viscous, slightly opaque, striated, alkaline solution, and it together with the suspended sperm is referred to as seminal fluid, or *semen*. The semen supplies nutrients for the sperm and curiously enough contains large amounts of the carbohydrate fructose, rather than glucose which is the normal sugar found in animals. When sexual excitement reaches a certain point, an intricate series of muscular contractions involving the prostate gland, the perineal muscles, the ejaculatory duct, and the penis, give the seminal fluid a propulsive force which carries it into the urethra and forcibly ejects it from the penis.

Semen

The volume of semen in a single human ejaculate is about 4 ml on the average, but it can vary from 1 to 11 ml depending on the individual and the circumstances. The average sperm count is about 120,000,000 per ml, with a range of about 45 to 200 million per ml. Although only one sperm is necessary to fertilize an egg, if the sperm count falls to about 50 million per ml the individual is likely to be infertile. Infertility is also probable if more than 25 percent of the sperm appear morphologically abnormal, although it should be noted that all ejaculates contain large numbers of abnormal sperm. During coitus the semen is usually deposited close to the female cervix, so much so that sperm have been demonstrated in the cervix within 90 seconds after ejaculation. They immediately start to swim up the female genital tract and, aided by peristaltic contractions, they can be well into the Fallopian tubes within one hour, but not many ever get that far. Once in the female genital tract, sperm may remain motile for two to three days (possibly longer), depending on the condition of the tract, but it is unlikely that many of them are capable of fertilizing an egg all this time. Since the human egg is only capable of being fertilized for 24 to 36 hours after being released into a Fallopian tube, it can be seen that fertilization is possible whenever sperm are deposited in the vagina from about three days before ovulation to three days after. That is about five or six days per month, but the real problem is to determine *which* five or six days.

WET DREAMS AND MASTURBATION

It should not be imagined that heterosexual coitus is the only normal time for ejaculation to occur. On the contrary, starting at puberty the vast majority of males usually experience erection and ejaculation during sleep or immediately on arousing from it. These are referred to as wet dreams, and they frequently occur during or at the termination of an erotic dream, even though the dream may not seem erotic. Wet dreams may occur as often as every night or only a few times a year, depending on the individual and the particular circumstances. Once sexual relations are initiated with another person the frequency of wet dreams usually declines considerably, but if for any reason sexual relations are temporarily suspended, their frequency will probably increase again. It is most important that prior to puberty young boys should have the phenomenon of wet dreams explained to them, so that they are not psychologically disturbed when they inevitably start.

Another very common and normal form of ejaculation is as a result of masturbation. Recent studies have shown that at least 80 to 90 percent of all males go through periods of masturbation, particularly in the years following puberty and prior to the initiation of other sexual outlets. However it may continue throughout life. Masturbation is probably one of the means by which young boys and girls learn the nature of sexual acts, and also probably supplies a necessary sexual outlet in the absence of other sexual relations. Considering the natural nature of masturbation, its enormous and almost universal frequency, it appears ludicrous and indeed tyrannical that it should have been, and indeed still is, considered such a terrible sin. There is no evidence whatsoever that it causes acne, sterility, blindness, madness nor any other disorder which has been ascribed to it.

SEXUAL GROWTH PATTERN

The mechanisms controlling both the growth and functioning of the reproductive organs are complex. They are partly influenced by the central nervous system, which may in turn be affected by a host of both external and internal stimuli, and also by internal secretions called *hormones* which are secreted by *endocrine glands* directly into the blood stream. The word hormone is derived from a Greek word meaning "to excite," and since the discovery of the first hormone, somewhat less than 100 years ago, a great deal of work has been done on them in both animals and plants. However, while a lot has been learned, it must be stressed that they are powerful physiological substances, not one of which is independent of the next, and that the factors controlling their production and their mode of operation are little understood. Furthermore new hormones and their effects are constantly being discovered.

It has already been pointed out that the sex of an individual is genetically determined at the time of fertilization, when the egg is fertilized by a male or female sperm. However, this is only the first of many factors which go into the production of a mature male or female. Much of our knowledge of these factors comes from work on rats and monkeys, since it is obvious that the human cannot easily be experimented on — though sometimes this is possible without potentially harmful effects.

In the human embryo there are no external indications of sex until about the eighth week after fertilization. These first eight weeks may be said to be a period of neutrality in which even the gonads show no signs of whether they will develop into testes or ovaries. At about the end of eight weeks, however, differentiation into one sex or the other normally starts. If the individual is destined to be a male, the crucial factor is that the fetal gonads (testes in this case) must start to produce the hormone testosterone. The production of testosterone is in turn initiated by a hormone called *chorionic gonadotrophin* that is formed in the placenta.

The testosterone then causes the embryo to produce the primary male sexual organs and the secondary male sexual characteristics. The production of testosterone normally continues until birth, at which time the effect of the chorionic gonadotrophin from the placenta ceases and the production of testosterone accordingly stops, no more being produced until the beginning of puberty.

From experiments on animals, it would appear that this embryonic secretion of testosterone has other profound physiological effects associated with the reproductive organs and with sexual behavior. One of the ways in which the reproductive physiology of the male and female differ is that in the female there is an obvious cycle, whereas no such cycle is evident in the male. Now, from the aforementioned experiments on animals (rats, guinea pigs and monkeys), it seems certain that the reproductive physiology as well as sexual behavior is under the influence of the brain, and particularly that part of the brain called the hypothalamus. What is more important is that whether the hypothalamus develops and functions sexually as male or female depends on whether it receives the stimulus of testosterone in the very early and crucial stages of embryonic development. To put it another way, it would appear that the embryonic brain of all mammals is essentially female, but if it is exposed to testosterone in its early stages of development (the particular stage varies with different mammals) it thereafter has male characteristics. If it is not exposed to testosterone it remains female. There is another good reason for believing that everyone's brain starts out essentially female. This is demonstrated by a genetic disease known as the "androgen insensitivity syndrome." Persons suffering from this hereditary disease are all genetic males, secrete normal amounts of testosterone, but due to cellular defects cannot utilize the testosterone. Such males have many of the secondary sexual characteristics of females, and tend to behave as females also.

So far as sexual matters are concerned, the characteristics of the brain exert their influence through the secretions of the anterior pituitary gland which lies at the base of the brain, and which in turn has profound effects on the body, both sexual and otherwise. In the human there is more than one male sex hormone, but testosterone is by far the most important. There are also several estrogens (female sex hormones), but by far the most important of these is *estradiol*. In view of the extraordinarily far reaching effects of these two major sex hormones, it is remarkable that their chemical composition is so similar (Fig. 3.11). It is also important to realize that in the post-pubertal state, testosterone and estradiol are not confined to male and female, respectively. All normal adult males secrete some estradiol, and all normal adult females secrete some testosterone, both of which in this case come from the cortex of the adrenal glands.

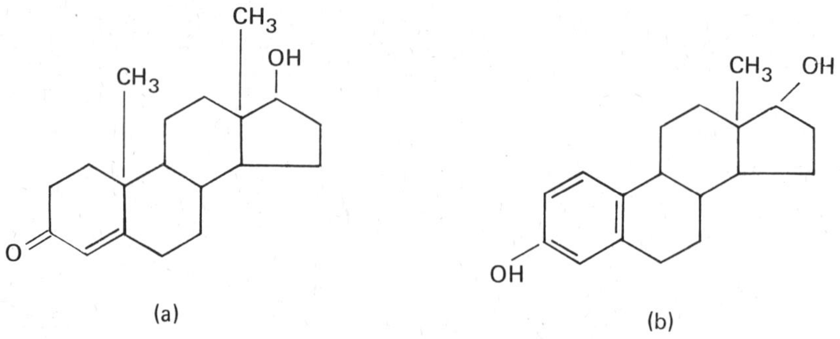

Fig. 3.11. Chemical composition and structure of (a) testosterone and (b) 17β-estradiol.

Hormonal Influences at Puberty

As puberty is approached in the male (at about age 13, but with large variations) a whole new set of physiological factors begin to function, but why they begin at this age is simply not known. Under the influence of the hypothalamus, with its nine known neurohumoral substances, the anterior pituitary gland starts to secrete three hormones, referred to collectively as *gonadotrophins*. They are produced in both male and female, but they have been named according to their effects in the female. This has given rise to a great deal of confusion which it will be well to avoid here by explaining the synonyms. (These and their functions are summarized later, in Table 4.1.) The three hormones are (1) the *follicle-stimulating hormone* (FSH), referred to by that name in both male and female; (2) the *luteinizing hormone* (LH), referred to as such in the female but as the *interstitial cell-stimulating hormone* (ICSH) in the male; (3) the *luteotropic hormone* (LTH), referred to as such in both male and female, but also as *lactogenic hormone* and *prolactin* in the female. These three hormones act on various parts of the sexual organs of both male and female, but their effects differ with the sex. Knowledge of this area is very limited, and the phenomena involved are very complex and little understood. In the male, FSH acts primarily on the seminiferous tubules of the testes, stimulating spermatogenesis. ICSH acts on the interstitial cells of Leydig, causing them to once more start the production of testosterone, which in turn stimulates the growth of the reproductive organs and the male secondary sexual characteristics. The mode of action of LTH is not at all clear. In the male it is thought to function in the same manner as ICSH, but it may also cause direct stimulation of the growth of both primary

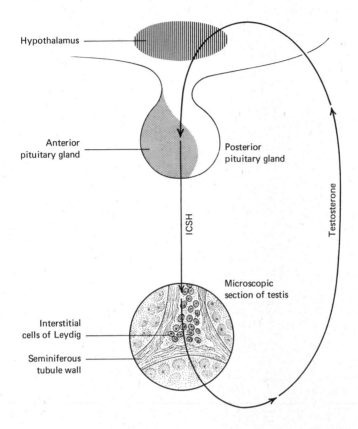

Fig. 3.12. Interaction of ICSH and testosterone in the human male.

and secondary sexual characteristics, i.e., it may act as a supplement to testosterone. There is a reciprocal feedback mechanism between ICSH (and possibly the other gonadotrophins) and testosterone. As the concentration of testosterone in the blood increases, it acts on the hypothalamus, which through a neurohumoral substance causes the anterior pituitary to secrete less ICSH — which decreases the production of testosterone. Similarly, a decreased concentration of testosterone will eventually cause an increased secretion of ICSH. However, there is no known cyclical or rhythmic system as in the female. The interplay of ICSH and testosterone is shown in Fig. 3.12. It can be seen from this brief discussion that the processes by which the male becomes a sexually mature individual and functions as such are very complex with a host of interacting factors. However, the one overriding aspect is the influence of the hormone testosterone, with all the varied effects for which it is mainly responsible. The vicissitudes of testosterone for the human male have been recently well expressed by a Canadian physician, D. W. Killinger.

> A hairy chest and hairy chin
> Are doubtlessly so masculine.
> With bulging muscles, hard as stone,
> It's all due to Testosterone.
>
> Receding hairline, loss of hair—
> They also have a manly air,
> With arteries as hard as stone
> A fickle friend, Testosterone.*

STUDY TOPICS

1. Explain the function(s) of the following: (a) testes, (b) scrotum, (c) interstitial cells, (d) seminiferous tubules, (e) epididymis, (f) vas deferens, (g) seminal vesicles, (h) prostate gland, (i) urethra, (j) ureter.

2. Draw a longitudinal and cross section of the penis, and label its major parts.

3. Explain the mechanism by which the penis becomes erect.

4. How does the temperature of the scrotal sac compare with normal body temperature, by what mechanism is this temperature regulated, and what is the biological significance of this?

5. Of what is semen composed, and where does each part come from?

6. How is the genetic sex of an individual determined?

7. Explain the importance of the reduction (meiotic) divisions in the production of sperm.

8. Explain what is meant by wet dreams and their significance.

9. Explain what is meant by gonadotrophins and where they originate.

10. Explain the significance of chorionic gonadotrophin.

---

*D.W. Killinger, "Testosterone," *Can. Med. Assoc. J.* **103**(7), 1970, p. 733. Reprinted by permission.

FOR FURTHER READING

Grollman, Sigmund, *The Human Body — Its Structure and Physiology*. New York: Macmillan, 1969.

Harrison, R. J., *Reproduction and Man*. New York: W. W. Norton, 1967, 1971.

Harrison, Richard J., and William Montagna, *Man*. New York: Appleton-Century-Crofts, 1969.

Netter, Frank H., *Reproductive System*, Vol. 2, The CIBA Collection of Medical Illustrations. Summit, N.J.: The CIBA Pharmaceutical Co., 1965.

Netter, Frank H., *Endocrine System and Selected Metabolic Diseases,* Vol. 4, The CIBA Collection of Medical Illustrations. Summit, N.J.: The CIBA Pharmaceutical Co., 1970.

Vander, Arthur J., James H. Sherman, and Dorothy S. Luciano, *Human Physiology*. New York: McGraw-Hill Book Company., 1975.

Film: *Achieving Sexual Maturity*, 16 mm, color, 21 min. New York: John Wiley & Sons.

CHAPTER FOUR

Female Sexual Anatomy and Physiology

The incredible swing from yesterday's Victorian repression to today's orgasmic preoccupation has taken the human female but a few decades, and the shock of the transition has been imprinted deeply on our society.

William H. Masters and Virginia E. Johnson,
Human Sexual Response,
Boston, Little, Brown and Co., 1966.

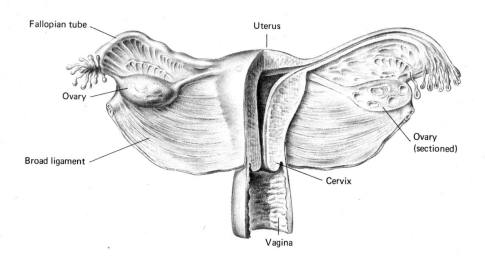

Fallopian tube

Uterus

Ovary

Ovary (sectioned)

Broad ligament

Cervix

Vagina

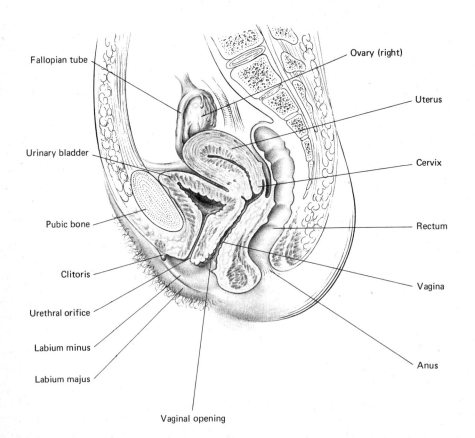

Fallopian tube

Ovary (right)

Uterus

Urinary bladder

Cervix

Pubic bone

Rectum

Clitoris

Vagina

Urethral orifice

Labium minus

Labium majus

Anus

Vaginal opening

FEMALE SEXUAL ANATOMY

The human female's internal sexual anatomy is shown in sectional view in Fig. 4.1, and the external sexual anatomy in Fig. 4.2. The primary sex glands, the *ovaries*, are paired, and like the testes of the male they have two known functions — the production of eggs and the production of steroid hormones called *estrogens* and *progesterone*. The ovaries are situated bilaterally toward the back of the pelvic portion of the abdominal cavity. They are suspended in a fold of peritoneum, called the *broad ligament*, which stretches out from the sides of the *uterus*. Arteries, veins, and nerves pass to the ovary through the folds and mesenteries of this broad ligament. In contrast to the male testes, the ovaries remain within the body cavity of the female throughout life. Each ovary is partially enveloped (though there is no attachment) by the frilled end of the Fallopian tube (Gabrielo Fallopius, 1523-1563), which then narrows and passes through the upper edge of the broad ligament to join the side of the uterus. Each Fallopian tube is coiled and about four inches long, and it is within this tube that fertilization of the egg normally takes place. The human uterus is somewhat pear-shaped, and lies above and behind the urinary bladder. The narrow lower end of the uterus projects into the *vagina*, and is referred to as the *cervix*. The wall of the uterus consists mostly of a powerful involuntary muscle called the *myometrium* and an internal lining of specialized tissue called the *endometrium* (Fig. 4.3). The myometrium, besides supplying protection for the developing embryo, also functions during parturition to expel the embryo through the mouth of the cervix into the vagina. The endometrium, the tissue in which the fertilized egg becomes implanted, supplies secretions for the egg, and in a nonpregnant female goes through a series of complicated changes on an approximately monthly basis during which it is eventually shed (menstruation). The vagina, which envelopes the neck of the uterus, is a muscular canal which extends to the cleft (*vestibule*) between the labia minora, and thence to the exterior. As can be seen from Fig. 4.1, the vagina is directed upward and backward a position probably associated with the evolution of the humans upright posture, which has in turn given rise to the usual copulatory position of front-to-front. Such a copulatory position is very rare in the mammalian class, and among the primates it is known to occur only in humans and the chimpanzee. Immediately in front of the vagina lies the bladder, with the urethra opening to the exterior.

◄ **Fig. 4.1. Internal structure of the female sexual organs.**

The external sexual organs of the female are referred to collectively as the *vulva* (Fig. 4.2). The outermost of these organs are the *labia majora*, two folds of skin which contain an abundance of adipose tissue, sebaceous glands and sweat glands. Together they enclose the vulval cleft. In front they join to form the *mons veneris*, a thick fatty prominence overlying the area of the pubic symphysis, and behind they terminate just in front of the anus. In the mature female both the mons veneris and the labia majora are covered with hair. Located within the cleft of the labia majora are two smaller folds of tissue, the *labia minora*. These folds of tissue enclose the area of the vestibule, and in front surround the clitoris. At the rear they join within the space between the labia majora. The labia minora have no hair, but are well supplied with sebaceous glands. The *clitoris*, located in front of the urethral opening, is a small organ consisting of a stalk and a

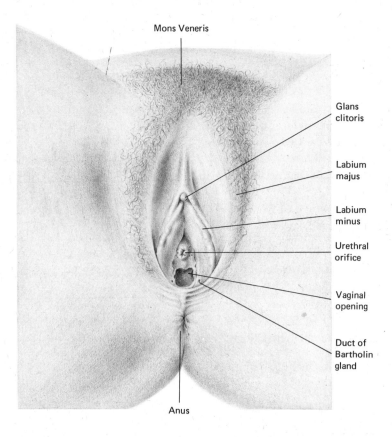

Mons Veneris

Glans
clitoris

Labium
majus

Labium
minus

Urethral
orifice

Vaginal
opening

Duct of
Bartholin
gland

Anus

Fig. 4.2. External structure of the female sexual organs.

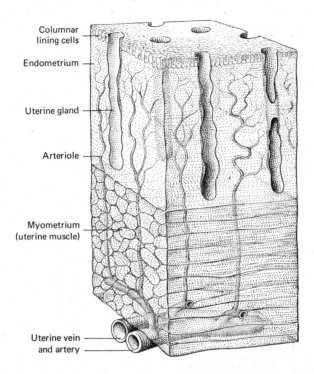

Columnar
lining cells

Endometrium

Uterine gland

Arteriole

Myometrium
(uterine muscle)

Uterine vein
and artery

Fig. 4.3. Structure of the uterine wall.

rounded terminal portion called the *glans clitoris*. It is composed mainly
of erectile tissue, and is the direct homologue of the male penis. It is very
sensitive to tactile stimulation, and normally becomes enlarged and
broadened during sexual excitement. Within the vestibule of the labia
minora and stretching across the opening of the vagina lies the *hymen*
(Greek god of marriage). It consists of a thin vascularized membrane, and
exhibits great variation from individual to individual both in thickness and
the nature of the hymenal opening. The hymen is peculiar to humans as a
species, has no obvious or known function, but is the subject of a host of
rituals, myths, cruelties, and superstitions which vary with the culture. By
the time adult life is reached, it is commonly the case that not much of
the hymen is left, and absence of an intact hymen does not necessarily
signify that the woman is no longer a virgin. After coitus and childbirth it
consists of only shrunken remnants. On either side of the vestibule, in the
groove between the hymen and the labia minora, lie the openings of
Bartholin's glands (Casper Bartholin 1655-1738), the glands themselves
lying somewhat deeper within the walls of the vagina. Just prior to orgasm

Fig. 4.4. External anatomy of the female breast.

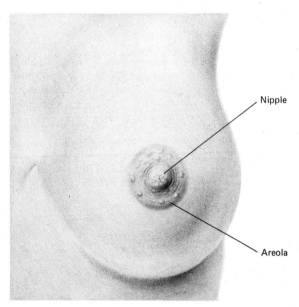

Nipple

Areola

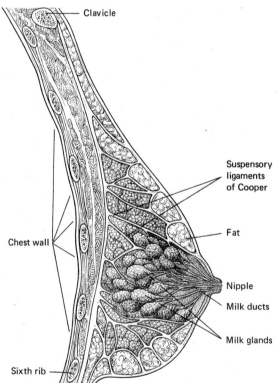

Clavicle

Suspensory ligaments of Cooper

Fat

Chest wall

Nipple

Milk ducts

Milk glands

Sixth rib

Fig. 4.5. Internal structure of the female breast.

these glands produce a tiny amount of mucoid secretion the function of which is not clear.

Although the female's breasts are usually classed as secondary sexual organs, they are so prominent and important that their anatomy and function will be discussed here. The external anatomy is shown in Fig. 4.4 and the internal anatomy in Fig. 4.5. The breasts, or mammary glands, of the female, like those of the male, are from an anatomical point of view modified sweat glands which do not start to enlarge until puberty and commonly take some years after that to reach their full size. In the center of the breast is a pigmented area called the *areola*, and within this is the nipple which contains the openings of the milk ducts. The nipple is also composed of erectile tissue and becomes noticeably erect during appropriate sexual stimulation. Within the substance of the breast are many milk glands, functional in the production of milk, which empty directly into the milk ducts leading to the nipple. There is also much fatty tissue within the breast, which helps to give it its characteristic rounded contour. Within each breast also are the suspensory *ligaments of Cooper* (Sir Astley Paston Cooper, 1768-1841). These ligaments consist of fibrous tissues which are anchored on the chest wall and lead through the breast where they are attached to the inner surface of the breast's skin. As Fig. 4.5 shows, they function in suspending the breasts from the chest and helping to maintain their shape. During pregnancy the breasts undergo marked enlargement with great proliferation of the milk glands.

FUNCTIONING OF THE GENITAL SYSTEM

The mechanisms by which the female's genital system functions are extremely complex, very delicately balanced by a host of interactions both external and internal, and of a nature quite different from those of the male. At the time of birth each human ovary (Fig. 4.6) contains about a quarter of a million *primary oocytes*, and all that a woman will ever have are there at birth. These specialized cells are all potentially eggs, and each is contained within an envelope of other cells which are collectively called a *primordial follicle*. These primordial follicles, each with their primary oocyte, are inactive until just before puberty. At this time, and for the rest of the woman's reproductive life (i.e., until menopause, when the ovaries become nonfunctional) usually one (but occasionally two or more) primordial follicles enlarge at the beginning of each reproductive cycle, and throughout this cycle of approximately 28 days both the follicle and its primary oocyte undergo complex changes. These changes are referred to collectively as the *ovarian cycle* (Fig. 4.7), which is closely related to and interacts with the menstrual or uterine cycle.

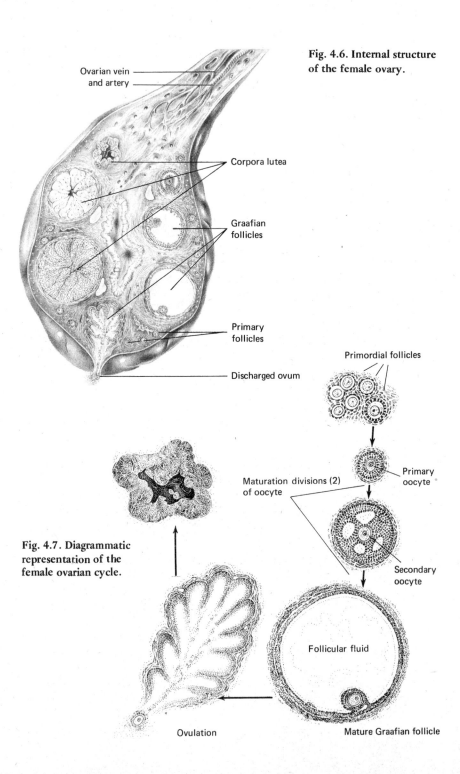

Fig. 4.6. Internal structure of the female ovary.

Ovarian vein and artery

Corpora lutea

Graafian follicles

Primary follicles

Discharged ovum

Primordial follicles

Primary oocyte

Maturation divisions (2) of oocyte

Secondary oocyte

Fig. 4.7. Diagrammatic representation of the female ovarian cycle.

Follicular fluid

Ovulation

Mature Graafian follicle

Ovarian Cycle

Initially the primordial follicle consists of a single layer of cells, but as it grows and the cells proliferate, a split in these develops, resulting in a fluid-filled follicular cavity. Jutting into this cavity is a disc of cells surrounding the primary oocyte. The growth of a primordial follicle is very rapid over a period of days and it may reach a diameter of one centimeter or more, dwarfing the contained oocyte which is only some 100 microns in diameter. At about the time the follicle develops its cavity, the primary oocyte starts its first maturation division, giving rise to a secondary oocyte and a small polar body. This division and the second maturation division together result in reduction of the 46 chromosomes to 23 and in the production of a mature ovum or egg which is about 1/175 inch in diameter. There is some doubt, however, whether the second maturation division takes place within the maturing follicle or only after the stimulus of fertilization, as is the case in most mammals.

The mature follicle with its mature egg is referred to as a *Graafian follicle* (Regnier de Graaf, 1641-1673). Under average conditions a mature Graafian follicle develops over a period of about two weeks, starting from the onset of the menstrual flow. In other words, it reaches maturity about half way through the menstrual cycle. At this point the follicle ruptures, and the egg is shed from the ovary in the process of *ovulation*. It is important to note that usually follicles mature alternately in the two ovaries, but sometimes more than one may mature at the same time. In addition, ovarian cycles can occur without ovulation (they are then called anovular) or the egg that is shed may not reach the Fallopian tube, but simply be absorbed in the abdominal fluids. However, most eggs probably do enter the Fallopian tube, gradually move along it by peristalsis and the movement of mucus by cilia, and are susceptible to fertilization. As previously pointed out, however, their life span if not fertilized is extremely short, perhaps 24 hours, after which they gradually degenerate. If fertilization occurs, it takes place in the Fallopian tube — usually at the upper end — and the whole complex process of pregnancy begins. This will be discussed in a later chapter.

After the egg is shed from the Graafian follicle, the follicle undergoes further development and growth, the rupture point heals over, and it becomes an endocrine organ — the *corpus luteum* — whose hormones affect the uterine endometrium, causing its glands to secrete. During the first four days after ovulation, blood vessels grow into the corpus luteum, and by the ninth day it may have reached a diameter of two centimeters. However, by the thirteenth or fourteenth day the life of a corpus luteum reaches a crucial stage, for if fertilization has not occurred it quickly begins to degenerate, and this in turn immediately starts the process of menstruation. Within the ovary the corpus luteum is replaced by a tissue scar called a *corpus albicans*, and within two months hardly a trace is left. But if fertilization has occurred, the corpus luteum persists as a functional endocrine organ for about the first three months of pregnancy, after which it degenerates, its functions having been taken over by the placenta. Providing fertilization does not occur, an ovarian cycle consists of about 28 days, but variations from female to female are very great, and there may be considerable variation in each successive cycle within an individual female.

Menstrual Cycle

Although the menstrual cycle is closely related to the ovarian cycle, we will describe it briefly and separately, and then consider the controlling and interacting mechanisms of both cycles (Fig. 4.8). As previously pointed out, the internal lining of the uterus consists of a tissue referred to as the endometrium (Fig. 4.3). This tissue is composed of three layers, two superficial layers which are shed at each menstruation, with a basal layer which remains and from which the two superficial linings are regenerated. For purposes of descriptive convenience the approximate 28-day menstrual cycle is divided into four phases: (1) the proliferative or follicular phase, (2) the ovulatory phase, (3) the secretory or luteal phase, and (4) the menstrual phase. It is a mistake to assume that these phases are of any set duration; on the contrary they vary considerably and one phase gradually changes into the next. Nevertheless some reasonable average times can be given, as shown in Fig. 4.8 where Day 1 is considered to be the beginning of the menstrual flow. On completion of the menstrual flow—which lasts about four or five days, but is often longer—the endometrial lining is relatively thin and its glands and blood vessels are small. During the next ten days (the proliferative phase), this lining grows at a rapid rate and at the end of it the endometrium is about 5 mm thick. At approximately this time (i.e., some 12 to 17 days after the onset of the menstrual flow) ovulation usually takes place (the ovulatory phase), and this may last only a few hours. The secretory phase is initiated almost at once, and this lasts some 12 to 14 days. During this time the endometrial lining continues to thicken, though at nowhere near the same rate as during the proliferative phase, and its glands secrete at a maximum rate. However, if fertilization of an egg has not occurred, the secretory phase terminates with the breakdown of the two superficial cellular linings of the endometrium and the menstrual phase is initiated. The total volume of the menstrual flow over a period of four or five days does not normally exceed about 8 fluid ounces, of which only about 3 fluid ounces are

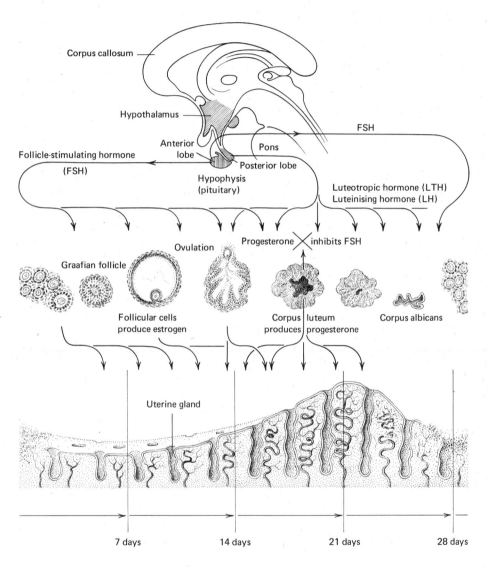

Fig. 4.8. Diagrammatic representation
of the relationship between the ovarian
and menstrual cycles.

actually blood, the remainder being discarded tissue. It is noteworthy that at this time the vagina has an abundant bacterial flora which naturally helps remove the remains of the menstrual flow.

Hormonal Control of Ovarian and Menstrual Cycles

As with the male, the regulation and control of the reproductive organs in the female are most complex, and subject to many influences both external and internal. They are principally controlled by the interaction of several hormones which undergo approximate monthly cyclical changes, which in turn have a major influence over the ovarian and menstrual cycles (Fig. 4.8 and 4.9). These phenomena, together with the development of the female secondary sexual characteristics, start at puberty when the ovaries come under the influence of the three gonadotropins secreted from the anterior pituitary, i.e., FSH, LH and LTH. Puberty usually occurs about age 13, but there are wide variations, and it is not uncommon for it to occur as early as age nine. Furthermore, there is good evidence to show that the average age of menarche (the onset of menses) has been progressively declining (at least in western societies) over the last hundred years at the rate of about four months in every 10 years. However a recent (1976) study supported by the National Institute of Child Health and Human Development clearly indicates that in the United States this trend has leveled off. It seems obvious that the onset of menses in a young girl's life is a major event, and it is of the utmost importance that she should be well prepared for it, otherwise it may well be a very traumatic experience for her. She will in addition require the utmost understanding, tact, and help from those closest to her.

Before the end of a menstrual flow, the anterior pituitary gland starts to secrete FSH directly into the bloodstream, and this has two direct effects; first, it causes one of the ovarian follicles to begin rapid growth, and second, it causes specialized cells of this follicle to secrete estradiol directly into the blood. As the concentration of estradiol in the blood increases, it acts directly on the endometrium, giving rise to the proliferative phase described previously. There is a reciprocal relationship operating via the hypothalamus (Fig. 4.9); as the concentration of estradiol in the blood increases, it gradually inhibits the production of FSH from the anterior pituitary. By the time the follicle has become a mature Graafian follicle, and the endometrium has enlarged to the end of the proliferative phase (about two weeks), the concentration of estradiol has reached a point where it triggers, again via the hypothalamus, the release of LH from the anterior pituitary, and inhibits even further the production of FSH. However, under the combined effects of FSH and LH the Graafian follicle ruptures and the egg is released.

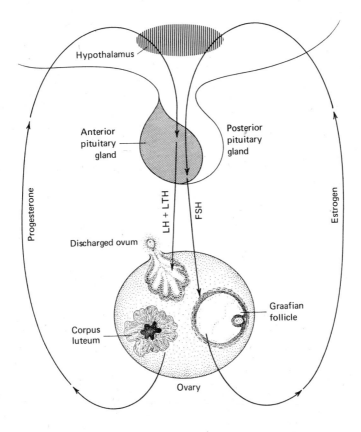

Fig. 4.9. Interaction of various sex hormones in the human female.

At about this time LTH is also secreted from the anterior pituitary, though its exact functions are not at all clearly understood. However, it probably acts with LH to stimulate production of the powerful hormone progesterone from the corpus luteum. The production of progesterone directly into the blood completely inhibits further production of FSH, and also acts directly on the endometrium of the uterus, causing the secretory phase. This phase lasts for the second half of the menstrual cycle, during which the endometrium thickens further and the glands produce copious secretions. There is also probably a reciprocal relationship via the hypothalamus between LH, LTH, and progesterone. As the level of progesterone increases in the blood, the production of LH and LTH is completely inhibited, which causes the corpus luteum to degenerate and the production of progesterone to eventually stop. This in turn causes the secretory phase to cease and menstruation to begin, and in a short time the production of FSH starts to initiate the next cycle. Table 4.1 summarizes the principal functions of the gonadotrophic hormones in the human male and female.

Table 4.1
Summary of the principal functions of gonadotrophins in the human male and female.

Gonadotrophic hormone from anterior pituitary gland	Function in male	Function in female
Follicle stimulating hormone (FSH)	Acts on seminiferous tubules of testes, stimulating spermatogenesis.	In ovarian cycle it causes a Graafian follicle to grow rapidly and secrete estradiol. It is also involved in the rupture of the follicle.
Luteinizing hormone (LH) in female, referred to as interstitial cell stimulating hormone (ICSH) in male.	Acts on interstitial cells of Leydig in the testes, causing production of testosterone.	Acts on mature Graafian follicle with FSH, causing its rupture and release of the egg. May also stimulate production of progesterone from the corpus luteum.
Luteotropic hormone (LTH), also referred to in the female as lactogenic hormone or prolactin.	Function not clear, but may supplement ICSH.	Function not clear, but may supplement LH.

In describing the mechanisms controlling the female reproductive cycle there is the problem that the student of the subject will assume that it is a rather simple and well documented phenomenon. Nothing could be further from the truth. First, it is not known how estrogens and other steroid hormones act. It is possible that they may alter the rates of synthesis of enzymes, or activate enzymes, or act as cofactors in an enzyme system. Yet again they may alter cellular permeability to various substances, or alter the genetic programming of cells which in turn will alter their entire metabolism. Second, it is well established that estrogens exert physiological effects way beyond those associated with the reproductive cycle. In addition, females also secrete some testosterone, and males some estrogens from the cortex of the adrenal glands. Estrogens also influence the production of pituitary hormones other than gonadotrophins, such as ACTH (adrenocorticotropic hormone), TSH (thyroid stimulating hormone) and GH (growth hormone). They also affect directly other endocrine glands such as the adrenals and the thyroid. In fact it is probable that no hormone is independent of any other. Estrogens also affect protein and carbohydrate metabolism, calcium balance, water and salt balance, and many other physiological processes. Thus it seems almost superfluous to add that interfering in any way with the female reproductive cycle should be done with great caution—and never without expert professional advice. Hormonal physiology is a constantly and rapidly evolving science, and while what has been said here is as up to date (albeit superficial) as circumstances permit, nevertheless it will inevitably become dated very quickly.

It has already been pointed out that the female reproductive cycle is a cyclical phenomenon of internal origin, whose control center is probably in the hypothalamus of the brain. However, despite its cyclic nature, the time span varies considerably not only from woman to woman, but from cycle to cycle within an individual woman. Furthermore, the cycle is commonly affected by many external factors, the affects of which vary from woman to woman. These external factors include anything which may cause an emotional disturbance, almost any illness, travel, or any sudden change in routine day-to-day activities. These and other factors, depending on their severity, may have very minor or no effects but depending on the individual they may cause gross disruption of the menstrual cycle.

Pain in Menstruation. Despite the fact that menstruation is a natural function, it may cause monthly pain, discomfort, or emotional disturbance in many women. Estimates of the frequency of monthly pain severe enough to interfere with routine daily life are difficult to obtain accurately, but a figure of 50% does not seem unreasonable. In fact many women describe a completely painless menstrual cycle as "a figment of male imagination." Certainly no male can hope to fully understand such a problem, and can only rely on womens' own descriptions of their feelings. It is of course possible that these problems may be partly of psychological origin, but this does not make them any less real to the individual concerned. Apart from the enormous variety of emotional disturbances which many women describe, they seem to experience two major forms of pain or physical discomfort. These are referred to as spasmodic pain and congestive pain, or the premenstrual syndrome. Spasmodic pain apparently occurs in some women on the first day of the menstrual flow. It is usually felt as a spasm in the lower abdomen, and may occur at rhythmic intervals. It may also extend to the back and thighs, but is usually confined to the lower part of the body. This seems natural, since it would be the nerves in the lower part of the body that were stimulated by what is physiologically taking place. This spasmodic pain does not appear to last long, perhaps one or two days at the most. Congestive pain, or premenstrual syndrome, consists of a group of symptoms which may occur some days before the onset of menstruation, and the time span may vary greatly. The symptoms also vary considerably and may comprise any or all of the following: backache, headache, tender breasts, and pains in the joints. The woman with premenstrual syndrome may also be irritable, depressed, lethargic, or have a general feeling of discomfort. It must be stressed however, that this is an individual thing, many women experiencing no such symptoms at all.

Cultural Factors and Menstruation. Unfortunately, menstrual problems are not helped by the many myths, ignorances, superstitions, and taboos associated with menstruation both in the past and the present. The orthodox Jewish taboos on the subject are fully described in Leviticus 15, and at one time or another in human recorded history a menstruating woman was supposed to cause almost any disaster from the souring of wine and the breaking of violin strings to the death of men. During the middle ages it was believed that menstruation demonstrated the essential sinfulness and inferiority of women, and they were accordingly forbidden to attend church or take communion while menstruating. And unbelievable as it may seem in this more enlightened time, this attitude still persists in some areas.

Menopause

Just as the causes of menarche are unknown, so also are the causes of menopause, that is the final cessation of the ovarian and menstrual cycles. This event does not occur abruptly but over a period of months or years. It usually takes place between the ages of 45 and 50, but it can occur considerably earlier or later. There is a high correlation between the age of the menarche and the age of onset of the menopause—the earlier the menarche the later the menopause (a common reaction to this fact is "how cruel can nature be"). There is also a strongly inherited pattern, daughters tending to follow the pattern of their mothers very closely. It is interesting that, so far as is known, the human female is the only mammal that lives long enough to exhibit the phenomenon of menopause.

Basically, menopause is due to a change in hormonal stimulation from the anterior pituitary to the ovaries which results in gradual atrophy of these organs. This inhibits production of mature eggs, estradiol, and progesterone. Eventually both the ovarian and the menstrual cycles are abolished and with them the ability to reproduce. There is evidence to show that the ovarian cycle is probably abolished long before the onset of menopause. It is important to note that with menopause it is only the faculty of childbearing which is lost. To the woman in good health, interest in sexual enjoyment remains and may even be increased with the fear of pregnancy gone.

Side Effects of Menopause. Considering the fundamental physiological changes involved with menopause, it is not surprising that there are commonly certain side effects associated with it. These side effects can usually be attributed to the lack of estradiol. The most common of them is apparently a slightly labile thermostat, causing so-called hot flushes which take the form of a sudden rush of blood to the head, with possible feelings of dizziness, and perspiration. These are due to dilation of the arteries in the upper part of the body and normally last about a minute. Unfortunately, women experiencing these become worried that they are very obvious to everyone else, when in fact this is simply not the case. In addition to hot flushes, any or all of the following may occur: irritability, depression, insomnia, headaches, and loss of appetite. As pointed out previously, that these may be of psychological origin does not diminish their reality. Over the years of menopause and thereafter, the external features of a woman tend to take on a more intersexual aspect. The skin becomes drier and less elastic, and it wrinkles more easily. There may be loss of some hair on the head and slight hair growth on the face, and the breasts commonly diminish in size. The so-called middle aged spread, often associated with menopause, in fact usually starts long before it. It is significant to note that most women go through this phase of their life quite naturally without adverse symptoms of any significance, and in modern industrial countries can look forward to another 25 years or so of active productive life. For those who have difficulties, replacement hormone treatment may be of great help.

ORIGINS OF FEMALE REPRODUCTIVE PHYSIOLOGY

In concluding this chapter on the reproductive physiology of the human female, it is pertinent to ask how the phenomenon of menstruation evolved. On the surface it would seem to be a very wasteful and inconvenient means of assuring reproduction of the species. Most mammals have a reproductive cycle called estrus, and depending on the species there may be one or more of these a year. There is no overt sign of bleeding. The outward characteristic of an estrus cycle is that the female becomes sexually receptive to the male only for a specific and usually short period of time, during which she is said to be "in heat." Typically, female mammals in the natural state will not sexually tolerate a male for most of the year. This is no doubt related to the necessity for mammals to produce their young at specific times of the year, usually in the spring. However, in some old-world monkeys (Catarrhines), the great apes (Pongidae) and the only surviving member of the Hominidae, i.e., humans, there is what can be termed a menstrual cycle of some 20 to 60 days, depending on the species, during which there is some overt bleeding. In these examples, including humans, the breeding season is all year, and the female is permanently sexually receptive to the male. It seems, therefore, that the advantage of a menstrual cycle is that the species can breed all year, which gives it enormous reproductive potential, providing it is relatively independent of the effects of a harsh seasonal environment. This of course is the case with humans—and to a greater degree than with any other mammal. Thus the menstrual cycle has great biological advantage and significance.

Despite its biological advantage, menstruation is a very obvious and inconvenient event which would certainly cause great consternation and concern in the natural state. However, it is reasonable to argue that in a natural state, such as the one in which humans undoubtedly evolved, virtually all females would be either immature, pregnant, lactating, about to ovulate, ovulating, postmenopause, or abnormal. Thus overt menstruation would in fact be a rather rare event. It is therefore really not surprising that there are a host of rites, superstitions, and taboos which are associated with the phenomenon, and the curious reader may wish to learn more about these by reading Sir James Frazer's work *The Golden Bough*. It is noteworthy also that some men still marvel that women accept this monthly bleeding with so little disturbance, when to them the mere sight of a drop of blood may cause severe shock!

STUDY TOPICS

1. Explain the function(s) of the following: (a) ovary, (b) Graafian follicle, (c) corpus luteum, (d) Fallopian tubes (e) clitoris, (f) vagina, (g) uterus, (h) cervix, (i) mons veneris, (j) hymen.

2. Sketch an external view of the female genital organs, and label the following: vaginal opening, clitoris, mons veneris, labium majus, labium minus, urethral orifice, anus.

3. Sketch a cross sectional view of the female breast and mark in the following: nipple, chest wall, milk glands, milk ducts, fat deposits, suspensory ligaments of Cooper.

4. Describe the ovarian cycle and trace the route of the ovum from a primordial follicle to its final degeneration (given no fertilization).

5. Summarize the principal known functions of gonadotrophins in the human male and female.

6. With the aid of a diagram explain the various events and their interaction in an average ovarian and menstrual cycle.

7. Many women experience pain and/or cramps during the menstrual cycle. Explain the nature of these.

8. Explain what is meant by menopause.

9. Explain the differences between the estrus and menstrual cycles, and their biological significance.

10. Are there differences in the brains of males and females? Explain.

FOR FURTHER READING

Grollman, Sigmund, *The Human Body—Its Structure and Physiology.* New York: Macmillan, 1969.

Harrison, R.J., *Reproduction and Man.* New York: W.W. Norton, 1967, 1971.

Harrison, Richard J., and William Montagna, *Man.* New York; Appleton—Century—Crofts, 1969.

Film: *Achieving Sexual Maturity,* 16 mm, color, 21 min. New York: John Wiley & Sons.

Levine, Seymour, "Sex Differences in the Brain." *Scientific American,* April 1966.

Netter, Frank H., *Reproductive System,* Vol. 2, The CIBA Collection of Medical Illustrations. Summit, N.J.: The CIBA Pharmaceutical Co., 1965.

Netter, Frank H., *Endocrine System and Selected Metabolic Diseases,* Vol. 4, The CIBA Collection of Medical Illustrations. Summit, N.J.: The CIBA Pharmaceutical Co., 1970.

Novak, Edmund R., Georgeanna Jones, and Howard W. Jones, *Gynecology.* Baltimore: Williams and Wilkins, 1971.

Zacharias, Leona, William M. Rand, and Richard J. Wurtman, A Prospective Study of Sexual Development and Growth in American Girls: The Statistics of Menarche. *Obstetrical and Gynecological Survey* 31 (4): Supplement: 325-337, 1976.

Vander, Arthur J., Sherman, James H., and Dorothy S. Lucian, *Human Physiology*. New York: McGraw-Hill Book Company.

CHAPTER FIVE

Male and Female Sexual Development and Precopulatory Behavior

An unresolved dilemma of our day is how to classify the pubescent or adolescent female. When a 10- or 12-year-old girl with menstrual problems is admitted to a hospital, she is either too old for the pediatric ward or too young for the gynecological ward.

James P. Semmens and F. Jane Semmens "Physical Growth and Emotional Adjustment of Adolescent Girls" from *The Adolescent Experience*. J. Semmens and K. Krantz, Editors. Copyright© 1970 by Macmillan Co., New York, p. 47.

Some of the factors involved in the embryonic growth and development of sex in humans have already been mentioned, and we must now consider how these factors fit into the developmental processes that occur between birth and maturity. This is complicated by the fact that sexual development is completely integrated with all the other growth systems, and all of these are controlled by a complex of factors, both internal and external. For example, genetic, neural, and hormonal factors on the one hand, and nutrition, socioeconomic status, climate, exercise, disease, and psychological environment on the other hand. Despite all this there is one period in human development which has overwhelming sexual importance, namely puberty. This is the age at which the reproductive organs become functional, while the rather more diffuse period between puberty and maturity is called adolescence. In girls the fundamental sign of puberty is menarche, or the first menstruation, while in boys it is the first involuntary seminal emission during sleep or in masturbation. In neither case, however, should it be assumed that these events necessarily imply the ability to produce offspring, for the whole process of puberty lasts about two years.

PUBERTY

Puberty is normally coincident with, but partly preceded by, a variety of profound physical changes which affect the whole body as well as the primary sexual organs. Perhaps the most obvious of these is the so-called adolescent spurt in rate of growth. This begins in girls at about the age of 10 or 11 and in boys about 12 or 13, though, of course, there are wide variations. The spurt usually lasts just over two years, and during this time girls gain about six and a half inches and boys about eight inches in height. After this there is a rapid slowing of growth, and by ages 17 and 18 respectively, the vast majority of girls and boys have reached 98% of their final height.

During the period of growth from birth to puberty there is little to distinguish the structural form of girls and boys (Fig. 5.1). But the secondary sex characteristics appear, including the sex differences in the skeleton, in association with the adolescent spurt in growth rate. In the female the secondary sexual fat pads are laid down, resulting in the typical female body form; the pelvis becomes wider and roomier, which is functionally related to childbearing. In the male the shoulders grow more than the pelvis, which is presumably related to the fact the male's body is generally more muscular.

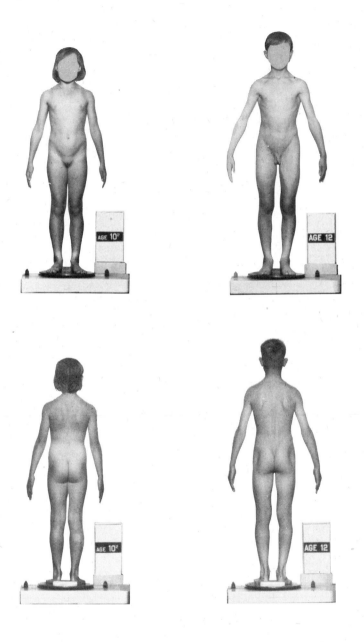

Fig. 5.1. Similarity of body form in the prepubescent stage of a 10-year-old girl and a 12-year-old boy. (Courtesy of Dr. J.M. Tanner, Institute of Child Health, University of London.)

Between the ages of 7 and 10 there is a marked and progressive increase in the internal secretion of sex hormones in both male and female, and it is noteworthy that in girls this secretion is cyclical even before the first menstruation. This increased secretion of androgens and estrogens is in turn brought about by an increased activity of the pituitary gland, in the production of both the gonadotrophic-hormones and the growth hormone. This enormous and combined increase in hormonal production is probably the immediate cause of all the complex physical and psychological changes that take place during puberty and adolescence. In girls the usual first external sign of the beginning of puberty is the enlargement of the breasts, followed closely by the appearance of pubic hair and rapid growth of the ovaries, uterus, and vagina. There is much thickening of the vaginal epithelium and great changes in its bacterial flora. Some months or years later the first menstruation will occur. In boys the earliest visible sign of puberty is the rapid growth of the testes. Until about the age of ten these have grown only to some 10% of their final size. This growth is usually concurrent with the appearance of pubic hair and enlargement of the penis, prostate gland, Cowper's glands, and the seminal vesicles. Usually, somewhat later, the larynx undergoes its characteristic changes, and the distribution of hair on the body changes, including the initial growth of facial hair. Common to both sexes are changes in the skin, which include enlargement of the pores and increased secretion of fat in the skin due to an increased secretion of the sebaceous glands. There is also increased activity of the sweat glands. All these changes commonly result in skin lesions such as acne or blackheads, which may become distressingly severe and cause severe psychological suffering.

Health at Puberty

Despite all these truly enormous physiological changes that take place during the years of puberty, there is no period of life when physical health is better. The sickness curve drops steeply during this time and rises again afterward, while accident is the only cause of death that takes a greater toll during puberty than at other stages of life.

The years of puberty and adolescence are often described as a conflicting and frustrating period of life, though perhaps it would be more accurate to say that conflict and frustration reach a peak during these years, and may at times become intense. However, it is thought that if a sense of security and self-reliance has been built up during the earlier part of life, then the individual will better withstand the destructive influences of these years. It is of the utmost importance to realize that the processes leading to physical maturity are governed primarily by the individual's genetic makeup, nutrition, and the general physical environment, while the processes governing the development of emotional maturity are largely learned. What is learned and how it is learned will naturally be greatly influenced by the general social environment.

Behavior at Puberty

Behavioral features typical of puberty and the years that follow include emotional instability, antagonism, worry, anxiety, fear of death, and concern for the health and development of the body, commonly to the point of mild hypochondria. Concurrent with these features are changes in sexual motivation which result in behavior patterns very different from those of the prepubertal child. The typical childhood development of heterosexual behavior patterns are of interest and can be fairly accurately divided into the following seven stages.

1. Infants: both sexes are interested only in themselves.
2. Early childhood: both sexes seek associations with other children regardless of sex.
3. About age 8: boys prefer to play with boys and girls with girls.
4. Ages 10 to 12: the sexes are commonly antagonistic to each other.
5. Ages 13 to 14: girls commonly show some interest in boys, but boys are typically disdainful or contemptuous of girls.
6. Ages 14 to 16: girls typically tend to pair off with older boys, while boys begin taking an interest in girls.
7. Ages 16 to 17: pairing off is common.

This classification is valid only generally of course, since the development of heterosexual behavior is influenced by a wide variety of cultural and social factors.

Curiosity about, and playing with, the sexual organs is an almost universal part of a normal child's behavior from very early years onward. Most parents are sooner or later confronted with the fact that their children have been engaged in some form of play (taking down pants, for example) which involves genital exploration. Parental reaction to such events is no doubt a major factor in determining the child's attitudes toward sex in general. It is known beyond reasonable doubt that such attitudes are formed very early in life, and once formed are not easily changed. An intolerant and repressive attitude toward sexual knowledge and behavior in the child will almost inevitably produce an adolescent and adult with serious psychological problems related to sex. On the other hand, a tolerant and open attitude will certainly give the child a better chance of accepting its sexuality as a natural and advantageous part of its whole being.

Masturbation. As the years of pubertal development progress, more overt forms of sexual behavior begin to manifest themselves, and the first of these is almost always that of masturbation (i.e., the use of the hand on the penis of the male and on the clitoris of the female to bring about sexual excitement). Initial experiences with masturbation may stop short of orgasm, but very quickly the practice will usually be carried through to orgasm. Accurate figures of the prevalence of masturbation among sexually developing young people are difficult to obtain, mainly because young people are reluctant to talk freely about the subject. This fact is confirmed by the recent "Sorensen Report" (1973) in which surveys in the United States found that there was no sex practice among adolescents which caused so many inhibitions and such deep embarrassment. Despite this, Sorensen's findings were that within the 13 to 19 age group, 58% of boys and 39% of girls had masturbated at least once. In all probability the reality is that the figures are much higher. Estimates are that in boys between the ages of 13 and 15, 75% masturbate to some degree, and by 16 and 17 the figure is over 90%.

The corresponding frequency figure for girls is somewhat lower, perhaps between 60 and 70%. This lower rate among girls is probably due to an interaction of sociological and biological factors. Girls generally receive a more antisexual training in childhood, which would tend to reduce their sexual expression and certainly to reduce their willingness to talk about it. In addition, experimental evidence from animals indicates clearly that sexual behavior in males is more easily activated than the corresponding behavior in females. There is no guarantee that the same is true in the human, but it would appear that to some extent this is the case. Thus both sociological and biological factors are involved in the frequency of masturbation as in all forms of sexual behavior.

Since masturbation is nearly always the first form of direct sexual expression which is commonly accompanied by elaborate sexual fantasies and dreams, and since it is something both new and intense in the individual's life, it is not surprising that it initially creates a considerable amount of psychological stress. Whether the individual copes with and overcomes this stress will depend in large part on the general background of attitudes that he or she has been taught regarding it. (Less than 20% of both boys and girls have been told anything about it by their parents before they experience it.) So far as is known, the only possible harmful effects that can result from masturbation are caused by the guilt feelings associated with it. It is probable that boys suffer more from these guilt feelings than girls, since (although girls' sexual training is usually antisexual) girls usually know more about the subject than boys—who are too often taught nothing. Consequently, when sexual expressions can no longer be suppressed, boys experience guilt feelings simply as a result of ignorance. They may even fear that something is seriously wrong with them if they have involuntary nocturnal emissions without any knowledge of what these mean. Boys should be prepared for this just as girls should be prepared for menarche.

It has already been pointed out that the moralistic prohibitions on masturbation, which are still widely held, are simply absurd from a biological point of view. Not only is it physically harmless, no matter how much it is practiced by an individual, but there are cases where it can be shown to have a beneficial effect. For example, it has been claimed that masturbation in the young tends to make later sexual adjustment with a partner difficult, especially for women. This simply is not the case. On the contrary, women who know through masturbation how they may be sexually aroused can teach their male partner how to do it, rather than go through a long period of trial and error which may lead to maladjustment. Despite all the terrible afflictions that until very recently have been attributed to masturbation, there seems little doubt that it is virtually universal, and that it is merely one of the primary ways by which young people both learn the nature of sexual acts and achieve sexual satisfaction.

Interest in the Opposite Sex

In most cases, though by no means universally, some form of physical interest in and association with the same or opposite sex will start during puberty or shortly thereafter—and will continue, with varying degrees of intensity, into adult life. These activities are all part of the learning processes by which girls and boys learn to familiarize themselves with each other, and at least one researcher (Michael Schofield, to be reported later) has found that they usually occur in a rather precise order though with enormous variations in time.

Dating is normally the first overt form of heterosexual behavior, and the first date in a boy's or girl's life is an important event, because it indicates not only the awakening of sexual interest, but also the departure from a form of life in which the boy's associates are primarily male and the girl's associates primarily female. It is a useful activity by which the opposite sexes start to learn about each other both physically and psychologically. Depending on a variety of social factors, there may not be any physical contacts at all during initial dating experiences, either the boy or the girl being too shy. However, physical contacts will start fairly quickly. Typically, girls start dating younger than boys, and teenage dating is probably always more important psychologically to girls than to boys. The second sexual activity which most teenagers experience is kissing, usually lip to lip initially, and commonly as a "goodnight kiss" at the end of a date. In future dates, however, kissing increases considerably, and the whole complex process of "petting" begins. This may lead to a third sexual activity which is quite specifically sexual in nature—namely deep kissing, in which the tongue of one partner enters the mouth of the other. This is by no means universal, and apparently many teenagers do not enjoy it.

Up to this point (i.e., kissing), society normally accepts the learning processes of sexual behavior with little restriction, and the partners are free to carry on in semipublic or even public places. However, as petting gradually increases, both in intensity and scope, the couple starts further explorations of each other's body. Since society usually frowns on this, the partners tend to seek privacy. This will lead to a fourth sexual activity, the boy's manual stimulation of the girl's breasts over her clothes. In due course this usually leads to the fifth sexual activity, stimulation of the girl's breast under her clothes. Compared to previous activities, this aspect seems to represent a rather significant degree of sexual sophistication.

As bodily exploration continues, active and passive manual stimulation of the genitals themselves will commonly occur. In the active case (the sixth sexual activity) the boy or girl stimulates the genitals of the sexual partner; in the passive case (the seventh), the boy's or the girl's genitals are being stimulated by the partner. The reality is that boys fondle girls' genitals more than girls fondle boys'. Finally, the eighth sexual activity prior to sexual intercourse is actual genital apposition, in which the sex organs of each partner are in immediate contact but there is no intromission. It is important to note that genital apposition does not inevitably lead to sexual intercourse, but is commonly a temporarily terminal sexual activity for many teenagers. In fact it seems quite probable that many young teenagers in a state of sexual ignorance mistake genital apposition for sexual intercourse.

Sexual intercourse itself does, of course, occur in quite young people, but the treatment of this will be left to following chapters. What is of interest here is the incidence of the aforementioned sexual activities, that is, how much sexual activity there is in young people, and at what ages it occurs. Once again, figures are difficult to obtain for a variety of reasons, and also there are large differences between socioeconomic groups and between those with different cultural backgrounds. Kinsey's figures on the subject are old and probably have little meaning today, and in addition were heavily weighted in the upper middle class U.S.A. On the other hand, the recent study by Dr. Robert C. Sorensen, *Adolescent Sexuality in Contemporary America*, (New York, World Publishing Company, 1973)—the Sorensen Report referred to earlier, gives a great deal of up-to-date information.

ADOLESCENT SEXUAL EXPERIENCE

Dr. Sorensen is an experienced social psychologist, and both he and his team prepared their study in great detail in order to minimize the errors which commonly occur in most questionnaire type surveys. Their sample of the adolescent population was large and nationwide, and was chosen from the age group of 13 through 19. Consent was obtained from both the adolescents and their parents before the questionnaires were submitted. It is important to note that the survey comprised simply the sampling of the 13 through 19 age group, and there was a minimum of breakdown within the group. Those without any sexual experience were included along with married adolescents, but two sizable groups were more or less omitted: so-called "institutionalized" adolescents—those in jails, reformatories, hospitals, boarding schools, college dormitories, and military service—and so-called invisible adolescents—runaways, drifters, and transients. As Sorensen points out, they did try to contact the latter group (though on a small scale) because it is rapidly increasing in numbers and may be having considerable influence on other, more stable young people. Despite these inevitable omissions, Sorensen's sample seems to be by far the most accurate of any survey in this country.

The Sorensen Report is very difficult to summarize because of the vast amount of information it contains on the attitude of adolescents to such diverse subjects as sex and parents, personal sexual values, homosexuality, marriage, venereal diseases, and contraception, to name but a few, and the reader can do no better than refer to the original work. What is pertinent here, however, is the actual amount of sexual activity which Sorensen found to be taking place within his 13 through 19 age sample. It was found that within this age group, 80% of boys and 75% of girls had experienced sexual intercourse or other sexual activities. It follows that 20% of boys and 25% of girls are sexually inexperienced, which Sorensen defines as "total absence of any sexual contact with another person, other than kissing, that either aimed at or resulted in pleasurable physical reactions." As might be expected, sexual inexperience declines as a person grows older, but 16 seems to be a crucial age, for it was found that at 15 years of age only 68% of adolescents had had some sexual experience, but at 16 years the figure was 90%. The figures for actual sexual intercourse within the 13 through 19 age group were that 52% had had sexual intercourse, 59% of boys and 45% of girls. In boys the figure rises from 44% (ages 13 through 15) to 72% (ages 16 through 19), while in girls it is 30% at ages 13 through 15 and 57% at ages 16 through 19. There are no earlier figures from this country with which to compare the figures from the Sorensen Report, but there is little doubt that young people today do

Table 5.1
Percentage of males who had participated in a sexual activity at least once;
by age groups (Michael Schofield, *The Sexual Behavior of Young People,*
©1965 Longmans Publishing Co., London; Little, Brown, and Co., Boston,
p. 29.)

Activity	Younger (15-17) %	Older (17-19) %	Total (15-19) %
Dating	78	93	85
Kissing	78	92	85
Deep kissing	43	67	54
Breast stimulation over clothes	49	74	62
Breast stimulation under clothes	36	63	49
Active genital stimulation	24	51	37
Passive genital stimulation	16	39	28
Genital apposition	14	38	26
Sexual intercourse	11	30	20
Sample no. (100%)	487	456	934

not share the traditional sexual attitudes or values of their parents—
though it is quite false to imagine that their lives are one long sexual orgy.

There is another highly pertinent study, done in England, which
contains far more detail regarding the sexual behavior of adolescents as
they grow older, and it will be of value to quote some figures from this.
Though there is danger in making direct comparisons between one society
and another, nevertheless, they give some indication of what the overall
situation probably is in most affluent societies. The study is *The Sexual
Behavior of Young People* (1965) by Michael Schofield, referred to
earlier. Michael Schofield is an experienced psychologist and his study was
characterized by large random sample size and the extreme care and skill
with which the questioning of young people was done. The major age
group with which he concerned himself was 15 through 19 years, and
these were divided into two groups, one called the younger (15 through
17) and the other called the older (17 through 19).

Table 5.2
Percentage of females who had participated in a sexual activity at least once; by age groups (*Ibid.*, p. 30)

Activity	Younger (15-17) %	Older (17-19) %	Total (15-19) %
Dating	91	96	93
Kissing	91	96	93
Deep kissing	64	81	72
Breast stimulation over clothes	60	79	69
Breast stimulation under clothes	38	61	49
Active genital stimulation	12	29	20
Passive genital stimulation	22	44	33
Genital apposition	13	29	21
Sexual intercourse	6	16	12
Sample no. (100%)	475	464	939

Table 5.1 shows the percentage of males who had participated in a sexual activity at least once, while Table 5.2 shows the same data for females. In Figure 5.2 the information from Tables 5.1 and 5.2 is plotted graphically, with the age groups added together. The figures speak for themselves and little if any elaboration is necessary. As Michael Schofield points out, however, it can surely be no surprise to anyone that as teenagers grow older their sexual experience increases. Thus, among the 15 through 19 year olds only 20% of males and 12% of females had experienced sexual intercourse. The increase in incidence with age, however, is better shown in Tables 5.3 and 5.4, where the accumulative incidence is shown as a percentage at a particular age. Thus in this sample, 34% of males and 17% of females had experienced sexual intercourse at age 18. It would appear likely that since these studies were done the incidence of sexual activities among the teenagers had considerably increased and may approximate those of this country.

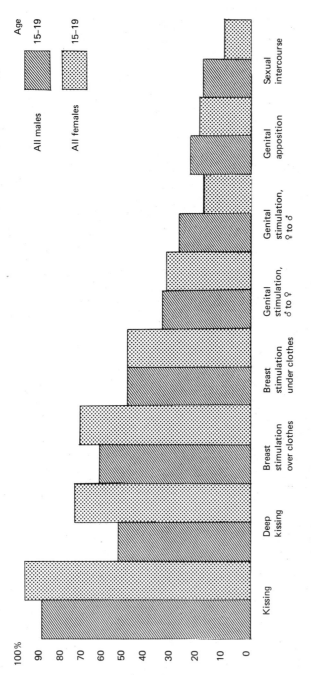

Note: Passive genital stimulation for females is placed with active genital stimulation for males in the fifth category. In the sixth category active genital stimulation for ♀ is placed with passive genital stimulation for ♂. In general ♀ take the passive role in most sexual activities; thus when the activities are put in this order, the overall pattern of sexual development for both sexes is followed.

Fig. 5.2. Diagrammatic representation of the incidence of eight sexual activities shown in percentages for young males and females (*Ibid.*, p. 31)

Table 5.3
Accumulative incidence of seven sexual activities among males showing
percentage with experience at each age (*Ibid.*, p. 33)

Activity	Age							
	Under 12	12	13	14	15	16	17	18
Kissing	3.2	8.9	23.0	47.7	70	82	90	92
Deep kissing	—	0.6	3.0	15.0	27	46	61	70
Breast stimulation over clothes	1.1	2.0	6.0	17.0	36	55	71	80
Breast stimulation under clothes	0.5	1.1	3.5	11.5	25	43	60	69
Active genital stimulation	0.4	1.1	2.1	6.7	16	30	45	56
Passive genital stimulation	0.2	0.9	1.6	4.4	10	22	37	44
Sexual intercourse	0.2	0.5	0.9	2.3	6	14	26	34

Table 5.4
Accumulative incidence of seven sexual activities among females showing
percentage with experience at each age (*Ibid.*, p. 34)

Activity	Age							
	Under 12	12	13	14	15	16	17	18
Kissing	2.1	6.5	25.0	54.0	80	94	95	96
Deep kissing	—	—	3.6	16.6	40	62	75	83
Breast stimulation over clothes	0.2	0.6	3.2	15.0	38	58	74	80
Breast stimulation under clothes	—	—	0.8	7.2	19	36	51	62
Active genital stimulation	—	—	0.1	0.9	4	11	19	31
Passive genital stimulation	—	—	0.1	2.2	10	21	33	46
Sexual intercourse	—	—	0.1	0.4	2	5	10	17

SOCIAL PROBLEMS

It has already been pointed out that in most western societies sexual maturity, as a biological phenomenon, has been occurring earlier and earlier with each generation, though this is now apparently leveling off. At the same time the economic demands of an increasingly technological society require that the young person obtain more and more education, which inevitably means longer financial dependence on parents and society at large, with the result that social maturity is only attainable at a higher and higher age. Thus for both biological and sociological reasons the period of adolescence has been considerably increased. This in itself is difficult enough, but unfortunately it is not all. As a result of our excessively rapid rate of social change, but with an always-lagging political accompaniment, the young adolescent of today is faced with a host of new learning processes, discontinuities, and difficult emotional adjustments and conflicts. Thus autocratic and moralizing parents (or other authorities) who adopt the theme "when I was your age" not only have rather short memories or highly embellished recall (or both!), but fail to realize that the sexual standards of their youth have little relevancy to the youth of today. In a less complex and more static society the demands made on the growing youth are more easily defined and are generally quite clear. In modern society, however, there are no clearly defined roles even between the sexes. This latter aspect is becoming increasingly complex with the new and rapid demands of women to be the social and sexual equals of men, and as a result our concepts of masculinity and feminity are undergoing reevaluation, by men as well as by women. This is particularly the case in sexual roles where the young woman of today is damned if she does and damned if she doesn't! In this respect the sociologist Dr. Clark E. Vincent has pointed out that the "ideal of premarital chastity is discontinuous with the idealization of the honeymoon and the expectation of full sexual responsiveness and enjoyment almost immediately after marriage."*

There are other highly pertinent problems which the growing young people of today face as they slowly and painfully progress from child to adult. Outer signs of adultness in the form of cosmetics and dress (both sexual in nature) are encouraged at an earlier and earlier age by a sophisticated commercialism, but this in no way means that the young are accepted into adult society. On the contrary, depending on the particular state or other political unit, they may not have a bank account or a driver's license until 16, or leave school until 18; they may be forced

---

*Dr. Clark E. Vincent, in *The Adolescent Experience*, p. 18.

into military service at 18 and now allowed to vote, but not to drink a glass of beer; they may enter into a marriage contract at 18 but not into a contract for a loan to buy a house! In fact, not until 21 can they carry out most legal and business transactions, and the body of knowledge required in some professions makes it inevitable that they remain as formal students (who are certainly not accepted as full adults) until age 30 or beyond. Finally, the Constitution forbids them to seek the office of Representative until 25, Senator until 30, and President until 35. Now, these age restrictions are not cited to imply that they are all invalid (though some of them certainly are), for it is true that in the human, as with other mammals, sexual maturity precedes emotional and mental maturity by an appreciable time period. But these instances do point up the fact that the business of growing up in a modern industrial society is a long, tortuous, frustrating, confusing, and conflicting process in which there is no single event or symbol which signifies maturity. Superimposed on these social aspects are the desires of younger and younger bodies for sexual experimentation and outlet, but official morality continues to say, "No, no, no!" As Dr. Lester A. Kirkendall so neatly puts it, "We have come to a time when a reevaluation of the place and meaning of sexuality and morality in our culture can no longer be postponed."*

In any case, traditional sexual morality simply no longer has much meaning to the young, for recent surveys show that one-half of all females and two-thirds of males experience sexual intercourse before marriage. (*Human Sexual Behavior*, Ed. Marshall and Suggs, p. 210.)

STUDY TOPICS

1. Explain the physiological changes that take place in girls at puberty.

2. Explain the physiological changes that take place in boys at puberty.

3 Explain the nature of psychological problems and general health at the time of puberty.

4. Explain the usual sequence of events in interaction between the sexes both before and after puberty.

5. Explain the sequence of sexual learning events which occur after puberty.

---

*Dr. Lester A. Kirkendall, in *The Adolescent Experience*, p. 23.

6. Explain the conflicting social forces at work on a young adolescent growing up in today's society.

7. Do you believe in sexual education from the earliest age possible? Why are people so afraid of it? Discuss this problem with your friends, parents, and teachers.

FOR FURTHER READING

MacCorby, Eleanor E. (Editor), *The Development of Sex Differences.* Stanford, Calif.: Stanford University Press, 1966.

Money, John, and Anke A. Ehrhardt, *Man and Woman, Boy and Girl. The Differentiation and Dimorphism of Gender Identity from Conception to Maturity.* Baltimore: Johns Hopkins University Press, 1973.

Pomeroy, Wardell B., *Boys and Sex.* New York: Dell, 1968.

Pomeroy, Wardell B., *Girls and Sex.* Baltimore: Penguin, 1971.

Sandström, C. I., *The Psychology of Childhood and Adolescence.* London: Penguin Books, 1966, 1970.

Schofield, Michael, *The Sexual Behavior of Young People.* Boston: Little, Brown, 1965, 1969.

Semmens, James, P., and Kermit E. Krantz, *The Adolescent Experience—A Counseling Guide to Social and Sexual Behavior.* New York: Macmillan, 1970.

Sinclair, David, *Human Growth after Birth.* London: Oxford University Press, 1969.

Sorensen, Robert C., *Adolescent Sexuality in Contemporary America.* New York: World, 1973.

Tanner, J.M., "Earlier Maturation in Man." *Scientific American,* January 1968.

Film: *Achieving Sexual Maturity,* 16 mm, color, 21 min. New York: John Wiley & Sons.

CHAPTER SIX

Sexual Intercourse and Response

In Nature's infinite book of secrecy
A little I can read.

William Shakespeare (1564-1616)
Antony and Cleopatra, Act I, Sc. 2

Sexual intercourse, coitus, and copulation are all words which mean essentially the same thing, namely, complete intromission in which the erect penis of the male is fully inside the vagina of the female. This usually results in the internal ejaculation of semen during the male orgasm, and orgasm in the female. It is considered to be the ultimate physical act of sexual relations.

IMPLICATIONS

It is important to note that sexual intercourse between a man and a woman usually has profound and far-reaching emotional implications, and also that it is learned rather than instinctive. Certainly a great deal of learning goes into what may be termed satisfactory and satisfying sexual intercourse. Many writers have pointed out that first experiences in sexual intercourse are likely to be a messy business, and very frustrating or even humiliating for both male and female. In these respects, it is interesting to note one or two facts about the copulatory behavior of our closest living relative, i.e., the chimpanzee. Young male and female chimpanzees raised in total isolation and then brought together when sexually mature cannot perform sexually. This is particularly true of the male, who will reach an advanced state of sexual excitement, but then (to speak figuratively) simply does not know what to do in relation to the female. In some cases they will eventually learn, but in other cases the deprivation of the sexual learning processes in their youth is so great that they cannot copulate when adult. It would be a mistake to automatically assume that exactly the same situation applies to the human, but certainly sexual intercourse is something which is the result of a long and complex learning process which is greatly influenced, for better or worse, by a host of biological and psychological factors. In addition, it should be an act of the utmost responsibility on the part of both partners. Like every other living thing, each human is an individual, and our discussion of sexual intercourse must therefore deal in generalities.

MOTIVATIONS

A human male and female do not simply "decide" to engage in sexual intercourse without previous social relations. There is usually an elaborate social and psychological build up to it. This may take only hours in some cases, but more commonly it takes days, weeks, or even years. The reasons for it, apart from the purely biological ones of desiring sexual activity and release, may vary all the way from what may be described as "dare-devil" exploration to deep emotional attachment between the partners. Particularly in the case of young people who are about to engage in sexual intercourse, it is worthwhile noting Dr. Mary S. Calderone's observation that "She will play at sex in order to gain love, he will play at love in order to gain sex." This is a generalization, of course, but it certainly contains an element of truth. This does not necessarily imply that the male's motivations are purely biological and devoid of emotion, but simply that biologically his sex drive, at least up to the age of about 25, is on the average more intense than the female's. Of course, the sex drive is conditioned to greater or lesser degree by a variety of religious, cultural, and social factors. Some modern feminists have argued that perhaps young males appear to have a greater sex drive than young females merely because most young girls are brought up with negative attitudes toward sex. While this is a difficult point on which to make a positive statement, it does seem that there are sound reasons for thinking there is a determining factor which is mainly biological. This is the behavioral influence of the hormone testosterone (chemically the same in a vast variety of male animals as well as man), which in animal experiments clearly indicates that it is responsible for the generally more assertive sexual behavior of males. It would appear likely that this is also the case in humans. In modern industrialized societies, males are said to reach the peak of their sexual drive at about age 19 or 20, on the average, while females do not reach it until about 25 to 30—at which time their sex drive may well exceed that of males of a similar age.

TACTILE STIMULATION

As sexual intercourse is approached, the overwhelming stimuli are tactile (touch), and they may become very intense. In courtship, or pre-copulatory behavior, much tactile stimulation may be carried out in a standing or sitting position, but as the sexual partners proceed toward sexual intercourse they almost always tend to a more and more prone position. The organs used for tactile stimulation are not just the hands, fingers, lips, and tongue, but also the legs and particularly the thighs. Kissing contacts typically are extended all over the body and the hands caress widely, eventually including the buttocks and the genitalia. The male usually pays particular attention to the female's breasts and nipples with both his hands and his lips. There is much intertwining of arms and legs, with body pressed close to body, and these movements can at times seem almost violent. But in partners who are emotionally well adjusted, these apparently struggling movements are really a form of play which increases the sexual excitement and helps to bring the partners to the point where intromission can be accomplished satisfactorily.

INTROMISSION

Intromission of the female's vagina by the erect penis of the male is a process which normally requires the active physical cooperation of both partners, and certainly both should be emotionally ready for it. It may be less obvious that both partners should also understand certain important psychological factors. The man who wishes to establish good sexual relations with his partner should realize that to be penetrated is quite a different matter than to penetrate. Initial intromission is likely to be painful to a woman, however temporarily, because the hymen may have to be ruptured and the vagina stretched. Also, for a woman to receive another person into herself involves psychological aspects—usually but perhaps not exclusively favorable—which are outside the scope of this book. The second factor the man should be aware of is that sexual intercourse presents to virtually every woman the risk of becoming pregnant. While it is true that in the proper circumstances the risk is vanishingly small, the man should be aware that a woman's fear of the consequences of an unwanted pregnancy is something that no male is likely to fully understand. Thus gentleness, patience, and consideration should be guidelines for the male.

For her part, the woman who wants to establish good sexual relations with her partner should be aware that it is precisely at the point of intromission that many men fail, particularly in initial sexual experiences. They may be so sexually excited that they are unable to withhold ejaculation, and so it takes place outside the vagina, with the following rapid loss of erection making intromission impossible. Or ejaculation and loss of erection may occur almost immediately after intromission. Either way, it leaves the female very frustrated. The humiliation of such failure (and men are usually well aware of it) is more intense than a woman is likely to realize. Thus sympathy and understanding should be her guidelines.

POSITIONS

In human beings the front-to-front position of sexual intercourse is by far the most common, and it is interesting that there are very few other mammals who use this position. Almost all other mammals copulate by the male mounting the female from behind, and this is true of our close primate relatives also. At one time it was thought that this front-to-front position in humans was culturally conditioned rather than biologically determined. However, this does not seem to be the case, for Ford and Beach (*Patterns of Sexual Behavior*, 1951) in their extensive cross-cultural surveys, found that the front-to-front position of sexual intercourse was almost universally the primary position. This position would seem to be biologically determined as a result of the human's upright posture and the angle of the female's vagina, which slopes up and back from its opening. This should not be taken to mean that there is anything abnormal or wrong in preferring to have sexual intercourse with male intromission from behind, but simply that the front-to-front position is by far the most common. Within this latter category there are many variations which every couple should experiment with until they find what is most satisfactory for them. Furthermore their desires in this respect may change as time goes by, just as their sexual desires in general will change. In western cultures, with which most readers of this book will be familiar, the typical and probably most common position is with the woman lying on her back, and the male lying on top facing her (Fig. 6.1). So common is this in our culture that it has even been described as "the American way—male on top," and it is certainly the way in which most couples probably start out. However, many variations are possible. The position can easily be reversed, with the male lying on his back and the female lying on top facing him (Fig. 6.2). It is not surprising that many women prefer this position; men are commonly larger and heavier than women—in some cases very much so—and consequently the male-on-top position may sometimes be very uncomfortable for the female. Another position that many women enjoy is with the male again lying on his back, but with the female partly kneeling and partly sitting astride his thighs (Fig. 6.3). In this position the female has much more control over intromission and movement of the penis within the vagina. In addition, it is simple for her to lower and stretch each of her legs in turn so that she may change to lying full length on top. Yet another popular position, and one which some prefer, is with both partners lying on their sides, front-to-front (Fig. 6.4). It is not difficult to change from this position to either of the prone positions, and vice versa, without interrupting coitus. Coitus may also take place with both partners kneeling face-to-face, or standing face-to-face, and there may of course be variations of any of the positions just described. Every couple desiring good sexual relations should experiment with the various positions, and try to work out what is satisfactory for each partner.

Fig. 6.1. Coital position with female lying on her back and male lying face-to-face on top. Both are in the plateau phase of the sexual response cycle. (Photograph by Wilbur Gregg.)

Fig. 6.2. Coital position with male lying on his back and female lying face-to-face on top. Both are in the plateau phase of the sexual response cycle. (Photograph by Wilbur Gregg.)

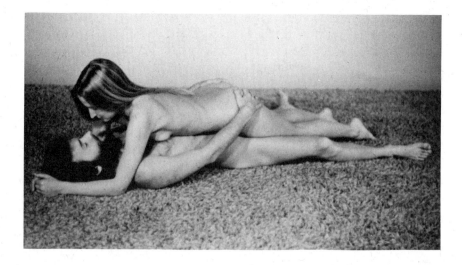

Fig. 6.3. Coital position with male lying on his back and female partly
kneeling, partly sitting astride his thighs and hips. Both are in the plateau
phase of the sexual response cycle. (Photograph by Wilbur Gregg.)

Fig. 6.4. Coital position with both partners lying on their sides, face-to-face. They are
in the plateau phase of the sexual response cycle. (Photograph by Wilbur Gregg.)

THE ORGASM

Once intromission has been accomplished, the male will usually, and more or less involuntarily, start a series of pelvic thrusts with the apparent desire to penetrate as deeply as possible. This no doubt has biological significance in that the deeper the intromission the more likely it is that the sperm will reach the opening of the cervix and thus eventually fertilize an egg. The female, particularly when experienced, may respond with pelvic thrusts of her own in a rhythmic manner, and thus the sexual partners acting in unison may experience a period of intense physical pleasure which, again in experienced partners, may be prolonged for some time. However, sooner or later, one or the other of the partners, and ideally both, will reach orgasm though not necessarily simultaneously. This latter fact should not cause undue concern, as it is certainly not essential for satisfactory sexual relations that both partners reach orgasm at the same time. The most common situation is that the male will reach orgasm first, though experienced males can often control themselves well enough to permit the female to reach orgasm before they do. If the male does reach orgasm before the female, there is the danger that she may be left without sufficient stimulation from her partner to reach orgasm. At such a time it is particularly important that the male (despite his natural desire to relax and sleep) continue to pay attention to the female—her breasts, lips, etc.—so that she is assisted to orgasm. It may also be necessary for her to do a certain amount of manual self-stimulation of the clitoris, depending on the circumstances. In any case the important thing is that each partner should be concerned and try to achieve understanding of the other's needs and desires. In these respects there are commonly serious communication barriers, and every effort should be made to overcome these in order that good sexual relations can be established. The attitudes of both partners should be of tolerance, experimentation, concern, and patience. If either partner ignores these attitudes, then deep hostility is likely to develop, and a mutually satisfying sexual relationship will be virtually impossible. This, in turn, is likely to lead to general incompatibility.

The sensations experienced in both male and female orgasm are difficult to describe for those who have not experienced it. The one major difference is that there is no equivalent in the female of the male's ejaculation, but in other respects the sensations of both are probably essentially the same. Orgasm commonly lasts only a few seconds in both male and female, though in some females there may be more than one, following immediately on the last. Orgasm is a short process of intense physical and emotional experience leading to the immediate release of sexual tensions. It is of biological interest that orgasm is a phenomenon peculiar to humans. No other mammal exhibits anything resembling orgasm in its sexual behavior. Male mammals ejaculate, of course, but there is apparently no equivalent of orgasm in either male or female. Both male and female monkeys, for example, walk away from copulation with apparent utter disinterest—though this is of course an anthropomorphic interpretation! Since from a biological point of view only ejaculation in the male is necessary, one might ask what the function of the orgasm is in humans. No precise answer to this is possible, but one can speculate that since orgasm is an extremely enjoyable physical experience it would tend to bring the individuals back for more, with obvious advantages for the chances of increased reproduction. It probably evolved in humans along with the menstrual cycle, which made the female continuously sexually receptive to the male, and also as a part of the human's enormous and complex emotional development.

THE SEXUAL RESPONSE CYCLE

The various biophysical changes which take place during the entire process of sexual intercourse have been called "the sexual response cycle" by Masters and Johnson (*Human Sexual Response,* 1966). They have rendered a great social and scientific service by accurately recording these changes in experimental subjects, and thus have enormously increased our knowledge of this overwhelmingly important biological process. They have arbitrarily divided the sexual response cycle into four phases: the excitement phase, the plateau phase, the orgasmic phase, and the resolution phase. These four phases occur progressively within the entire response cycle, but it should be clearly realized that there is no sharp dividing line between any two; one gradually progresses into the next. Also, the total time of the entire cycle, as well as each phase within it, may vary considerably from individual to individual and depending on the particular circumstances. Likewise the intensity of the response cycle may vary, as well as its duration, and it seems that both of these aspects (as well as others) are more variable in women than in men. Masters and Johnson refer to the "infinite variety in female sexual response,"* while pointing out that men tend to follow a more standard pattern with less individual variation. Nevertheless, in both male and female there are two major physiological responses which are apparent during sexual stimulation leading to the response cycle; these are generalized congestion of the

---

*William H. Masters and Virginia E. Johnson, *Human Sexual Response*. Boston: Little, Brown and Co., 1966, p.4.

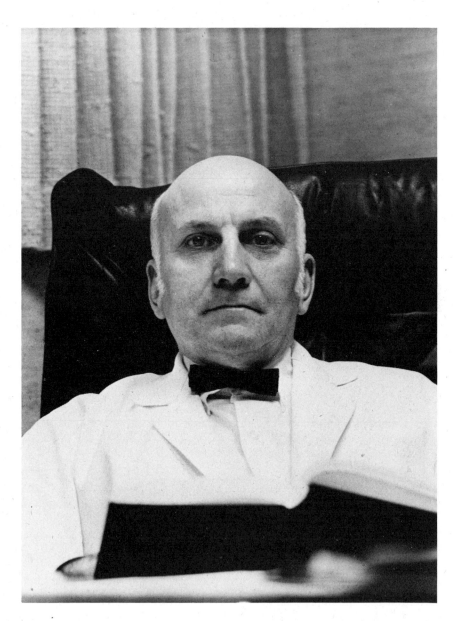

William H. Masters (Photograph by Howard
Earl Day, reproduced by courtesy of the
Reproductive Biology Research Foundation.)

blood vessels and increased muscular tension. Within the framework of these two major responses there are a host of bodily changes which take place, more or less in sequence, during a complete sexual response cycle, and these will now be described for each sex in turn, starting with the female.

Female Sexual Response Cycle

The sexual response cycle of the female has been divided into four phases: Excitement, Plateau, Orgasmic, and Resolution.

Excitement Phase. This phase is said to be initiated by any effective sexual stimulus. The stimulus may be purely psychic, or it may be more directly sensual, such as the sight, sound, or touch of the sexual object, or a combination of these stimuli. Regardless of how the excitement phase is initiated, the physiological responses are the same. In the female the first observable reaction is vaginal lubrication, which occurs within seconds after any effective sexual stimulation. It was formerly thought that the source of this lubrication was the cervix or Bartholin's glands, but it has now been conclusively demonstrated that neither of these plays any effective lubricating role. The mucoid lubricating fluid in fact comes directly from the walls of the vaginal barrel. It is usually profuse in quantity and has the obvious biological function of preparing the vagina to engulf the erect penis. Once this initial response is underway, a variety of other changes lead to the excitement phase (compare Figs. 6.5 and 6.6). The inner two-thirds of the vaginal barrel begins to lengthen and distend from its normally closed condition, and in time this increase in distension is truly remarkable. It is even further increased by the fact that the cervix and body of the uterus are pulled upward from their normal position, projecting into the vaginal barrel. As this distension proceeds, the walls of the vagina become congested with blood, darkening their color. At this time there is also a slight thickening of the outer one-third of the vaginal barrel.

In addition to the changes in the vagina during the excitement phase, other organs respond as well. The shaft of the clitoris increases in diameter, though rarely in length, and there may be a slight increase in the tumescence of the glans clitoris. In the past these slight changes in the clitoris have been interpreted as corresponding to erection of the penis in the male, but this interpretation does not seem to be correct. Concurrent with the increased tumescence of the clitoris, the labia minora become engorged with blood, increasing their diameter considerably. At the same time the labia majora tend to flatten somewhat and retract away from the midline of the vulva. The nipples of the breasts become erect and there is

an actual increase in the size of the breasts. There may also be a so-called
sex flush, a rash (described as measles-like) which starts under the rib cage
and spreads over the breasts. Finally, there is an overall increase in
muscular tension.

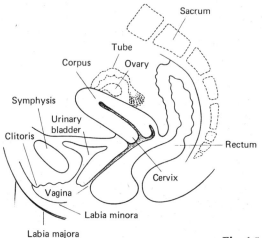

Fig. 6.5. Female pelvic organs during the
unexcited or normal phase. (Figures 6.5
through 6.14 are reprinted by permission
from William H. Masters and Virginia E.
Johnson, *Human Sexual Response.* Boston: Little, Brown and Co., 1966.

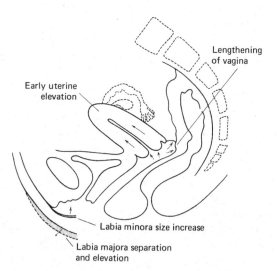

Fig. 6.6. Female pelvic organs
during the excitement phase.

Plateau Phase. As sexual tensions mount, the female reproductive system enters the plateau phase (Fig. 6.7). The walls of the outer one-third of the vagina become greatly engorged with blood, so much so that the internal space is actually reduced from what it was in the excitement phase. The labia minora also become further engorged with blood, greatly increasing their diameter and length. In the state of plateau-phase vasocongestion this whole area, the outer one-third of the vagina and the labia minora, develop a tension reaction called the "orgasmic platform," so called because it is from here that the physiological phenomena occurring during orgasm seem to emanate. During the plateau-phase, the labia minora also undergo color changes which depend on whether the woman has had children. In those women who have not had children the change is from pink to bright red, while in women who have had children the change is to a deeper red. At this time in the response cycle the clitoris undergoes marked changes, in that the entire organ retracts from its normally exposed situation to a position completely covered by the tissue of the clitoral hood, and at the same time the length of the clitoral body decreases by about one-half. It should not be inferred from this retraction of the clitoris that it can no longer be sexually stimulated, but simply that continued stimulation will be indirect through the tissue of the hood. The nipples of the breasts become further engorged with blood, and the sex flush may spread to the abdomen and even to the thighs and the back of the body, as well as reaching a peak in color. There is further muscle tension, breathing tends to become deeper, and both the heart rate and blood pressure increase markedly as the tensions rise toward orgasm.

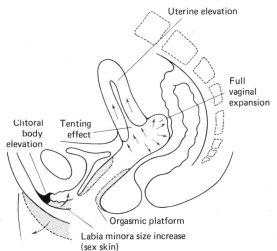

Fig. 6.7. Female pelvic organs during the plateau phase.

Orgasmic Phase. The orgasmic experience is commonly described as an explosive physiological event of short duration. The sensations accompanying it are intense, which is not surprising when it is realized what is occurring. Fortunately, we now have both subjective and objective accounts of this experience from the work of Masters and Johnson, and before proceeding to the actual physiology of the event a few words are in order concerning the female's subjective experience, which has been divided into three stages. During the first stage of orgasm women describe a sensation of "suspension" which lasts only an instant, and is followed immediately by a feeling of "intense sensual awareness, clitorally oriented, but radiating upward into the pelvis" (Masters and Johnson, p. 135). Simultaneous with this there is usually a decrease in the acuteness of sensory perception. As the subjective progression of orgasm proceeds into the second stage, virtually all women describe a sensation of "suffusion of warmth," specifically in the pelvic area but rapidly spreading to the rest of the body. Finally, in the third stage, there is a feeling of "pelvic throbbing" and this sensation seems to have its focus in the vagina or lower pelvis.

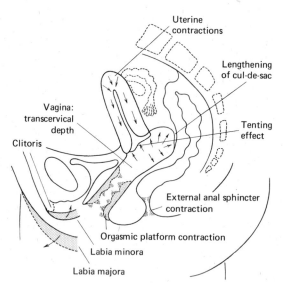

Fig. 6.8. Female pelvic organs during the orgasmic phase.

The physiological events accompanying orgasm (Fig. 6.8) start with strong muscular contractions in the outer one-third of the vaginal barrel, i.e., the orgasmic platform. The first contraction may last two to four seconds, but thereafter the contractions are rhythmic and are at intervals of about 0.8 second. Depending on the individual woman and her particular orgasmic experience, these rhythmic contractions may range from 3 to 15, and their intensity is greatest at the beginning, gradually dying away. There is little change in the inner two-thirds of the vagina, except perhaps for a tendency to expand. There are, however, distinct contractions of the muscles of the uterus which occur only in the orgasmic phase. Neither the labia majora, labia minora, clitoris, nor breasts show changes of any appreciable significance. The sex flush is already at a peak of color intensity and distribution. There may be strong muscular contractions, both voluntary and involuntary, in many parts of the body, including the rectal sphincter muscle which often contracts rhythmically at the same rate as the orgasmic platform. The respiratory rate may reach a peak of two or three times normal, the heart rate may be twice as high as normal, and the blood pressure as much as one-third above normal. Finally, it is important to note that some women have the ability to achieve multiple orgasms—that is two, three, or even more orgasms without appreciable loss of plateau phase excitement levels—and in rare cases may actually have a prolonged orgasm of up to a minute's duration.

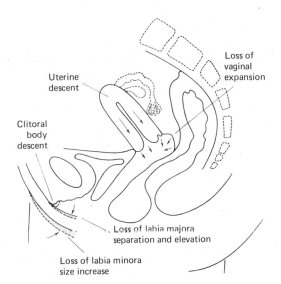

Loss of vaginal expansion

Uterine descent

Clitoral body descent

Loss of labia majora separation and elevation

Loss of labia minora size increase

Fig. 6.9. Female pelvic organs during the resolution phase.

Resolution Phase. As orgasm terminates and the resolution phase starts, changes begin (Fig. 6.9) which will gradually return the sexually responding female to the normal or unexcited stage. The blood which engorged the walls of the outer third the vagina disperses rapidly, slightly increasing the internal space of this part of the vagina. The inner two-thirds of the vaginal barrel gradually shrinks back to its unexpanded state and its color returns to normal. Simultaneously the uterus descends toward the vaginal barrel with the cervix again projecting into it. The labia minora quickly change to their normal color and decrease in size, while the labia majora return to their normal thickness and close toward the midline. The clitoris rapidly returns from under the clitoral hood to its normal exposed position, though its return to normal size may take considerably longer. The nipples and the breasts themselves gradually decrease in size, and the sex flush disappears from the different parts of the body in almost the reverse order in which it appeared. The body muscles relax quickly; breathing, heart rate, and blood pressure return to normal. Finally it is common for a film of perspiration to cover the body, and there is commonly, though not always, an urge to sleep.

Before going on to our discussion of the male sexual response cycle we should correct some of the long-standing misconceptions about the female orgasm. In the first place it is important to stress that the clitoris is the primary organ involved in the attainment of erotic sensations, and that the stimulation of the clitoris may be psychological or directly tactile, though it is not easy to separate the two. But despite the primary importance of the clitoris in erotic sensations, it is now well established that the size of neither the clitoral shaft nor the glans has any known influence on female sexual response. While there are great variations in the size of the clitoris, the historical view that women with a large clitoris were more sexually responsive is in fact just one more myth associated with our phallic fallacy. It has also long been held that the exact positioning of the clitoris was important to the female's sexuality, some positions making penile stimulation during coitus easier and more probable and therefore presumably making sexual response greater. The fact of the matter is, however, that during normal coitus the penis very rarely comes in direct contact with the clitoris—especially when the latter withdraws under the clitoral hood—and thus this concept also is still more phallic fallacy. As Masters and Johnson once again so neatly put it "sexually responding women achieve orgasmic levels of sexual tension without regard to variables in the basic anatomy and physiology of the clitoris."* On the other hand, both the method and amount of direct clitoral stimulation do seem important in the attainment of sexual tensions. It is well established that masturbating women choose to stimulate the clitoral shaft, not the glans. The latter is in fact rather painfully sensitive to touch immediately after orgasm and is thus avoided during any restimulation. Tactile stimuli of the clitoris may also be painful

---

*Ibid., p. 58.

if applied for too long or with too much pressure. More important however, is that women usually prefer to stimulate the entire mons area rather than the clitoral body itself and reach orgasmic states in this way. Male sexual partners would do well to bear these facts in mind when learning appropriate techniques of female sexual stimulation. Above all, men should listen to and learn the wishes of their individual female partners rather than what "marriage manuals" state as effective techniques. It is obvious that in this respect at least, the individual woman knows best.

It has long been held that there are really two forms of orgasm—clitoral and vaginal. However, Masters and Johnson have conclusively shown that regardless of the method or area of stimulation, the organs involved respond in the same way. Though there may be greater variation in intensity and duration, depending on the individual and the circumstances, from a biological point of view there is just one type of orgasmic experience.

The different attitudes in our culture toward male and female orgasm (the former having by far the higher status) are perhaps due to both biological and sociological factors. Biologically, the one major difference between them is the male's ejaculation; it is essential for the reproductive process, whereas female orgasm is not. The human species has always been concerned with survival, so it is not surprising that until very recently the reproductive role of ejaculation was considered more important than female orgasm. Furthermore, in our male-dominated cultural background, female sexual expression in the form of orgasm— indeed, female sexual well-being in general—has not been considered as important as that of males, and the generally more repressive sexual attitudes which women have been taught have no doubt played their part in denying women full sexual responsiveness. Despite the undeniable effect of attitude on female orgasm (which will be discussed further in another chapter), the reason that orgasm is so difficult for some women to achieve, and is never achieved by others, cannot at this time be ascribed wholly to negative social and cultural conditioning. There do seem to be biological factors of an hereditary nature involved. From their eleven years of research Masters and Johnson (p. 138) have become convinced that while in females, just as in males, sexual expression does respond to changes in social status and life style, the measurable intensity of orgasmic response does *not* seem to be influenced by psychosocial factors.

Male Sexual Response Cycle

The sexual response cycle of the male has been conveniently divided into the same four phases as the female: Excitement, Plateau, Orgasmic, and Resolution.

Excitement Phase. In the male, just as in the female, this phase is said to be initiated by any effective sexual stimulus. In the male the first known response is the beginning of the erection of the penis (Figs. 6.10 and 6.11), which involves an increase in both the length and the diameter of the penis. Depending on the intensity of the stimulus, and whether or not it is interrupted, the penis may become partially erect, then lose part of that erection, and repeat this pattern several times before complete erection is achieved. On the other hand, if the stimulus is intense, complete erection may be very rapid. At the same time that erection is proceeding, changes in the scrotum and testes begin. The scrotal skin becomes congested and thick, which decreases the internal diameter and the free movement of the testes within the scrotal sac. The testes become elevated by contraction of the cremasteric musculature, and one process reinforces the other in this elevation. At this time there may be some erection of the nipples of the breasts, but this phenomenon varies greatly in men (with women it is almost universal) and is without direct manipulation. (Stimulation of the male's breasts is not usually part of heterosexual activity, though it does commonly occur in homosexual activity.) The same sex flush occurs as in females, though it is less common. It starts under the rib cage and may spread over the chest, neck, and face, and even to the shoulders, arms, and thighs. It may start late in the excitement phase when sexual tension has been rapid, but commonly does not become established until the plateau phase. Both the heart rate and blood

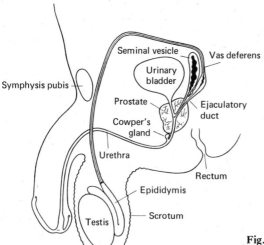

Fig. 6.10. Male pelvic organs during the unexcited or normal phase.

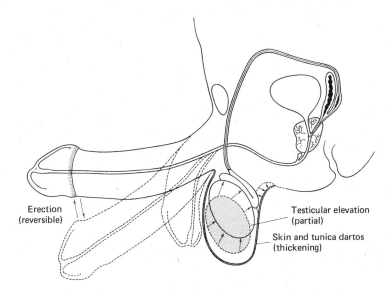

Erection
(reversible)

Testicular elevation
(partial)

Skin and tunica dartos
(thickening)

Fig. 6.11. Male pelvic organs during the excitement phase.

pressure begin to increase, and there is generalized increase in muscle tension with a tendency toward involuntary muscular contractions.

Plateau Phase. As the excitement phase gradates into the plateau phase (Fig. 6.12), there is a slight further increase in the size of the area of the glans penis, and sometimes color changes which apparently correspond to those in the female's labia minora. Also at this time there is a so-called preorgasmic emission of two or three drops of a mucoid substance. This is thought to come from Cowper's glands, and despite many theories as to what it does, its function (if any) is quite unknown. It does normally contain active sperm, but whether these are sufficient in number to cause fertilization is also dubious. The testes continue to be elevated in the scrotal sac until, at the end of plateau phase, they are held close up against the body. This elevation of the testes has been shown to have physiologic importance in that if it does not occur there is a considerable loss of ejaculatory pressure. In addition to the testicular elevation, there is actually an increase in the size of the testes by as much as 50% or even more. If there is a sex flush, it spreads rapidly in the plateau phase. There is further increase in heart rate and blood pressure and also an increase in the rate of respiration. Further muscular tension, both voluntary and involuntary, occurs as the orgasmic phase is reached.

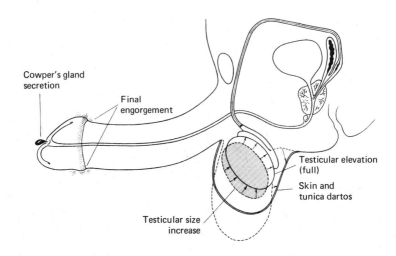

Fig. 6.12. Male pelvic organs during the plateau phase.

Orgasmic Phase. As with the female, the male's orgasmic experience is intense, both subjectively and objectively. Subjectively, men experience a sensation of "inevitability" which occurs just prior to ejaculation and lasts about two or three seconds. This is a very real sensation during which there is the feeling that there is no holding back now, and that self-control is no longer possible. As this feeling of inevitability gives way to the ejaculatory process, the male is aware of the presence of fluid in the urethra, and as ejaculation actually proceeds, he experiences a subjective feeling of intense physical pleasure radiating from the pelvic area throughout the body. The physiology of the actual ejaculatory process (Fig. 6.13) is something about which there is still much to learn. Actual contractions occur as far back as the testis, and continue through the epididymis into the vas deferens, the seminal vesicles, the prostate gland, the urethra, and the penis itself. The first three or four ejaculatory contractions are by far the most powerful and are capable of expelling semen up to 24 inches. They are also rhythmic, occurring at intervals of about 0.8 second (the same as those in the orgasmic platform of the female). Both the frequency and the expulsive force are rapidly reduced, the entire ejaculatory process lasting no more than a few seconds.

During orgasm the testes are held at their maximum elevation, the sex flush (if any) reaches its peak, the heart and respiratory rates may reach two to three times normal, and the blood pressure one-third above

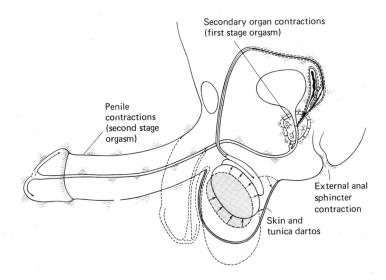

Fig. 6.13. Male pelvic organs during the orgasmic phase.

normal. There is a general loss of voluntary muscle control, with an increase in involuntary contractions including, as in the female, rhythmic contractions of the rectal sphincter, also at intervals of 0.8 second. The phenomenon of multiple orgasms experienced by some females does not occur in males. Neverthless some males, particularly young ones, are able to reach second and third orgasms after very short intervals, even though the volume of semen at each orgasm is progressively reduced. Masters and Johnson (p. 213) record one male who ejaculated three times within 10 minutes. He should be considered exceptional, however, for much longer refractory periods are normal, and they increase considerably as the individual ages.

Resolution Phase. Immediately after ejaculation is finished, a two-stage process begins by which erection is eventually lost and the penis returns to the flaccid state (Fig. 6.14). In the primary stage some 50% of the erection is lost rather rapidly; in the secondary stage, which lasts much longer, the penis returns to its normal unstimulated size. Many factors may affect the rate at which the penis returns from the erect to normal size, but the principal one is simply the degree to which close physical contact is maintained with the sexual partner after ejaculation. Maintaining the penis within the vagina for some time, followed by intimate

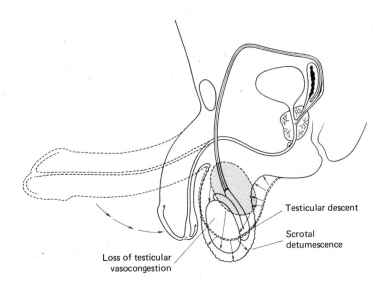

Fig. 6.14. Male pelvic organs during the resolution phase.

physical contact, will slow the process of the return to normal size. If the penis is removed from the vagina immediately after ejaculation, then loss of erection will be much more rapid. If the male subsequently removes himself from close contact with the female, then loss of erection will be more rapid still. It is quite common for the male to desire urination soon after the orgasmic experience, and since urination with a full erection is normally physiologically impossible, the concentration of trying to urinate will rapidly increase the rate of return to normal. In fact, the rate is so rapid that by the end of urination it is commonly complete. Concurrent with the return of the penis to normal size, the scrotum gradually loses its congested and thick nature, allowing the testes to descend and return to normal size, with the end result of a fully relaxed scrotum and free movement of the testes within it. If there has been breast nipple erection, this subsides rather slowly; if there has been a sex flush, this disappears rather rapidly. Similarly the heart rate, blood pressure, and respiration rate all rapidly return to normal. There is a general relaxation of muscles, the individual sometimes breaks out in a profuse sweat, and finally there is a strong desire to sleep. The whole resolution phase may take anything up to two hours, depending on the circumstances and the individual.

INTERCOURSE AND THE HEART

Sometimes people wonder (and not only young people) whether the increase in blood pressure and heart rate observed during sexual intercourse are potentially dangerous to those suffering from various heart diseases. In other words, is sexual intercourse an added strain on the heart? Also, our culture and tradition has always been convinced that orgasm is a far greater physical strain for the male than for the female. Teachers are not uncommonly asked questions such as "Is it true that sexual intercourse for the male is as strenuous as running a four-minute mile?" Well, consider the fact that vast numbers of men engage regularly in sexual intercourse to the point of orgasm, whereas very, very few are capable of running a four-minute mile. The two simply are not comparable. Furthermore there is no evidence that sexual intercourse in the male is more taxing than in the female; Masters and Johnson have shown that the physiological processes are very similar in both sexes. Thus if there are adverse effects on the heart due to sexual intercourse, they probably apply as much to either sex. Very little is known regarding possible detrimental effects of sexual intercourse, and it is an area ripe for thorough investigation. Nevertheless, anyone with serious heart problems should seek professional advice on the matter, for it would seem highly probable that excessive amounts of sexual intercourse in persons suffering from severe heart ailments cannot be in the best interests of their physical health.

EMOTIONS

In this chapter the physiological aspects of sexual intercourse have been described on a somewhat impersonal and purely biological basis. This approach facilitates the discussion and learning process, but it should not be inferred that in humans, above all animals, sexual intercourse is a purely biological process. Almost all human behavior is conditioned in one way or another by the enormous evolutionary development of the emotions in humans, and sexual behavior is literally permeated by the emotions. Furthermore, humans are not primarily promiscuous animals. In some modern communes it is the rule that everyone sleep with a different partner each night, but this simply doesn't last long. Sooner or later partners "pair off," and usually sooner. Of more importance still is one of the main conclusions of the recent (1976) Hite Report. From questions posed to over 3,000 women, from ages 14-78, it is quite clear that for women at least, what the overwhelming majority want is a loving relationship with a sexual partner. Sex relations by themselves are just not enough. The Hite Report has a wealth of modern information on women's attitudes and desires towards sex, and readers would do well to consult it.

Quite apart from any moral considerations, it is simply in the best interests (both physically and emotionally) of sexual partners that they learn from each other how to achieve good sexual relations. This takes time, practice, patience, understanding, communication, compassion, and above all—love. The aim, which inevitably will be achieved only in part, should be to reach a satisfying sexual relationship which can change and grow with time, without either partner making demands on the other. The Beatles put it very well. "In the end the love you take is equal to the love you make."* Sexual relations and love go hand-in-hand; both are fragile and both need great care.

STUDY TOPICS

1. Why is sexual intercourse said to be learned in men and women?

2. What fears and/or anxieties are commonly found in both men and women prior to first experiences in coitus?

3. What are the main coital positions? Are these culturally or biologically determined?

4. Discuss the possible benefits of the various coital positions.

5. In what ways does orgasm differ in the male and female?

6. What is the biological significance of orgasm in males and females?

7. What is meant by the "sexual response cycle" and what are its various stages?

8. Describe the "sexual response cycle" in the human female.

9. Describe the "sexual response cycle" in the human male.

10. Discuss the various problems of achieving orgasm during sexual intercourse.

11. Discuss the problems of sexual intercourse in relation to heart disease.

12. What do you consider to be important ethical and moral considerations in sexual intercourse?

---

*John Lennon and Paul McCartney, The End. ©Northern Songs, Ltd., 12 Bruton St., London W1X 7AH. Reproduced by permission.

FOR FURTHER READING

Brecher, Ruth, and Edward Brecher, (Editors), *An Analysis of Human Sexual Response*. New York: Signet Books, 1966.

Hite, Shere, *The Hite Report*. New York: Macmillan, 1976.

Masters, William H., and Virginia E. Johnson, *Human Sexual Response*. Boston: Little, Brown, 1966.

McCary, James Leslie., *Human Sexuality*. New York: D. Van Nostrand, 1973.

SIECUS, Editors., *Sexuality and Man*. New York: Charles Scribner's Sons, 1967.

Film: *The Sexually Mature Adult*, 16 mm, color, 16 min. New York: John Wiley & Sons.

CHAPTER SEVEN
Sexual Difficulties and Failures

No sooner met but they look'd; no sooner look'd but they lov'd; no sooner lov'd but they sigh'd; no sooner sigh'd but they ask'd one another the reason; no sooner knew the reason but they sought the remedy.

William Shakespeare (1564-1616)
As You Like It, Act V, Sc. 2.

Like all things biological, the differences in the ability and desire of individual humans to engage in sexual relations are enormous. Similarly, the variations in the quantity of sexual relations are great too. Thus some men and women, for one reason or another, are unable to engage in sexual intercourse throughout their entire lives, while on the other hand some may experience coitus and/or orgasm several times a day over long periods of time. Furthermore, some people look forward to and experience sexual relations with the utmost pleasure and satisfaction, while others view them with apprehension and horror, and experience them with reluctance and even disgust. More distressing still is the fact that sexual difficulties frequently cause serious psychological problems, hostility between sexual partners, and even complete breakdown of a person's ego and personality. What can be described as normal or abnormal is purely arbitrary; nevertheless, there are various rather easily defined sexual difficulties which create serious problems in people's lives, and some of these will be discussed now.

FEARS OF PERFORMANCE

In western cultures there are certain traditional attitudes which have had grave effects on the sexual functioning of both male and female. In the case of the male the overwhelming belief has been that he is the dominant member of the two sexes, and that it is up to him to perform sexually and to satisfy the female (though it was somehow her fault if he didn't!). This has generated in the male the so-called fear of performance, the fear that in some way he will be sexually inadequate. In the case of the female, on the other hand, the overwhelming belief has been that she is the passive sexual partner, not really supposed to enjoy sexual relations, but to supply the outlet for the dominant male's sexual desires and of course to produce children. Such ignorance and dogmatic belief has wrought havoc for centuries, and has survived too far into our own age. It is one of the brighter signs of our times that ignorance in sexual matters is gradually being overcome, and that the basic sexual nature and functioning of both males and females are undergoing thorough examination. It seems unlikely that anything but good can come from this.

Regardless of the nature of any particular sexual inadequacy, fears of performance are almost bound to affect both partners adversely. For example, if the male tends to be impotent, he will approach any opportunity for sexual intercourse with the fear that he will fail to obtain an erection, or that if he does he will be unable to retain it long enough to achieve coitus. This fear can be so intense that as such a man approaches a sexual situation, he loses all sense of the pleasure associated with this naturally occurring event, and may even break out in a cold sweat. Thus the fear itself destroys the nature of the sexual situation, and an erection becomes virtually impossible. On the other hand, the female partner of such a man is constantly worried not only on his behalf, but also that she will do something or behave in such a way as to embarrass him or aggravate his problem. Thus the sexual partners turn what should be a pleasurable and natural part of their relationship into a fear-ridden emotional nightmare. The same sort of situation can develop in reverse if the female has difficulty achieving orgasm—whatever the reason may be. She starts to worry that something is wrong with her, or that she is sexually inadequate. During sexual intercourse her fear of performance becomes the dominant aspect of the event, which of course only aggravates her problem. The concerned male partner, on the other hand, fears that it is his inadequacy which is responsible for her failure to reach orgasm.

These are only examples of how the culturally stereotyped "behavioral norm" causes such traumatic misery in so many couples. Much of this, though perhaps not all, could be averted if people could learn to cast off the culturally imposed ideal sexual image, and realize that they are individuals with individual needs, desires, and problems which may not at all fit the "ideal." Yet again, sexual partners with fear-of-performance problems would do well to cultivate an atmosphere of open and complete communication with each other, rather than trying to bottle up their fears. With our cultural hangover of the Puritan belief that "sex is sin," this is not easy, but perseverance will surely help to overcome the fear of inadequacy, which Masters and Johnson identify as "the greatest known deterrent to effective sexual functioning."* While fear of inadequacy no doubt is the biggest problem, this only begs the question as to what causes the fear. The answer is not easy to come by, since a person's sexual behavior and attitudes cannot be separated from the whole person, who is a result of the entire biological, psychological, social, and cultural complex which has molded him or her. Despite this there are certain well established biological and environmental aspects which may be wholly or partially responsible for any or all sexual failures. These include the purely biological factors which may cause sexual failure in a multitude of ways: anatomic deformities; cardiorespiratory diseases; endocrine, urogenital, vascular, hereditary, neurologic (especially those with spinal cord injuries), and infectious diseases; and an enormous variety of drugs (including alcohol). At the psychological and social level, causes of sexual malfunction include the severely damaging effects of religious

---

*William H. Masters and Virginia E. Johnson, *Human Sexual Inadequacy:* Boston: Little, Brown and Co., 1970, p. 12.

Virginia Johnson (Reproduced by courtesy of the
Reproductive Biology Research Foundation.)

orthodoxy and suppression, maternal or paternal dominance (or both) with concurrent repression, influences of a one-parent family, and homosexual orientations, to name but a few. It is quite impossible in a book of this nature to attempt a description of the many pathological causes which may result in sexual malfunction, but certainly they should be recognized and professionally treated as far as is possible. However, some of the primarily environmental causes of sexual failure are now quite well documented, and a consideration of these is in order.

SEXUAL PROBLEMS OF THE MALE

The major problems of male sexual malfunctioning are several, and indeed a book could be written on that subject alone. Space limitations preclude the attempt in this work, and so we will discuss only what are perhaps the two most common of such problems: premature ejaculation and impotence, primary and secondary.

Premature Ejaculation

Perhaps the most common form of sexual failure in the male is premature ejaculation—which is simply ejaculation any time prior to the female partner's orgasm. It may even occur before the penis is inserted into the vagina—possibly even during preliminary sex play, before the woman herself is sexually aroused. This may not greatly concern some men, and even some women, for it is a rather sad fact that both male concern for the female's sexual well-being and the female's own feeling of frustration seem to be in direct correlation to the degree of formal education. Males with the least education show the least concern for the female, and females with the least education show the least frustration at the male's inadequacy. In fact, a woman who may simply be a subservient sexual object to a dominant male may welcome his premature ejaculation as a means of minimizing the time spent in sexual intercourse.

Of course, if a woman takes an inordinately long time to achieve orgasm, then even a male partner with quite good control is likely to have a premature ejaculation. Nevertheless, for many males it is a very real problem to delay ejaculation long enough to gratify the needs of a normally responsive woman. This is a serious condition, for when a woman becomes highly sexually aroused during sex play, and her sexual tensions are elevated still further by intromission of the penis into the vagina, to have the male ejaculate at once and then lose his erection literally leaves her "in the lurch." If this becomes the established pattern of sexual intercourse, her frustration will be intense, giving rise to serious problems with far-reaching ill effects to both sexual partners. Thus it behooves the male to learn to control his timing, and as always this will be helped by an understanding and sympathetic female partner.

Although our knowledge is scanty, and though there may be purely biological factors involved, there is fairly good evidence to indicate that males who have too little ejaculatory control have acquired this failing as a result of the particular nature of their first coital experiences. In such males first experiences typically include intercourse with prostitutes, intercourse in semi-private situations such as the back seats of cars, intercourse which involves withdrawal, and situations where male ejaculation takes place without intercourse but in the presence of a female partner. All these first experiences have in common the rapid rise and release of male sex tensions with little concern for the female. Female prostitutes, for example, commonly want coitus to be as quick as possible, and encourage the male in that direction—the quicker the turnover the more profit! It apparently does not take much of this for the male to establish a pattern of rapidly reaching plateau phase tensions and ejaculation, and this certainly involves little concern for the female. Similarly, first experiences in semi-private situations, where an accompanying fear of sudden discovery is almost inevitable, also tend to encourage the male to be as quick as possible with the same undesirable results. Intercourse which involves withdrawal is a little different, for here the usual pattern is some form of sex play until the male reaches plateau phase tension, then intromission with a few quick pelvic thrusts before withdrawal and immediate ejaculation. Withdrawal is, of course, a means of contraception (still the most widely used method in the world), and shows concern for the female to the extent that she should not become pregnant. However, the disadvantages are that the whole coital act is hurried and permeated with fear that the male will not withdraw in time, and there is little incentive for the male to learn ejaculatory control or to aid the female in reaching her orgasm. Finally, there is another type of first experience (usually in teenagers) which apparently leads to premature ejaculation. In this case the sexually excited—but fully clothed—male mounts the female in the male superior position but with no attempt at intromission and rapidly reaches orgasm simply by friction. This releases his sexual tensions, of course, but not hers, and if repeated often is likely to establish a pattern of premature ejaculation. These first experiences are very common, as Masters and Johnson have found, in the histories of males who suffer from lack of ejaculatory control, and while they are no doubt contributary causes it would be folly to assume that they are anything more than that. Our understanding and knowledge of this problem is minute, but at the same time many men who want to can successfully learn ejaculatory control. They must, of course, have the incentive and will to do this, but given these, many men—perhaps a large majority—can succeed, and the results are bound to be worth the effort.

The Squeeze Technique. In order to assist men with this sexual problem, Masters and Johnson have devised a treatment which any sexual partners can carry out without professional help. It is simple, though it may require certain changes in the couple's normal sexual pattern, and when properly carried out with patience and persistence, it has been proven extraordinarily successful. It can be described as follows: The female should sit at the head of the bed with her back against the wall and with her legs apart. Then the male should lie on his back facing his partner, and placed in such a way that his legs are between hers and astride her thighs (Fig. 7.1). This will allow the female easy access to the male's genitals, and simply by direct fondling she should bring the male to full erection. When the male reaches an overwhelming desire to ejaculate the female then employs what is referred to as the "squeeze technique." She places her thumb on the underside of the erect penis just where the glans penis joins the shaft, and the first two fingers on the upper side opposite the thumb (Fig. 7.2). The exact position of the thumb and fingers is important. She then squeezes the penis for about three or four seconds, which will normally cause the male to temporarily lose his ejaculatory urge. The female should not be afraid to apply considerable pressure, in which the male should guide her, for the erect penis can withstand a great deal of pressure without discomfort. After a short interval, the process of fondling and squeezing is repeated, and this may be done several times. By this method the male will gradually gain control. Perhaps even more important, he will gain confidence that it is possible for him to change his pattern of rapid excitement and ejaculation. This whole process should be repeated over a period of days (even weeks or months, if necessary).

Once the male feels he has gained some control the next step should be attempted. This consists of the male lying flat on his back with the female in the kneeling-sitting position, facing him and astride his thighs (Fig. 6.3). After the male has been brought to full erection, the female applies the squeeze technique a couple of times, and then the penis is inserted into the vagina. Both partners should then remain as motionless as possible without any thrusting. This allows the male to learn further control, but if he feels that he is reaching ejaculation too soon, the female can simply raise her body on her knees, which will remove the penis and

Fig. 7.1. Male and female positioned so that female may fondle male's genitals during treatment for premature ejaculation. (Photograph by Wilbur Gregg.)

enable her to apply the squeeze technique again. This whole process of penile insertion with no thrusting, removal, squeeze technique, and insertion again may be carried out several times and repeated over a period of days. Once the male has mastered control under these conditions, or with just enough pelvic thrusting to maintain his erection for some minutes, then the thrusting of both partners can gradually be increased. Finally it should become possible for both partners to change from the female superior position to that of both lying on their sides, if they wish,

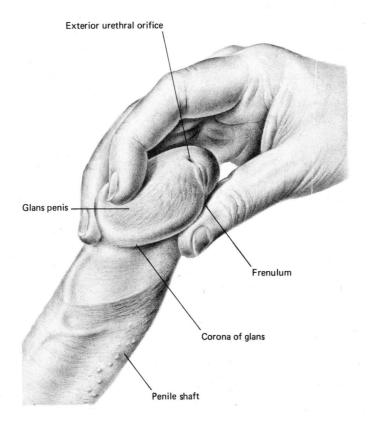

Exterior urethral orifice

Glans penis

Frenulum

Corona of glans

Penile shaft

Fig. 7.2. "Squeeze technique" used during treatment for premature ejaculation.

where coitus can be completed and, ideally, both reach orgasm. The male superior position should be avoided, as it is most difficult for the male to control his ejaculatory urge in this position. The whole process by which the male learns ejaculatory control may take months, and perseverance and patience on the part of both partners is essential. There may even be relapses where the techniques will have to be applied afresh, but the sexual rewards and satisfaction to the couple who achieve success are of inestimable value to their lives.

Impotence

While the problem of ejaculatory control is of great importance in people's sexual lives, it is not likely to have anywhere near such profound effects as that of impotence, i.e., the inability of a male to achieve an erection, or to maintain it long enough for coitus to take place. By its very nature complete impotence will deprive both sexual partners of any sexual intercourse, and it is certainly one of the most distressing things that can afflict a male, for from a psychological point of view it deprives him (rightly or wrongly, but almost inevitably) of what he sees as a very basic part of his manhood. Technically, impotence is divided into two types, primary and secondary. In primary impotence an erection sufficient to achieve coitus has never been obtained. In secondary impotence the male has been able to achieve coitus once or many times, but has then lost this ability.

As pointed out previously (p. 99), impotence, either primary or secondary, may have direct organic causes, and these can only be treated medically where possible. However, it is now well established that in many cases, perhaps a majority, the causes of impotence are due to environmental influences which have a profound psychological effect on the individual. These environmental influences may be multiple and of long duration (perhaps going back into childhood), and commonly result in primary impotence. Or a single traumatic sexual experience may result in impotence either primary or secondary. Some examples taken from the documented clinical work of Masters and Johnson will help to establish the nature of the environmental influences which are thought to be responsible for impotence in individual cases, though there is no guarantee that the same environmental influences will have the same effect on all.

Primary Impotence. Masters and Johnson have observed cases of primary impotence in young males for whom maternal influence and interest had apparently been sexual up into the teenage years. In these cases there was a record of an absentee father and a situation where the sons slept in the mother's bedroom both before and after puberty. In some cases they actually slept in their mother's bed well into the teenage years, and while there were no recorded instances of either actual or attempted incest, there were instances of the mother stimulating the son's genitals right through to ejaculation. Later in the young man's life erective failure developed and coitus became impossible.

A second example involved several cases of primarily impotent men who had had childhood backgrounds of strict religious orthodoxy (though from various sects), and who lived with an excessive burden of "thou shalt-nots." Their sects taught that virtually any form of sexual expression, particularly in the teenage years, was immoral and/or harmful to physical or mental health, and they grew into mature males with a wealth of sexual misinformation and taboos. Unfortunately young males from such repressive religious backgrounds tend to associate with and eventually marry females from like backgrounds. Thus, when attempts at sexual intercourse finally become psychologically (if not biologically) inevitable, both partners are so wrapped in fear and apprehension that the male is physically unable to engage in coitus, and his condition may become permanent.

A third example of primary impotence emerged in men who had a background of homosexual behavioral patterns in their teenage years. The homosexual relationships ranged from only a few months in some cases to a few years in others, but in all cases they were terminated before heterosexual relationships were attempted. Although the range of heterosexual relationships included marriage for many years, sexual intercourse was never possible for the males. It was noted that in these impotent males with homosexual backgrounds, there was great variation in religious training, but in half the cases there was a history of an excessively dominant mother in the family unit.

Finally, a fourth example of primary impotence was found in men who had a history of what may be termed severe "psychological shock" associated with their first attempt at sexual intercourse, which in these cases was with a prostitute. The young men involved were apparently so revolted by the crude and squalid aspects of prostitution that they immediately developed severe fears of performance and an accompanying inability to obtain an erection.

It must be stressed that these are only examples of apparent major causes of primary impotence in men. Masters and Johnson point out, however, that the environmental causes are multiple and by no means clearly understood. Furthermore, any or all such factors as maternal dominance, repressive religious control, or teenage homosexual experiences may cause primary impotence in some males while others survive such experiences without apparent sexual harm. Thus at this stage of our very inadequate knowledge it is extremely dangerous to over generalize about such a complex subject as the causes of primary impotence.

Secondary Impotence. Like primary impotence, secondary impotence may have multiple causes and may develop suddenly or very gradually. Many men have occasional erective failures due to excessive mental or physical fatigue, illness, the use of various drugs, or other factors. These episodes should not be classed as impotency, as they will normally disappear with the temporary cause. Situations arise however, when the rate of failure gradually increases, usually accompanied by fears of performance, and a more or less permanent state of secondary impotence will develop. This of course may also have far-reaching psychological effects on the individual concerned.

On the basis of their extensive clinical experience in treating secondarily impotent males, Masters and Johnson have established at least six major factors which are commonly associated with the development of secondary impotence. These factors may be dominant or only minor contributory causes, while in other cases men may survive them without any apparent sexual malfunctioning. The contributory factors are (1) a history of premature ejaculation, (2) acute alcoholic consumption, (3) maternal dominance, (4) paternal dominance, (5) religious orthodoxy, and (6) homosexuality. Each of these will be discussed briefly, with some actual clinical examples.

1. Premature ejaculation. Many secondarily impotent men have a history of an established pattern of premature ejaculation going back to their first hurried sexual experiences, with little if any subsequent control being learned with a more permanent sexual partner during marriage. Gradually (and not surprisingly) the female partner becomes frustrated with the situation and begins to make her frustrations known by appealing to the male to consider her sexual welfare. These requests to the male may become demands to cease his "selfishness," and eventually may turn into contempt for his whole sexual behavior. A sensitive male partner may easily respond to this by attempting a host of diversionary tactics which are intended to delay ejaculation but which, in one way or another, blunt the physical and emotional input from the female partner. Masters and Johnson consider this to be the first step toward secondary impotence, for from this situation the male may derive fears of performance, and "Once the premature ejaculator develops any in-depth concept that he is sexually inadequate, he is ripe for psychosocial distraction during any sexual encounter."* Finally the male, now under pressure, tries to avoid sexual intercourse, communication with the female declines, and he may literally become disinterested in any sexual advances from her. His disinterest may well include no erective response, and this in turn leads first to more serious fears for his sexual adequacy and eventually to impotency. This whole complex process may take years to develop, and obviously every case will be different, but there seems little doubt that premature ejaculators who do not successfully learn control are predisposed to possible secondary impotence.

---

*Ibid., p. 162.

2. Acute alcoholic consumption. Both the short-term and long-term effects of alcoholic consumption on the human body are legion, though perhaps not as well understood as most people imagine. Thus it is not surprising to find that alcohol can have adverse effects on sexual functioning, and can be an initial causative factor of secondary impotence. The ways in which this may occur are no doubt many, but typically the problem begins in middle life with a male who has a background of regular daily drinking, and who on some particular occasion has entirely too much. On such an occasion he decides, against the obvious wishes of his sexual partner, that he is in the mood to satisfy her sexually, but finds to his amazement that he is unable to achieve an erection. This does not necessarily alarm him at the time, for the alcohol has in any case dulled his mind, and the hangover may last a couple of days anyway. However, he is usually aware of this failure and so is determined to demonstrate to himself and his sexual partner that he is still very much a man. So shortly afterward (well fortified by two or three drinks) he again attempts to perform sexually, only to find that he is a total failure—due probably as much to his conscious concern as to the alcohol. From this point onward the individual may be in a state where "fears of sexual performance have assumed full control of his psychosocial system."* He worries, and the worries may be transferred to his sexual partner. He begins to avoid potential sexual situations. He feigns tiredness. Communication between the sexual partners becomes strained and generally declines with adverse effects on their whole lives. The impotence is not necessarily complete, but may be sufficiently severe to permanently damage his sexual functioning, and with it his concept of himself as a male. It must be stressed that while this kind of situation with heavy alcoholic consumption as a causative factor may lead to secondary impotence, it is by no means the rule. Many men can continue to consume large quantities of alcohol throughout their lives without apparent ill effects on their sexual performance.

3. Maternal dominance. A specific case history of secondary impotence with maternal dominance as an apparently causative factor will explain the phenomenon better than any generalized theory. The following is from Masters and Johnson.

> Mr. B, a 34-year-old man, was referred with his wife for treatment of secondary impotence. He could remember little in family structuring other than a totally dominant mother making all decisions, large or small, controlling family pursestrings, and dictating, directing, and destroying his father with harsh sarcasm. He remembered the paternal role only as that of an insufficient paycheck, and

---

*Ibid., p. 167

of a man sitting quietly in the corner of the living room reading the evening newspaper. When he reached midteens, the parental representative at school functions was always the maternal figure, for both the young male and his younger sister (two siblings only). The same situation applied to church attendance, and, eventually, to all social functions. The family matured with the concept that only three people mattered.

Masturbatory onset was in the early teens with a frequency of two or three times a week during the teenage years. As would be expected in a maternally dominated environment, dating opportunity for the boy was delayed, in this case until the senior year in high school. Through college there were rare commitments to female interchange, all of them of a purely social vein. The young man was insecure in most social relationships, particularly those having orientation to the male sex. He had been forbidden participation in athletics by his mother for fear of injury. He rarely pursued male companionship, feeling himself alternatively totally insecure in, or intellectually superior to, the male peer group.

Finishing college, the young man, particularly interested in actuarial work, joined an insurance firm. Although mainly withdrawn from social relationships, at age 28 he met and within three months married a 27-year-old divorcee with a 2-year-old daughter. The divorcee, a dominant personality in her own right, was the mirror image of his mother. The two women were, of course, instant, bitter, and irrevocable enemies. The marriage, accomplished in spite of his mother's vehement objections, was a weekend justice-of-the-peace affair.

The sexual experience of the courtship had been overwhelming to the physiologically and psychologically virginal male. The uninitiated man literally was seduced by the experienced woman, who manipulated, fellated, and coitally ejaculated him within three weeks of their initial meeting. The hectic pace of the premarital sexual experience continued for the first 18 months of the marriage with Mr. B awed by and made increasingly anxious by his wife's sexual demands. Coitus occurred at least once a day. Following the pattern established during the courtship, opportunities, techniques, positions, procedures, durations, and recurrences, in fact, all sexual expression in the marriage, was at his wife's able direction.

For the first year of the marriage the wife thoroughly enjoyed overwhelming her fully cooperative but naive and insecure husband with the force and frequency of her sexual demands. As the marriage continued unwavering in the intensity of her insistence upon sexual and social dominance, his confidence in his facility for sexual functioning began to wane. He sought excuses to avoid coital connection, yet when cornered tried valiantly to respond to her demands. Finally, there were three occasions when sudden demand for coital connection forced failure of erection for the satiated male. Her comments were harsh and destructive, and the sarcasm struck a familiar chord.

The fourth time he failed to satisfy her immediate sexual needs, his wife's denunciations reminded him specifically of his mother and of her verbal attacks on his father. For the first time in his life he identified with the man sitting in a corner of the living room reading the newspaper, and within a month's time he had withdrawn to a similarly recessive behavioral patterning within his own home.

There is only one subsequent recorded episode of erection sufficiently succesful for intromission with his wife. Aside from this, the man was totally impotent and had been so for three years when seen in therapy.

On an occasion when his wife was out of town he followed the time honored response pattern of the secondarily impotent man. There was attempted coition with a prostitute to see whether he could function effectively with any other woman. For the first time in several months there was a full erection, but when he attempted to mount, the concept of his mother's disapproval of his behavior disturbed his fantasy of female conquest. He immediately lost and could not recover the erection. This was his only attempt at extramarital sexual functioning.*

4. Paternal dominance. Another case history, this time of paternal dominance, will illustrate how this may cause secondary impotence.

Mr. C was 39 years old when seen with his 37-year-old wife in therapy. He had been married for 13 years. There were three children, the youngest of whom was 5 years old. The environment of his formative years as one of three children was dominated by a de manding, selfish, insensitive, but brilliant father, who brought into the home from a successful business career his executive impatience, impersonal demands for efficiency, and stringent standards of performance. The mother, an attractive woman, created an impression of always being overwhelmed—by the demands of the home, by the demands of the children, and above all else overwhelmed by her hus-

*Ibid., pp. 170-171.

band whom she alternately obviously adored and passionately hated. The father made little effort to hide his interest in other women outside the marriage, a particularly disturbing element to the son.

Mr. C does not remember any family social commitments, entertainment, or vacation times conducted other than under the direction of and in the interests of his father. Since the father was a devotee of classical music, his was the only type of music permitted in the home.

When seen in therapy, he had no concept of his mother's preferences in music. He presumed them to be classical also. His personal taste in music was more of the popular variety; rarely had he the courage to indulge his listening pleasure even with the father absent from the home.

His father's demand for adherence to excellence of performance was directed toward grades in school, social functions, and athletics. Since the boy was not well coordinated, there were countless hours of physical torture as he tried and failed to make several of the school teams, always at his father's direction.

Bitterness and resentment but, at the same time, pride and awe were constantly conflicting emotions concerning his father during his teenage years.

Starting at 13 years, he masturbated regularly two or three times a week during the teenage years. His dating pattern (suggested by his father) was fully acceptable socially, and he first had intercourse when a junior in high school. He continued with occasional coital experiences through college but gave no evidence of in-depth identification with any female partner. There was no evidence of any functional sexual distress. At the age of 26, he married after a six-months' engagement. The courtship was current standard American, with initial petting moving into coital activity during the last few months before marriage.

In the first six years of the marriage there were three children and an established regularity of coital expression. A multiplicity of job opportunities became available, and an equal number of job changes occurred. His ventures into the business world were without specific identification of direction. In several of his professional opportunities he failed to perform satisfactorily; in others he lost interest. Mr. C found it hard to maintain any long-continued level of productivity.

As his fears for performance in the business world increased, he became less secure at home. Frequency of sexual functioning fell off when tensions created by less than effective work production left him tired and irritable during the evening hours. He spent less and less time with the children and drank progressively more than had been his previous pattern.

Finally he went to work in his father's business. After more than a year on the job, he still worried about his effectiveness of performance, panicked at the thought of losing his position, resented his father's demands, and in general was made grossly insecure in interpersonal relationships by his fears for performance. An error in judgment caused distress to a valued customer. This was reported to his father, who reprimanded him severely. His session with his father left him with a feeling of total inadequacy. He could not eat supper, paced angrily about the house, finally going to bed but not to sleep. Seeking to lose his tensions and reestablish some ego strength in sexual release, he turned to his wife and during routine precoital play achieved a strong erection. As he moved to position, the image of his bungled business performance and the scene of his father's denunciation flooded his consciousness. As he was attempting intromission he lost and was not able to regain the effective erection.

To this disturbed man, it seemed the end of the world. His sexual failure was only further evidence of the fact that he was not and never would be as good a man as his father, whose success both in business and in bed appeared legendary. With this concrete evidence of sexual failure, his frustrations were overwhelming. His fears for performance in business only amplified his fears for performance in bed and his erective incapacity continued essentially without relief.

Three months after the initial episode of erective failure, he awoke with an erection, quickly mounted and ejaculated. His unprepared wife became pregnant. Once the diagnosis of pregnancy was established, he had a reliable excuse to avoid the recently developed pressures of sexual performance, and intercourse was voluntarily contraindicated for the duration of the pregnancy, much to his wife's chagrin. When his wife demanded coital opportunity after birth of the child, Mr. C was totally impotent and continued so until referred for therapy. His fears for sexual performance and, for that matter, almost any measure of performance were overwhelming. His discussions in therapy were mixtures of praise and damnation for his father. His consistently hopeless personal comparisons with presumed levels of paternal performance were indeed sad to behold.*

———————

*Ibid., pp. 172-174.

In summing up the role of unbalanced parenthood as a potential factor in causing secondary impotence, Masters and Johnson conclude, "Unopposed maternal or paternal dominance, regardless of how created, can destroy any susceptible young man's confidence in his masculinity."*

5. Religious orthodoxy. The adverse effects of religious orthodoxy on sexual functioning in general, as well as a potential causative factor of secondary impotence will be indicated by a final case history.

> Mr. and Mrs. D were married in their early twenties. He was the product of a fundamentalist Protestant background, she of equally strict Roman Catholic orientation. The man had the additional disadvantage of being an only child, while the wife was one of three siblings. The marriage was established over the firm and often expressed objections of both families.
>
> Prior to marriage the wife had no previous heterosexual, masturbatory, or homosexual history, and knew nothing of male or female sexual expression. She had been taught that the only reason for sexual functioning was for conceptive purposes.
>
> Similarly, the husband had no exposure to sex information other than the vague directions of the peer group. He had never seen a woman undressed either in fact or in pictures. Dressing and toilet privacy had been the ironclad rule of the home. He also had been taught that sexual functioning could be condoned only if conception was desired. His sexual history consisted of masturbating during his teenage years with only occasional frequency, and two prostitute exposures. He was totally unsuccessful in each exposure because he was presumed a sexually experienced man by both women.
>
> During the first episode the prostitute took the unsuspecting virginal male to a vacant field and suggested they have intercourse while she leaned against a stone fence. Since he had no concept of female anatomy, of where to insert the penis, he failed miserably in this sexually demanding opportunity. His graphic memory of the incident is of running away from a laughing woman.
>
> The second prostitute provided a condom and demanded its use. He had no concept of how to use the condom. While the prostitute was demonstrating the technique, he ejaculated. He dressed and again fled the scene in confusion. These two sexual episodes provided only anxiety-filled examples of sexual failure. Since he had no background from which to develop objectivity when con-

*Ibid., p. 174.

sidering his "sexual disasters," inevitably the cultural misconception of lack of masculinity was the unfortunate residual of his experiences.

There was failure to consummate the marriage on the wedding night and for nine months thereafter. After consummation sexual function continued on a sporadic basis with no continuity. The wife refused contraception until after advent of the third child.

Sexual success was never of quality or quantity sufficient to relieve the husband of his fears of performance or to free the wife from the belief that either there was something wrong with her physically or that she was totally inadequate as a woman in attracting any man. They rarely discussed their sexual difficulties, as both husband and wife were afraid of hurting one another, and each was certain that their unsatisfactory pattern of sexual dysfunction was all that could be expected from indulgence in sexual expression at times when conception was not the prime motivation. With no appreciation of the naturalness of sexual functioning and with no concept of an honorable role for sexual response, the psychosocial pressures engendered from their negatively oriented sexual value systems left them with no positive means of mutual communication.

The failure of this marriage started with the wedding ceremony. There was no means of communication available for these two young people. Trained by theological demand to uninformed immaturity in matters of sexual connotation, both marital partners had no concept of how to cope when their sexual dysfunction was manifest. Their first approach to professional support was to agree to seek pastoral counseling.

Here their individual counselors were as handicapped by orthodoxy as were their supplicants. There were no suggestions made that possibly could have alleviated the sexual dysfunction. When sexual matters were raised, either no discussion was allowed, or every effort was made to belittle the importance of the sexual problem.

Without professional support, the marital partners were again released to their own devices. Each partner was intimidated, frustrated, and embarrassed for lack of sexual knowledge. The sexual dysfunction dominated the entire marriage. The husband was never as effective professionally as he might have been otherwise. He withdrew from social functioning as much as possible. The wife was in a constant state of emotional turmoil, which had the usual rebound effect upon the children. By the time this marital unit arrived at the Foundation, she was well on the way to earning the title of "shrew."

The unit was first seen after a decade of marriage. As expected from individuals so handicapped in communication, each partner had established an extramarital coital connection while individually searching for some security of personal identity and effectiveness of sexual performance. The wife had been successful in establishing her own security of psychosexual performance; the husband, as would be anticipated in this instance, had not. After ten years of traumatic marriage, both individuals gravely questioned their religious beliefs. Although no longer channel-visioned, the wife continued church attendance, the husband rejected all church affiliations.*

The serious damage caused by various religious indoctrinations to any form of natural sexual behavior seems too obvious to warrant elaboration. The time is past when religions can escape responsibility for such disasters simply on the grounds that their teaching is "religious belief."

6. Homosexuality. Just as with primary impotence, so secondary impotence may have as a causative factor homosexual behavior usually starting in the teenage years. The pattern of sexual behavior may subsequently vary enormously. The homosexually oriented young male may be unable to successfully establish any heterosexual relationship due primarily to a basic fear of them, and consequently secondary impotence appears at once. On the other hand the young male may establish good heterosexual relations, marry and have children, only to find that after some years he has a compelling desire to engage in homosexual behavior again. The pattern henceforth can again vary enormously, but the end result may simply be that he loses all sexual interest in the opposite sex, and becomes secondarily impotent.

Treatment for Impotence. It is important to realize that the factors that apparently cause secondary impotence are multiple and affect one individual quite differently from another. Furthermore, there are probably many other environmental factors about which we know little, if anything. It is of the utmost importance that those suffering from impotence should receive good professional advice. Unfortunately, this is not easily obtained, and indeed much professional advice is bad and may well do more harm than good. However, at least a brief outline is in order of the broad principles involved in present day treatment of impotence.

---

*Ibid., pp. 177-179.

Masters and Johnson point out that it is the causes of impotence that should be dealt with, rather than the symptoms, and that the goals in treating it should be to remove the male's fears of inadequate sexual performance, to change his sexual behavior so that he becomes a participant rather than a spectator, and to relieve his female partner of her fears for his sexual performance. This is easier said than done, for an impotent male is usually a very insecure and fear-ridden person. However, the psychosocial causes of the impotence must be identified, and above all the individual must learn to come to terms with these causes in such a way that he will gradually get rid of his fear, which is probably the immediate cause of his inability to achieve an erection.

Once the basic causes of the impotence are recognized, and the male is taught to overcome them, he is then encouraged to reopen communication with his sexual partner. This step includes the education of both partners in what should be the natural, uninhibited nature of sexual functioning, rather than in the usual hodge-podge of misinformation, fears, and taboos. All this, of course, will require skilled guidance by well-trained professionals, as well as patience on the part of the sexual partners. If these first, primarily psychological, steps are successfully accomplished, the couple is then encouraged to start touching and fondling, but at the same time specifically avoiding the genital areas and also not attempting coitus.

As Masters and Johnson explain, this allows the couple to experience sexual feelings and emotions without any demand to perform, and this can go a long way in removing the male's fear of performance since he is initially forbidden to perform. In this way, communication becomes established and the partners not uncommonly find that erection occurs without any direct contact with the genital areas. This is a big step, since it initiates confidence in both male and female. Furthermore both partners should realize that the attainment of any male's erection is something entirely natural; it cannot be willed nor can he be trained to achieve it.

As the couple proceeds, the fondling process is gradually extended to the genital areas, and they are encouraged to literally teach one another what pleases them most, by guiding each other's hands over the appropriate parts of their bodies and explaining exactly the best method of fondling. All this may take days or weeks, and if there is erective success the couple may then gradually proceed toward sexual intercourse. Masters and Johnson explain that the technique by which this is initially done is vital. First, the whole act should be under the control of the female, who should exercise that control in a nondemanding manner. With the female in control, yet not demanding male response, the male is relieved of more responsibility (and so some fear). He is under no pressure to respond, which makes the whole act a relaxing process for him.

Next, the female is encouraged to mount in the superior kneeling position, giving her maximum control, and in a slow, gradual, and nondemanding manner. She should control the insertive process, thus relieving the male of yet another responsibility. Many men suffering from impotence, and often just plain ignorance, find insertion difficult to perform, and consequently their erection may fail at this point. With the penis inserted it is important that the female avoid pelvic thrusting, as this is very demanding on the male. Gradually, over a period of days, this whole coital technique is repeated, and the couple can build to mutually rewarding sexual intercourse and to a natural male ejaculation.

Needless to say, this whole procedure for the treatment of male impotence requires the full and wholehearted cooperation of a sympathetic and understanding female partner—and in these respects women have proven to be remarkably cooperative. In the experience of Masters and Johnson, over 90% of women give full cooperation once they realize that it is their marital partnership which is being treated, rather than just the male's sexual failure. Despite all this, success is by no means assured, for the causes of impotence are obscure, multiple, and deep-seated. Currently, and even under guidance by the best professionals, the failure rate is about 40% for primary impotence and 25% for secondary impotence, with the environmental cause of religious orthodoxy causing by far the highest failure rate.

SEXUAL PROBLEMS OF THE FEMALE

The female, just like the male, may be subject to a variety of purely biological factors which may cause her various degrees of sexual difficulties, from minor pain to the complete impossibility of sexual intercourse or orgasm. These of course should be treated professionally where possible, but unfortunately identification of the environmental factors that cause female sexual difficulties and failures is not as easy as in the case of the male. The reasons for this are complex, but they are certainly rooted in the cultural taboos which until very recently more or less forbade direct scientific research on sexuality, or the dissemination of information so obtained. Cultural bias has also virtually eliminated female investigators, who are most likely to understand female difficulties. And another obstacle to identification of environmental causes of female sexual malfunction is that "man has had society's blessing to build his sexual value system in an appropriate, naturally occurring context and woman has not."* By and large society has demanded that the growing

---

*Ibid., p. 135.

girl repress her sexual feelings, which in turn tends to inhibit the development of a meaningful and satisfactory sexual value system. Unfortunately, society has been helped in this respect by the biological fact that female sexual response is not necessary for conception! It is therefore true that, in comparison to the male, sexual expression has been partially repressed in almost all women. This fact, together with woman's undeniably more intricate sexual physiology, makes it extremely difficult to sort out the interaction of the biological and the psychosocial. Thus it follows that discussion of the environmental causes of sexual malfunction in the female must inevitably be shorter and less explicit than the preceding discussion of the male. We simply know less about the causes of sexual difficulties and failures in the female, and are less certain of what we do know. This does not mean that such environmental factors as religious and parental repression, ignorance, guilt feelings (particularly as a result of masturbation), lack of sexual education, fear (imagined or real), etc., do not inflict havoc on women just as they do on men, but simply that they are not as easily categorized.

Inability to Achieve Orgasm

The inability of some women to respond sexually in such a way that they reach orgasm is perhaps the most common and one of the most severe of female sexual inadequacies. Some women never achieve orgasm during their entire lives, others only very occasionally, or in dreams, while others may reach it by masturbation though not through coitus, or vice versa. As is pointed out however, in the Hite Report (referred to earlier), over 80% of the women interviewed said they masturbated, and of these 95% said they could easily reach orgasm this way. Shere Hite goes on to explain that our traditional concepts regarding this problem may be quite wrong. Why have we insisted that women should orgasm from intercourse? There is no law, biological or otherwise, which says this must be so, and that if she did not, something was wrong with her. The reality seems to be that in fact most women do not experience orgasm from intercourse. However by continuous masturbatory stimulation of the clitoris, either by the woman herself, or by her sexual partner, orgasm can usually be achieved. It must be remembered also that during coitus successful female sexual response is in large part dependent on a sexually effective male. Thus in addition to whatever biological difficulties and/or psychosocially imposed inadequacies the female may have, her response is partly dependent on an effective male performance. If her sexual partner cares only for his own gratification, for example, or if he is a premature ejaculator, then her chances of reaching orgasm on any kind of regular basis are almost nonexistent. In such a case the problem is really the male's inadequacy rather than hers. But whatever her problems, the solution will inevitably require the male partner's cooperation and understanding.

Despite the difficulties of identifying the multiple causes of some women's inability to reach orgasm, Masters and Johnson do point out that one of the major causes is religious orthodoxy.* It is not necessary to quote a long case history regarding this, but it may simply be said that where the atmosphere of the formative years equates sex with sin, and/or insists that the only reason for sexual intercourse is to procreate, then the female is likely to become so inhibited sexually that she may be unable to achieve orgasm. To correct such a situation requires complete reeducation of the individual so far as her sexual and social value systems are concerned. In view of the often severe nature of the psychological damage and the difficulty of reversing it, it is remarkable that success is sometimes possible. With the help of a cooperative male sexual partner, some women can indeed be helped to a natural sexual life, including orgasmic release.

Another major cause of the nonorgasmic situation is that of homosexual relations during the teenage years. Many young girls tend to form homosexual relations—though few continue into later years—and on turning from homosexuality to heterosexuality may find great difficulty in adjusting sexually to a male partner. This difficulty may include the loss of ability to reach orgasm.

The inability of some women to reach orgasm is also commonly due to failure to either identify or establish a happy emotional relationship with the male partner. As previously mentioned, the male may simply be sexually inadequate—a premature ejaculator, impotent, or perhaps totally inept. These problems may be overcome in part if the woman can successfully use masturbation as a means of orgasmic release. However, it is also possible that he may simply not meet her standards of a male partner in a host of subtle ways—as a result of her previous relations with other men, or the fact that the male is not faithful to her, or just because of the day-to-day irritations of what she sees as his inadequacies. It must also be noted that some women are nonorgasmic, or only rarely orgasmic, for no apparent biological or psychosocial reason. Perhaps future research will solve this rather distressing fact.

Treatment to Achieve Orgasm. Just as the impotent male may be helped to recover and lead a normal and satisfying sexual life, so in many cases can the nonorgasmic female achieve the same. In fact, Masters and Johnson's truly preeminent efforts have been more successful with nonorgasmic females than impotent males. Their successful approach to

---

Ibid., p. 229.

the female problem is not fundamentally different to that of the male problem, but it is necessary to describe their treatment procedure quite separately.

The first step, of course, is an attempt to find the causes for the woman's inability to reach orgasm. This is done by investigating her past history, and also her attitude, sexual values, and problems with her present sexual partner. This investigation is continued, and its findings constantly evaluated, as the treatment proceeds. The sexual partners must of course be made to understand the problem and to realize that orgasm cannot be just willed—that it must occur naturally. Furthermore, they must learn to communicate freely, both verbally and by touching and fondling. If this can be accomplished satisfactorily and sexual feeling returns to the woman, they are then guided into the next step.

This consists of encouraging direct stimulation of the female's genitals by the male, but in a very precise, nondemanding way with as much guidance as possible from the female. The male sits on the bed with his back against the wall and legs apart. The female sits between his legs with her back against him and her head resting on one of his shoulders, and her legs astride his. This allows the male direct approach to almost all of his partner's body, and the woman is encouraged to place her hand over the male's so as to guide it (and "explain" to it) what is most pleasing to her. The basic idea is that the male should learn from the female, and above all that he should avoid clitoral stimulation except exactly as the female desires it. All this permits the female to establish sexual response without demand, direct or presumed, from the male. It is not expected that the woman will reach orgasm in this manner, but it is hoped that as each session goes by her sexual arousal will increase and that she will enjoy the experience. If and when her enjoyment reaches an appropriate level, the couple are advised to proceed to the next step.

When the female reaches a high level of sexual excitement, coitus can be attempted in the female superior position, she kneeling across the male. Once again there should be no demand from the male and he should particularly avoid pelvic thrusting. The woman should be left free to simply absorb the pleasure of an erect penis within her vagina. The male must of course establish ejaculatory control, but with the proviso that he will inevitably need and should have periodic ejaculations over a period of days. Masters and Johnson also stress that during these sexual sessions the female should alternate between the superior coital position and simply lying in the arms of the male—i.e., mount and dismount. Furthermore it is important that "at least every fourth day is declared a holiday from physical sexual expression."*

---

*Ibid., p. 310.

As confidence is gradually gained, the couple are advised to change from the female superior position to the lateral one. This may take a little practice, but it allows the greatest freedom for sexual movement and experimentation by both male and female. In due course, and provided the male is understanding, cooperative, sympathetic, and patient, many women become able to reach orgasm. Unfortunately there is no guarantee of success, and even under the expert guidance of Masters and Johnson the overall failure rate is about 20%. It may be hoped, however, that with increased knowledge this figure may be lowered. It is even more to be hoped that with a less sexually inhibiting psychosocial environment and better education the problem can be avoided in the first place.

Vaginismus

Another major sexual problem which some women experience is that of vaginismus. In this situation the pelvic musculature in general, but the outer third of the vagina in particular, goes into a severe spastic contraction which effectively blocks any normal entrance to the vagina. It is an involuntary reflex in response to any imagined or real attempt at vaginal penetration, and is apparently of deep psychological origin. It may be surprising to realize that many women are unaware of it, and it can only be diagnosed for certain by a professional pelvic examination. As might be expected, the environmental causes are multiple in origin, but some of the major ones include a sexually inadequate male partner, an upbringing of religious orthodoxy, any unpleasant sexual event which may bring about severe psychic shock, painful sexual intercourse, and a background of homosexuality (particularly in the formative years). It is not necessary to cover each of these in turn, as the pattern (though with infinite variety) is already familiar to the reader. However, it may be of help to quote just two short case histories simply to show the severe effect, in these cases vaginismus, of appalling environmental events which some young women are unfortunate enough to experience. Both cases are taken from the files of Masters and Johnson. The first deals with the effects of religious orthodoxy.

When the unit was first seen in consultation, Mr. and Mrs. A's marriage had existed unconsummated for 4-1/2 years. The wife, from a sibling group of four females and one male, was the only one not to take the vows of a religious order. Her environmental and educational backgrounds were of strictest parental, physical, and mental control enforced in a stringent disciplinary format and founded in religious orthodoxy.

She was taught that almost any form of physical expression might be suspect of objectionable sexual connotation. For example, she was prohibited when bathing from looking at her own breasts either directly or from reflection in the mirror for fear that unhealthy sexual thoughts might be stimulated by visual examination of her own body. Discussion with a sibling of such subjects as menstruation, conception, contraception, or sexual functioning were taboo. Pronouncements on the subject were made by the father with the mother's full agreement. Her engagement period was restricted to a few chaste, well-chaperoned kisses, for at any sign of sexual interest from her fiancé, the girl withdrew in confusion.

Mrs. A entered marriage without a single word of advice, warning, or even good cheer from her family relative to marital sexual expression. The only direction offered by her religious adviser relative to sexual behavior was that coital connection was only to be endured if conception was desired.

Mrs. A's only concept of woman's role in sexual functioning was that it was dirty and depraved without marriage and that the sanctity of marriage really only provided the male partner with an opportunity for sexual expression. For the woman, the only salvation to be gained from sexual congress was pregnancy.

With the emotional trauma associated with wedding activities, and an injudicious, blundering, sexual approach from the uninformed but eager husband, the wedding night was a fiasco quite sufficient to develop or to enhance any preexisting involuntary obstruction of the vaginal outlet to a degree sufficient to deny penetration.

The husband, of the same orthodox background, had survived these traumatic years without developing secondary impotence. His premarital experience had been two occasions of prostitute exposure, and there was no reported extramarital experience. He masturbated occasionally and was relieved manually by his wife once or twice a week. His wife had no such outlet. Her only source of effective relief was well-controlled psychotherapy.*

---

*Ibid., pp. 254-255.

The second case discusses the effects of rape—incredibly, rape sponsored by male relatives.

> The remaining two rape experiences were family-oriented and almost identical in history. In both instances young girls were physically forced by male members of their immediate family to provide sexual release, on numerous occasions, for men they did not know. In one instance, a father, and in another, an older brother, forced sexual partners upon teenage girls (15 and 17 years of age) and repeatedly stood by to insure the girls' physical cooperation. Sexually exploited, emotionally traumatized, and occasionally physically punished, these girls became conditioned to the concept that "all men were like that." When released from family sexual servitude each girl avoided any possibility of sexual contact during the late teens and well into the twenties, until married at 25 and 29 years of age. Even then, they could not make themselves physically available to consummate their marriages, regardless of how strongly they willed sexual cooperation. Severe vaginismus was present in both cases.
>
> The husbands' physical and psychosexual examinations were within expected limits of normal variability. Neither husband had been made aware of the family-oriented episodes of controlled rape that had occurred years before their association with their wives-to-be. Once apprised of the etiology of their wives' psychosomatic illness, both men offered limitless cooperation in the therapeutic program.*

Treatment For Vaginismus. Like other treatments for sexual malfunctions, the treatment for vaginismus consists of identification of both the malfunction and the causes, and making both sexual partners aware of them. A cooperative male partner is, of course, absolutely essential. Then, under the guidance of a professional, but in privacy, the male partner is taught to gradually insert gradated dilators into the female's vagina. She, in turn, is taught to retain them in place for several hours at a time. The number of times this has to be done varies with the individual, of course, but it is remarkable that "in many instances, however, the simple clinical demonstration of the existence of the vaginal constriction and the

---

*Ibid., p. 257.

subsequent controlled usage of the dilators for a few days is quite sufficient to remove permanently this involuntary obstruction to vaginal penetration."* It is perhaps even more remarkable that a successful cure can be virtually guaranteed.

In concluding this chapter on both male and female sexual difficulties and distress, it must be emphasized that only a few of the most major problems have been mentioned at all, and these treated in barest outline. However, the dissemination of basic knowledge on the various problems is perhaps the most urgent task, for ignorance and superstition in sexual matters breed dire consequences.

STUDY TOPICS

1. Explain the meaning of the following: (a) impotence, (b) premature ejaculation, (c) squeeze technique, (d) sexual therapy, (e) vaginismus.

2. Name four common situations which are known to contribute to sexual failure in the male and female.

3. Describe the various factors that can be responsible for premature ejaculation.

4. What technique is offered by Masters and Johnson for the treatment of premature ejaculation?

5. Describe the basic treatment offered by Masters and Johnson for male impotence.

6. Why is communication between sexual partners so important in sexual therapy?

7. What are some of the causes associated with the inability of many women to achieve orgasm during coitus?

8. Describe the basic treatment offered by Masters and Johnson for the nonorgasmic female.

9. Explain the possible causes for vaginismus, and the treatment of it.

---

*Ibid., p. 263.

10. Discuss the guidelines parents might follow in giving their children the best chances of avoiding serious sexual problems.

FOR FURTHER READING

Belliveau, Fred, and Lin Richter, *Understanding Human Sexual Inadequacy*. New York: Bantam Books, 1970.

Hite, Shere, *The Hite Report*. New York: Macmillan, 1976.

Katchadourian, Herant A., and Donald T. Lunde, *Fundamentals of Human Sexuality*. New York: Holt, Rinehart and Winston, 1972.

Masters, William H., and Virginia E. Johnson, *Human Sexual Inadequacy*. Boston: Little, Brown, 1970.

CHAPTER EIGHT

Sexuality and Aging

*Will you still need me, will you still feed
me when I'm 64?*

John Lennon and Paul McCartney,
When I'm 64, ©Northern Songs, Ltd.,
12 Bruton St., London WIX 7 AH.
Reproduced by permission.

It is obvious to even the most casual observer that as human beings age, changes gradually take place in their bodies. Thus it should come as no surprise to realize that sexual anatomy and physiology are also subject to transformations. As a result of these, modifications of sexual behavior and desires inevitably take place. Sexual relations among young people are certainly more frequent on the average than among older people, but this is simply a reflection of the fact that as people age they tend to slow down in almost everything. It is quite false to imagine, however, that men and women who, in their younger years, have established a good and active sexual life cannot carry this on well into their seventies and even eighties. All this, of course, assumes that they are in good physical and psychological health, though unfortunately, in our urban civilizations, the vast majority of people do not take the trouble to keep themselves in good health as they age. Nevertheless, an active sexual life for post-menopausal women, and for men of similar age, is not only entirely feasible but also highly desirable. In this chapter we will examine some of the factors affecting sexuality in older people, an aspect which until very recently has been almost totally neglected.

EFFECTS OF AGING ON THE REPRODUCTIVE SYSTEM

Aging is, of course, a gradual process from birth to death, and it is impossible, as well as unnecessary, to define exactly what is meant by "younger" or "older" or "aging." These terms are purely relative, and in any case there are enormous variations in the aging process from individual to individual. Nevertheless, a major transitional phase in reproductive physiology takes place in women in the form of menopause, which occurs about the age of 45 to 50. This has already been described in Chapter 4, and here it is only necessary to point out that the phenomenon is primarily due to a natural depletion of the sex hormones which eventually stops the ovarian and menstrual cycles, making the woman infertile. Since there is nothing in the human male that resembles the cyclical nature of ovulation and menstruation, there is of course nothing directly comparable to the menopause. However, it is highly pertinent to ask whether there is in men, at approximately the same age (45 to 50), some sexual hormonal depletion which may cause physiological and psychological changes which are of a nature comparable to those occurring in women after menopause. At the present time there is really no satisfactory answer to this, since techniques to accurately measure the hormonal levels have only recently become available and may still be questionable. But what little evidence we have enables us to give a guarded judgment that there is some hormonal depletion in men which starts about this time, and there are certainly changes in male sexual response which start to develop around the age of 45 to 50. Of course, just as in the female, there are wide variations. In any event, for purposes of convenience only—and fully recognizing their inadequacy—we will use the terms "younger" in referring to men and women under 50, and "older" in referring to those over 50.

It is important to realize that after menopause, other changes take place in the female reproductive organs besides the reduction in size of the ovaries and the loss of the ovarian and menstrual cycles. These other changes also are probably directly due to hormonal depletion, though they may take years to complete. In particular the following should be noted. The walls of the vaginal barrel of older women gradually lose their thick corrugated nature and become thin. In addition there is an actual decrease in the size of the vagina, both in length and width, and a loss of expansive capacity. The breasts and clitoris may slightly decrease in size, and the uterus considerably so, and there is also a general decline in the elasticity of tissues making up the vagina, the labia majora and minora, and the breasts. Despite these changes it is significant that these organs do not lose their ability to respond to sexual stimulation. In older males there are generally no such obvious anatomical changes in the reproductive organs, though as in the female the tissues may become less elastic.

Once again Masters and Johnson have supplied us with direct observations of the nature of the sexual response cycle in both older men and women. Their findings are of great value since they dispel the myth (once and for all, it is hoped) that older women in particular have little interest in, or capacity for, sexual activity. Likewise older men are fully capable of leading an active and satisfying sexual life.

Sexual Response Cycle of the Older Female

The phases of the sexual response cycle of older women usually differ from those of younger women (described in Chapter 6) in the following relatively minor ways. These are generalizations only, for in some women any or all of these differences may not in fact appear.

Excitement Phase. In this phase older women tend to have a somewhat delayed onset of vaginal lubrication (i.e., 2 to 5 minutes, rather than seconds for the younger woman), and there is actually less of the fluid as well. This is no doubt the result of the thinning of the walls of the vagina. The expansion of the inner two-thirds of the vagina, while still taking place, is reduced in size, and delayed in time. The uterus elevates only slightly, if at all. The clitoral response of older women is much the same as in younger ones, but the labia minora exhibit a reduced amount of vasocongestion, and the labia majora do not separate and retract away from the midline as in younger women. This is probably due simply to the loss of tissue elasticity, which in this case is also accompanied by loss of fat in the labia majora and indeed in the mons area in general. In older women the erection of the breast nipples is the first response to sexual excitement, and this occurs much as in younger women. However any actual increase in breast size becomes less common with aging. The sex flush also becomes less common, and muscular tension tends to be reduced.

Plateau Phase. In older women the expansion of the inner two-thirds of the vagina may be delayed until this phase, but the development of the orgasmic platform occurs much as in younger women. The clitoris retracts under its hood, and there is further engorgement of the breast nipples. If there is a sex flush it is somewhat restricted, while just as in younger women breathing becomes deeper and the heart rate and blood pressure rise.

Orgasmic Phase. Orgasm in an older woman is very similar to that in younger women. The only differences worth mentioning seem to be that the orgasmic platform contractions tend to be reduced in number and intensity and the duration of the orgasmic phase itself is somewhat shortened. Otherwise orgasm is the same intense and satisfying event.

Resolution Phase. In older women this phase is marked by a very rapid return of the vagina to normal size, and of the clitoris from under its hood. In older women the loss of nipple erection is sometimes delayed considerably, but blood pressure, heart rate, and muscle tension all swiftly return to normal.

In summary it may be said that in older women the physiological reactions to effective sexual stimulation are somewhat delayed in time and are not quite so vigorous. However, providing the woman is in good health and has established good sexual habits during her younger years, it is highly probable that as she ages she will continue to be fully capable of sexual response to the point of orgasm.

Sexual Response Cycle of the Older Male

The typical sexual response cycle of younger men was described in Chapter 6, and the changes as men age are mainly relative. Their responses tend to become slower, but they do not seem to show any biological change of a fundamental nature.

Excitement Phase. Older men typically respond to effective sexual stimulation by taking longer to achieve penile erection, and generally speaking the older the male the more delayed the response. However, once erection is obtained, it commonly can be maintained without ejaculation for considerable periods of time, so much so that older men have a distinct advantage over younger ones in the matter of ejaculatory control. There is considerable reduction of scrotal vasocongestion in older men, and less muscular tension.

Plateau Phase. Full erection may not take place in older men until late in the plateau phase, while erection of the nipples of the breast (if it takes place at all) is delayed until this phase. Similarly, the sex flush is uncommon in older males. Testicular vasocongestion is also uncommon, and though the testes usually elevate in this phase, they do not do so to anywhere near the degree that they do in younger men.

Orgasmic Phase. As men age the physiology of ejaculation undergoes distinct but gradual changes. The sensation of "inevitability," so characteristic of impending ejaculation in younger men, tends to be lost in older men or perhaps lengthened to a point where there are several sensations of inevitability. The penile contractions occur at the same intervals of 0.8 second, but in the aging male there are fewer of them and the entire ejaculatory process is shorter. In addition there is less seminal fluid, and the expulsive force is reduced. Muscle tension, breathing rate, heart rate, and blood pressure all reach their peak in orgasmic phase in much the same way as in younger men.

Resolution Phase. It is not necessary to describe for older men, as has been done for younger ones, the various changes taking place which return the body to a sexually unstimulated condition. The process is much the same in both cases except that in older men the loss of erection and testicular descent are extremely rapid, while the entire resolution phase-refractory period is considerably lengthened. Older men usually do not develop an erection for 12 to 24 hours after an orgasm, and they are usually well satisfied with less frequent ejaculations than in their younger years.

Thus in older men, as in older women, aging gives rise to generally delayed and less vigorous responses to effective sexual stimulation. In older men there is usually not the need for such frequent ejaculations as in younger men, but providing there is good health and a background of good sexual habits, males can have an active and satisfying sexual life well into the eighties.

Sexual Problems of Older Women

Despite the basic capacity of older men and women for sexual relations, they nevertheless may be subject to a variety of problems which may well negate their potential capabilities for an active sexual life. The psychosocial environment both past and present is of course of enormous importance, and will be considered later, but there may be purely physical factors causing serious problems, particularly in the case of women who undergo some rather pronounced physical changes as a result of menopause. The important changes from a sexual point of view are general thinning of the vaginal walls and the reduction in size of the vagina and the uterus. As a result of these, many older women suffer varying degrees of discomfort both during and after sexual intercourse. This discomfort may take the form of some pain during male intromission, vaginal burning, pelvic or abdominal aching during coitus, or some pain during orgasm as a result of contractions of the smaller uterus. The clitoris also may be more sensitive to irritation, but no less sensitive to sexual stimulation by an experienced and considerate male. All these discomforts are extremely variable from female to female; they may never occur at all or they may be so severe that the woman will avoid sexual relations at all costs. Since the physical changes giving rise to these discomforts are a direct result of sex hormone depletion, the problem may in many cases be relieved by artificial supplementation of various hormones under professional guidance. However, by far the most important factor is to keep up a regular sexual life prior to menopause and after it. Such regularity will in most cases help to keep the organs in good condition, and thus avoid the problems which will inevitably result from disuse. Masters and Johnson explain this aspect as follows, "There is tremendous physiological and, of course, psychological value in continuity of sexual exposure, as expressed by the physical efficiency of vaginal response to sexual stimulation. To a significant degree, regularity of sexual exposure will overcome the influence of sex-steroid inadequacy in the female pelvis."* In older women who, over the years, have not maintained effective sexual exposure, sex hormone treatment will be almost a necessity if they are to have not only satisfactory sexual intercourse, but also any sexual desires at all.

Aging women, depending on their past and present psychosocial background, are of course subject to any of the sexual difficulties and failures of their younger counterparts, referred to in Chapter 7. Nevertheless many of them respond to the same treatments already described. Even if a post menopausal woman has never experienced

*William H. Masters and Virginia E. Johnson, *Human Sexual Inadequacy*. Boston: Little, Brown and Co., 1970, p. 341.

orgasm in all her life, some can still learn by appropriate treatment to become fully orgasmic during coitus. As with younger women, ignorance, fears, taboos, and bad social and psychological experiences will all have adverse effects on sexual functioning in later years. In addition, the belief is still widespread that post menopausal women cannot or should not engage in sexual activities. Unfortunately, professionals have done little to dispel such ideas, with the result that many older women believe there is something wrong with them if they have sexual desires or engage in sexual acts. Nothing could be further from the truth, and such beliefs continue to cause untold distress.

There is one significant factor in our society that is more acute for older women than younger ones, namely that as they age male partners become less and less available. This is due simply to the fact that in our society women live longer than men, and unfortunately they may well be deprived of a partner while still fully sexually active. Thus it is not surprising that masturbation as a form of relieving sexual tensions may become quite common in older women deprived of a male partner, and this indeed seems entirely desirable. As women reach an older and older age, their sexual desires and functioning will inevitably decrease both in amount and vigor from what they were in their sexual prime, but even then there is no basic reason why women should not continue to enjoy to the full the physical pleasure and emotional aspects of the presence of a male's body and companionship. Above all, however, as Masters and Johnson stress, there are two basic needs for an effective sexual life in aging women, "These necessities are a reasonably good state of general health and an interested and interesting partner."*

Sexual Problems of Older Men

The sexual problems and inadequacies of aging men are partly physical, as in the case with women, but tend to be far more of a psychosocial nature in origin. The natural changes in the sexual response cycle taking place as a result of aging have already been described, and there can also be no doubt that sexual desires, frequency of erection, ability to achieve full erection, and frequency of ejaculation all tend to decline as part of the normal aging process. In addition, almost any kind of illness, temporary or progressive, will tend to inhibit sexual behavior. It is, however, an absurdity to believe the widely held myth that men over fifty are sexual nonentities. This myth unfortunately reinforces the ever-present fear of the male about his ability to perform.

*Ibid., p. 350.

As in women, perhaps the most important factor for effective sexual functioning in older men is the maintenance of good sexual relations and habits established in the younger years. Both the sexual organs and the whole body should be kept in good, healthy, active condition if sexual well-being is to prevail. This is not the place to give lectures on the importance of physical health in the older male, but not much can be expected without it, sexually or otherwise. There is some evidence that effective sexual functioning in a male's later years is particularly closely related to a healthy and active sexual life in the formative years.

Perhaps the most common and severe sexual problem that the aging male faces is that of secondary impotence. Assuming good physical health, this can arise from much the same variety of psychosocial reasons as in younger men (see Chapter 6). However, due to the fact that the older man is commonly at the peak of his career, with social responsibilities very different from those of younger men, he is subject to additional factors which may bring about secondary impotence. These include preoccupation with his career at the expense of his sexual partner (whom he may also find boring), mental or physical fatigue, excessive eating and drinking, and inability to adjust to changed social circumstances.

Masters and Johnson have shown quite conclusively that if secondary impotence does occur in an aging male, it can respond to the same kind of treatment as has been worked out for similar cases in younger men. However, it cannot be overstressed that secondary impotence is *not* necessarily part of the normal aging process in males.

In concluding this consideration of the sexual problems in the aging, it should be stressed that only the most preliminary kind of research has been done on the subject, and that our ignorance is profound. It is hoped that future investigations will not only give us more concrete knowledge, but will help to dispel the incredible ignorances and myths that surround us. Every part of a person's life from birth to old age is important to that person (and others) at that time, and sexual well-being is important on a day-to-day basis throughout life. Aging men and women are no exceptions, and their later years can be much more satisfying and fulfilling if they can maintain sexual desires and interests and carry on satisfactory sexual activities. Barring poor physical health, there is no fundamental reason why this should not be the case. What is needed is the right attitude and an appropriate sexual partner.

Our society is neither very considerate nor kind to our aging population, and we must realize that our older citizens value their lives just as highly as younger people value theirs. One can hope that increased understanding will help the generations to be more tolerant of each other, and sexual understanding can go a long way to achieving this end. On the other hand, as men and women age they attempt to remain young simply by using cosmetics and inappropriate clothing to enhance their outward physical appearance. They would do better to keep their bodies in good physical health and their minds young and active, to maintain interest in the world about them, and thus to age gracefully.

STUDY TOPICS

1. What is the end result of menopause in women, and how does this come about? (See also Chapter 4.) Is there any equivalent of menopause in men?

2. What sex-related physical changes occur in the female with aging?

3. What age-related changes in the sexual response cycle can interfere with normal sexual enjoyment in men and women?

4. With aging, coitus may become painful for some women. What is the cause of this?

5. How does the frequency of sexual intercourse normally change with age?

6. What age-related change in male sexual response is considered to be advantageous?

7. What external factors can add to sexual difficulties in men as they become older?

8. Do the treatments suggested by Masters and Johnson for sexual difficulties change in their applicability with age?

9. Discuss the benefits of a continued regularity in sexual activity throughout the later years.

10. What do you think society might do to improve relations between the young and the old? Do the young need the old and the old the young?

FOR FURTHER READING

Belliveau, Fred, and Lin Richter, *Understanding Human Sexual Inadequacy.* New York: Bantam Books, 1970.

Masters, William H., and Virginia E. Johnson, *Human Sexual Inadequacy.* Boston: Little, Brown, 1970.

CHAPTER NINE

Variations of Sexual Behavior

*The truth of it is the first rudiments of
education are given very indiscreetly by
most parents.*

Sir Richard Steele (1672-1729).

INCONSISTENCY OF SOCIAL STANDARDS

Throughout recorded history there has never been any shortage of authorities who are not only eager to tell us right from wrong in matters of sexual behavior, but who are also well prepared to inflict the most savage penalties on those who deviate from their concept of right. It is reasonably safe to say that in some place and at some time almost every form of sexual behavior has been condemned. And yet, in some other place or at some other time, almost every form of sexual behavior has been condoned. Even incest, perhaps the most universally condemned sexual behavior of all, was considered highly desirable by the ancient Egyptian pharaohs. Indeed, Cleopatra was the last of a long line of brother-sister matings, and from all account she was no insignificant woman.

However, a glance at the laws of modern countries and states regarding sexual behavior—usually lumped under the heading of "crimes against nature"—serves to show that man is not only irrational in this regard, but ruthless as well. For example, in France homosexuality between consenting adults has not been a crime since the "Code Napoleon" of 1804, whereas in some Islamic countries the penalty (though rarely imposed) is death by stoning. In the United States, Illinois was the first to abolish statutes governing homosexual acts between consenting adults, and fortunately other states are gradually following suit, though we still have a long way to go.

Unfortunately, we are inevitably on dangerous ground when discussing sexual behavior because the civil laws governing it are nearly always based on religious dogma, taboos, and superstition, which in turn are compounded by plain ignorance. In the minds of most people, if not all, heterosexual intercourse is considered the norm and the only form of acceptable sexual behavior. Anyone whose sexual desires and behavior vary from this is considered abnormal, deviant, or perverted—or all three—and depending on the circumstances is treated as sick, a social outcast, or an outright criminal. A more candid and objective survey, as Kinsey and others have shown, would conclude that most people desire and need many outlets for their sexuality—and that at one or more times in our lives virtually every one of us behaves sexually in some manner condemned by society and probably by laws as well. Kinsey estimated that if the laws governing sexual behavior were strictly enforced, over 95% of American males would be in jail! Regrettable also is the generally held view (well fostered by daily newspapers) that sexually variant behavior is closely associated with violent crime. Nothing could be further from the truth. The majority of people whose sexual behavior varies from the heterosexual form are rather calm, unassertive people who are in fact actually less likely to be violent than the heterosexual. Of course, society may well harass them to the point where they are driven into the arms of criminal elements, but the vast majority of what we commonly term sexual deviates are not at all of a criminal or violent nature.

It is unfortunate that in modern societies mass advertising media pour forth an "ideal" sexual image which is in no way related to the reality of ordinary men and women. Superficially this might appear amusing and harmless, but to the highly impressionable adolescent struggling with his sexual development it may be neither. To the adolescent or any other insecure person, the television screen, magazines, and billboards portray a world of men and women of absolute sexual confidence. Tall, lean, well groomed, well proportioned, and impeccably dressed young men are shown striding through life convinced that every woman finds them highly desirable. Similarly beautiful, sophisticated, and charming women are portrayed as sexual paragons confident that no male can resist them. More experienced and more secure people have usually learned that this is a false picture, but adolescents or insecure adults may well imagine they are inferior or abnormal because they are not like that. Despite external appearances almost every real man and woman harbors insecurity, guilt, and fear that they may fail sexually or that their desires and behavior will not meet with the approval of their fellows. Unfortunately, in some cases their difficulties are almost insurmountable, because it is well known that the various factors conditioning a person's sexual desires and behavior are usually very deep-seated, and are determined by little-understood and very complex relationships in early childhood. It is not within the scope of this book to attempt any psychological analysis of the conditioning processes leading to various forms of sexual behavior, and to which almost every child in our society is subjected. However, a few brief remarks are in order simply as an aid to understanding the origins of the varieties of sexual behavior.

EFFECTS OF PARENTAL SEXUAL STANDARDS

It is now well established that a baby and developing child will require far more than food, drink, shelter, and clothing if it is going to grow up into a confident, productive individual with all the potential that implies. Babies who are denied proper parental and emotional care, or have other unsatisfactory parent relationships, develop more slowly than their more fortunate counterparts, and if the situation is bad enough it may result in permanent psychological damage of such a nature that the resultant adult may be incapable of forming any emotional ties with other humans. This fact in itself will affect sexual behavior simply because of the close link between sex and many emotions. More important still is the attitude of parents to various behavior patterns which a growing child will inevitably follow. In the child's mind, good and bad, right and wrong, will be determined primarily by the parent's reactions in the form of reward or disapproval. Standards of good and bad are established very early in life, and there are peculiar reasons why sexual desires tend to be categorized as bad, and thus elicit feelings of guilt: There is the general religious inhibition toward sex which the parents will very indiscreetly pass on; there is society's general taboo on the child's developing sexual interest—to which the parents will almost certainly conform; the sexual organs are closely associated with the organs of excretion, and since the latter are commonly considered "dirty," so also will there be a tendency for the sexual organs and sexual behavior to be considered "dirty."

It is important also to realize that the incest taboo greatly restricts children from learning the nature of sexuality and sexual acts, since it prohibits them from sexual experimentation within the family. This does not mean that the incest taboo is bad, for there are a number of sound reasons for it. Even setting aside moral, psychological, and genetic considerations, there is a very pragmatic reason for the incest taboo. As a species, humans have an extremely long period of childhood, during which the sexually developing child is dependent on the parents. This long and close association makes it difficult enough as it is for the child to break the parental bonds and establish itself as an independent adult. If, in addition to the inevitable partial dependency, the child has also established a sexual relation—with all the emotion which that implies—then it will probably be impossible to successfully break the parental bonds. It is because parents are "forbidden" that children are forced to look outside the security of the family for sexual partners and eventually make the break.

From this brief and very incomplete discussion it is obvious that people's sexual desires and behavior will vary according to the particular attitudes and relationships with which they were brought up, and that what seems natural and right to one person may seem quite unacceptable to the next. In any case, almost all authorities are agreed that sexual desires and behavioral patterns are primarily determined very early in life by the complex interreactions of children with other members of society—usually their parents, but also brothers, sisters, playmates, uncles, aunts, etc.

FORMS OF VARIANT SEXUAL BEHAVIOR

The many forms of sexual behavior have been categorized under special names and some of the more common of these will be considered here. However, it is important to realize, as previously noted, that no individual is likely to desire one form of sexual behavior to the exclusion of all others. Variations occur in us all to greater or lesser degree, and we will discuss some of these variations under their common names.

Homosexuality

This form of sexual behavior is simply that of erotic love between two persons of the same sex. They may be two males or two females, though the latter situation is commonly referred to as lesbianism (derived from *Lesbos*, an island which was the home of Sappho, a poet of ancient Greece who was herself a homosexual).

Before proceeding further, it will be of value to ask whether such behavior occurs in the animal world or is confined to man. Quite simply the answer is that homosexual behavior is found in various forms almost throughout the entire animal kingdom. In fish, sex discrimination is probably quite poor. Guppies and sticklebacks, which have both been well studied, display extensive homosexual behavior in both sexes. Going further up the evolutionary scale to amphibians, toads and frogs have very poor sexual discriminatory powers. In the American toad only the males croak and exhibit a peculiar body vibration, but the male toad will grasp and mount any other toad. If the toad he mounts is another male, it will croak and vibrate and the mounting toad lets go. If on the other hand, it grasps and mounts a female, there is no croak or body vibration in response and the two will continue their sexual activity.

Going still further up the evolutionary scale, lizards exhibit extensive homosexual behavior and indeed masturbation as well. Birds also are sometimes homosexual, though not as commonly as lizards.

So far as mammals are concerned, it is safe to say that in all species that have been studied homosexual activity has been observed and is indeed common. In the domestic cow, for example, females mount females, particularly when in estrous, and bulls mount bulls; young bulls are actually used as "teasers" to sexually arouse more mature bulls so that semen may be collected from them. Homosexual behavior is also common in more highly developed mammals such as the dolphin. Likewise in primates, including the baboon and chimpanzee—the latter being our closest living realtive. From the foregoing we may conclude that from a biological point of view homosexual behavior is common in virtually all animals; it is not in any way a uniquely human practice. Studies done on animals have determined that it is behavioral conditioning that results in homosexuality, with sex hormones playing a secondary and little-understood role.

Virtually all authorities on homosexuality agree that it is not an entity, that there are as many different types of homosexual behavior as there are heterosexual, and that in addition to society's taboo on this form of behavior, homosexuals have to contend with the same kinds of problems as those found between heterosexuals. Thus it is clear that this discussion, like our earlier discussion of heterosexual practices, can only be in generalities. It is also most important to realize that large numbers of people are bisexual, and can establish an erotic relationship with members of either sex. It is not at all unheard of for a happily married man or woman with children to carry on a homosexual relationship outside the family.

Apparently both male and female homosexuals have a great deal in common so far as causes and behavior are concerned, though the latter usually have the more stable relationships. Both sexes, for example, have the capacity to find homosexual satisfaction where members of the opposite sex are excluded from their daily lives, under such circumstances as sexually segregated schools and religious institutions, armed forces, and jails. So far as the incidence of homosexuality is concerned, Kinsey estimated that 37% of American males have had some form of homosexual experience during their lives, and that 5% have beeen exclusively homosexual during their entire lives. For women the incidence of exclusive homosexuality is much lower, perhaps 1 to 2%. Also much more is known about male homosexuality, and thus this discussion will inevitably be weighted in that direction.

The popular conception that male homosexuals are physically weak and behave in effeminate ways is quite misleading. While it is true of some (and true of some heterosexuals as well), male homosexuals are frequently strong and masculine and admire other masculine men (also true of heterosexuals). They may be found in all walks of life, from the roughest to the most aesthetic, and usually cannot be visually distinguished from other men. They tend to find women sexually threatening and are afraid of them, and therefore cannot make erotic advances to them. They find other men much easier to approach sexually, and do not consider this to be at all abnormal or unnatural. However, some homosexual males often get along well with women so long as sex does not enter their relationship.

Since two homosexuals cannot, because they lack the anatomical organs of the opposite sex, carry out sexual intercourse in the hetero-sexual sense, it is appropriate to ask just what sexual acts they usually perform. In lesbians these may vary all the way from what appears as a purely psychological or emotional attachment, through physical embraces and kissing (which society so commonly accepts among women but generally disapproves among men) to the inducing of orgasm by genital manipulation, oral-genital activity, and mutual masturbation. In male homosexuals much the same applies, but mutual masturbation is very much more common and in some cases there is anal penetration (which sometimes occurs in heterosexual behavior also).

Theories about the causes of homosexuality are legion, and despite a great deal of very good and meticulous research into the subject there are still great gaps in our knowledge and indeed much disagreement even among experts. Only a few years ago it was widely believed that homosexuality was almost wholly hereditary. This point is still not finally settled, in that some professionals still believe there are hereditary factors. However, the evidence is now quite conclusive that genetic factors play only the minutest of roles, if any at all. It has been observed that there is a tendency for male homosexuals to be late arrivals in a family, and it is generally true that the chromosomes in the eggs of an older women have more abnormalities than those of a younger woman. But that these might give rise to homosexual tendencies in the offspring is by no means proven (or even very strongly supported). The psychological relationships between a youngest son and an older mother are often very tense, and this could cause eventual homosexual behavior quite independent of any hereditary factor.

While homosexual behavior is probably a potential within every man and woman, the best evidence is that certain patterns of family background produce a much greater incidence of homosexuality than others. Even so, great caution must be observed in equating cause and effect. One of these patterns is the situation in which the father shows little affection for son—or worse, is actually hostile and even cruel toward him. A young growing boy needs a male model with which to identify, and of course this is usually the father. If the father-son relationship is poor the son may reject the father (his male model) and form a close emotional relationship with the mother. For reasons not clearly understood, though possibly through identification with the nurturing parent, such a family situation often produces a homosexual son. Another such pattern is one in which the father is (from a behavioral point of view) a rather weak, submissive individual in comparison to the mother, who not only "rules the roost" but treats the father as if his only function was to bring in the paycheck—which is never enough! Again for reasons not understood, but possibly through identification with the power figure, a son in such a family often grows up to be a homosexual. It has also been observed that children who eventually grow up to be homosexuals begin erotic behavior at an earlier age than their heterosexual counterparts.

In the case of lesbians little is known about the background family relationships, though some authorities believe that the young girl deprived of maternal love for any reason may have a tendency towards later homosexuality. It must be borne in mind that parental relationships are certainly not the only factors; brother, sister, peer, and teacher relationships are all involved but very little understood.

Wherever future research may lead us, it seems certain that sexual attitudes and behavior, at least those of a homosexual, bisexual, or heterosexual nature (and probably others to be discussed later) are determined very early in life, perhaps by the age of seven or eight. Almost all students of the subject are agreed that sexual attitudes are pretty well determined by the age of puberty, and that they are not likely to be changed either voluntarily or by various medical treatments except perhaps with great difficulty. In view of what is now known, it seems not at all unreasonable to put people's sexuality in a continuum, with a few highly heterosexual individuals at one end and a few exclusively homosexual individuals at the other end. The vast mass of people in the middle can be classed as bisexual, and they will tend to heterosexual or homosexual behavior, depending on their background and other circumstances.

In recent years, many countries and states, though not all, have relaxed their laws relating to homosexual behavior. Nevertheless, the homosexual is generally looked on as sick and/or a criminal, and often treated as both. Most people cannot hope to understand the fear and loneliness that many homosexuals experience year in and year out, and one may well ask what right society has to harass them in such a way. Two opposing views on this question have recently been given by different distinguished psychiatrists. The first, Dr. Manfred Guttmacher has written: "I have great faith in the democratic process. If it is the considered will of the majority that large numbers of sex offenders, most of whom admittedly have a high social nuisance value, be indefinitely deprived of their liberty and supported at the expense of the state, I readily yield to that judgment"*to which Dr. Thomas Szasz has replied:

> There is little meeting ground between those who "readily yield" to such a judgment and those, like myself, who repudiate such democracy as the quintessence of totalitarian oppression.

---

*Dr. Manfred Guttmacher, *Sex Offenses*, New York, W.W. Norton, 1951.

The importance of the political aspect of the problem of homosexuality cannot be exaggerated. Guttmacher stated that, if sex offenses—among them homosexuality—are condemned by the majority, one's loyalty to the group requires supporting that condemnation and the legal sanctions backing it. Why stop at homosexuality? If the majority finds Jews, Negroes, or atheists offensive, should it be free to harass them also? This logic is behind many of our present views and practices concerning homosexuality. As long as attorneys, legislators, and psychiatrists find this logic acceptable, their protests against specific measures, on the grounds that they are "unscientific," are doomed to fail.

There is, of course, another conception of democracy. According to it, democracy is not simply a political organization in which the majority tyrannizes the minority but one in which the freedom of minorities from such oppression is a foremost consideration. John Stuart Mill (1859) was one of the ablest champions of this classic idea:

"There is a limit to the legitimate interference of collective opinion with individual independence; and to find that limit, and maintain it against encroachment, is as indispensable to a good condition of human affairs, as protection against political despotism (p. 7)."*

In my view, the opinion expressed by Dr. Szasz is wholly commendable. There does not seem any rational reason why society should have the right to incarcerate homosexuals for their sexual behavior, which is as natural to them as heterosexual behavior is to others. Nor in my view, should society have the right to attempt to "reform" or "cure" them unless it is their specific desire. On the contrary, what needs to be reformed is society's attitude toward the homosexual. In recent years much progress has been made, but there is still a long way to go.

Transvestism

In this form of behavior the individual derives sexual pleasure by dressing in the clothes of the opposite sex, and may also actually think of himself or herself as feeling more like the opposite sex. Like so many other variant forms of sexual behavior it is more common among males than among

---

*Dr. Thomas S. Szasz, "Legal and Moral Aspects of Homosexuality," in *Sexual Inversion: The Multiple Roots of Homosexuality*, edited by Judd Marmor. © 1965 by Basic Books, Inc., New York.

females. Variations of transvestite behavior are wide, running all the way from a male who occasionally dresses in female clothes to small boys who simply cannot think of themselves as anything but girls and insist on behaving that way right into adult life.

Transvestites are normally heterosexual, though very occasionally there may be one who tends to homosexuality. They commonly derive great sexual pleasure from dressing in the tight and restrictive clothes worn by women, (corsets, bras, garters, etc.) and will often masturbate while so dressed. Psychoanalysts have attempted to understand what goes on in the mind of a transvestite while he behaves in such a manner, and it seems that many of them are creating a fantasy woman to their own special desires of the moment. At one time this fantasy woman may be of an extremely seductive nature, providing the creator with optimum sexual excitement and a feeling of extreme masculinity. At other times the fantasy woman may be kind, gentle, cruel, or dominant, depending on the desires of the man. Cross-sexual fantasizing is found in virtually everyone, of course, and the transvestite is simply carrying it a little further than most.

It has already been pointed out that a young child commonly learns its initial sexual role by identifying itself with the parent of the same sex. There is, of course, enormous cultural and social conditioning involved in this, but generally speaking boys learn to dress and behave like their fathers, and girls like their mothers. Occasionally this learning process somehow breaks down, and the small boy simply chooses to dress, play, and behave like a girl—a practice which quickly becomes the normal way for him. Attempts have been made, with little success, to change such behavior back into the typical male pattern, so that the individual will grow up without the transvestite characteristics. Once again the question has been asked whether there is moral justification for attempting to change young boys so inclined. One answer is that it is justified simply because of society's intolerance of transvestism, and if his behavior is changed it will make his life much happier. This is a valid argument, but is it valid to require that the boy conform to society's concept of what is right in this matter? It is an open question.

There are of course many women who dress in what are considered masculine clothes. However, this is very rarely done for the transvestite's reasons—to achieve erotic satisfaction. Young girls and women often wish to be of the opposite sex, but apparently not for erotic reasons.

Dress has great sexual significance, of course, and this will be discussed in a later chapter, but skirts are certainly not the sole domain of women (Scotsmen wear kilts) any more than trousers are the domain of men. In most societies men and women may legally dress as they please, but the prejudice and double standard of our society is once more evident in the fact that it tolerates women dressed as men far more easily than men dressed as women.

Pedophilia

This form of behavior is the sexual love of children. Although very occasionally a woman may display sexual interest in a young girl or boy, pedophilia in our society is almost exclusively found in males, and their sexual approach may be to either boys (homosexual) or girls (heterosexual).

The varieties of pedophiliac behavior are enormous, and may range all the way from assult by a sexually mature man on a young girl—even to the point of murder—to simply a preference for the company of children. By far the most common form of pedophilia is that in which a male (often heterosexual and happily married) makes advances to a child, particularly at the age of puberty, in an attempt to fondle or expose the childs genitals, buttocks, etc. This may progress to an attempt to persuade the child to manipulate the adult's genitals but actual sexual intercourse is rare. It should be noted that occasionally a man who has never had any previous pedophiliac tendencies may feel compelled to make sexual advances to children after he has suffered some severe personal loss.

As previously indicated, the great majority of pedophilia causes no physical damage at all, and indeed the child may well enjoy it and return for more. It is assumed, of course, that such experiences will be extremely harmful to the child. However, there is little evidence to support such a view, and certainly very large numbers of children do have some form of sexual experience with adults. While it is certainly not suggested that such sexual behavior be condoned or encouraged, parents should be reassured that any emotional or psychological damage is most unlikely, unless of course there has been something like actual physical rape. In fact, Kinsey has pointed out that the common aftermath of such sexual contacts in the form of hysterical condemnation by parents, police investigations, court appearances, and social ostracism may be far more damaging to the child than the actual sexual experience!

Adults who commit acts of pedophilia are to be pitied, for they are either physically ill or psychologically disturbed. They are usually in great need of emotional understanding and medical treatment. No amount of time spent in jail is likely to decrease their sexual desires and behavioral tendencies toward young boys and girls.

Sadism and Masochism

Because of their close association these two forms of sexual behavior are best treated together, and indeed they are often found in the same individual. A sadist is a person who obtains sexual pleasure from inflicting pain on someone else, usually by means of some kind of whip or cane or stick. The word is derived from the name of a Frenchman, the Marquis De Sade (1740-1814), who not only practiced sadism to excess, but wrote about it in great detail, arguing that it was an acceptable and indeed desirable form of behavior. It is perhaps not surprising that most of his works were written while he was in jail! Masochism, on the other hand, is the behavioral pattern in which the individual derives sexual pleasure from either self-inflicted pain or pain inflicted by someone else. This word comes from the name of the distinguished Austrian writer, Leopold von Sacher-Masoch (1836-1895), who was himself a masochist.

To those not familiar with the complexities of the human emotions and behavior it may seem absurd to think that the intimate and highly pleasurable acts associated with erotic love could be reinforced by the intentional infliction or receiving of pain. However, many of the human emotions are closely linked at the psychological level, and love and cruelty, pleasure and pain are often not so far apart. Some people at the height of orgasm respond as if in pain. In any case, both sadism and masochism are widespread, and as with so many other forms of sexual behavior, the seeds are within all of us. Indeed, millions of sexual partners engage in minor sadistic rituals as routine before sexual intercourse. It is only when such practices are carried to extremes and physically harm one of the partners—or cause them any degree of displeasure—that the urges must be curbed. Of course, no practice should be indulged in that is not desired by both partners.

It is said, though with little evidence to back it up, that men tend to be more sadistic, and women more masochistic! Whether this is true or not (and some men and women are certainly both), it is commonly the case that sadistic men cannot find a masochistic female partner. Thus they will often resort to houses of prostitution, which are experts at satisfying their customers' most eccentric needs. One of the most famous of these, the Moulin Rouge in Paris (immortalized by the painter Toulouse-Lautrec), actually had a "torture chamber" with a fine assortment of whips, where the sexual needs of their wealthy and distinguished customers were satisfied. The classic eighteenth century novel, *Fanny Hill,* by John Cleland, also contains accurate descriptions of sadism and masochism in practice.

Any judgment or condemnation of sadism or masochism must be tempered by the fact that such individuals are, in their own minds, behaving in a ritualistic way aimed at obtaining sexual satisfaction, and that they genuinely hope the partner will derive sexual pleasure in the same way that they do. If this happens not to be the case, severe antagonism will develop.

Exhibitionism

This is an exclusively male form of behavior in which the individual publicly exposes the genitals, usually with the penis erect, and usually in the presence of a young woman. His aim is to achieve sexual excitement and self-assurance from the young woman's reaction, and the exposure is usually followed by masturbation rather than by any advance to the woman. Exhibitionists are almost invariably very insecure, lonely individuals, often sexual failures who are, in their minds, simply trying to draw attention to themselves and establish their masculinity. The exhibitionist thinks that his erect penis will greatly impress the woman, and this gives him reassurance. (Men in general imagine that the larger the erect penis, the more of a man one is likely to be and the more women will admire it. However, the reality of the situation seems to be that women are seldom impressed by the size of the penis! Other male characteristics are apparently more important to them.)

A man may resort to exhibitionism once in a lifetime or habitually. The penalties for such behavior are usually very severe, which seems unnecessary when one realizes that such persons are suffering from great insecurity, and that in fact their actions do little if any harm to anyone.

Fetishism

The fetishist, usually male, becomes erotically obsessed with an object (a fetish) which is not sexual in the usual sense (e.g., gloves, shoes, pictures, furniture, a car, etc.) He may symbolically fall in love with it and perform ritual sexual acts in its presence. As with so much sexual variation, fetishism is potentially within everyone, and a person who for any reason cannot achieve satisfactory sexual relations with a member of the opposite sex may well seek gratification by turning to some other object with which success is more easily assured.

Buggery

Quite simply, buggery is sexual intercourse via the anus rather than the vagina. The word is sometimes used to signify sexual acts with an animal. However, anal intercourse is also called sodomy, while human sexual relations with animals is referred to as bestiality.

Anal intercourse is most common among homosexuals, though it certainly occurs among some heterosexuals as well. To the well informed it should come as no surprise that some people derive sexual pleasure from anal stimulation, and as previously pointed out the muscles surrounding the anus contract powerfully during orgasm. The law normally attaches the most severe penalties to sodomy, though once again this is not likely to stop those so inclined, and indeed it is difficult to see what harm such behavior does between consenting adults.

Kinsey estimated that some 5% of American males, mostly farm workers, engaged in sexual acts with a whole variety of farm animals. Though there is little scientific knowledge on the subject, it seems not surprising that young men in lonely areas and deprived of female company might well resort to animals for sexual gratification.

There are many other forms of sexual variation besides these mentioned, most of which are more common than is generally realized. There is voyeurism, in which the voyeur (or "Peeping Tom") obtains sexual satisfaction by observing others having sexual relations. There is fellatio, which is oral contact with the penis, and cunnilingus, or oral contact with the vulva. Society usually abhors oral sex, but it is certainly widespread and some people find it very desirable. It is hard to understand what harm is involved where there is mutual consent.

In general it may be said that our aim should not be to condemn sexual behavior of a variety we do not choose to participate in, but rather to understand and tolerate it where possible.

PORNOGRAPHY

Pornography (from the Greek *pornographos,* the writing of harlots) consists of writings or visual materials of a sexual nature which are considered obscene. Some members of society have always regarded any distribution of pornography as potentially extremely dangerous and corrupting, particularly to younger people. Both the laws and public attitude regarding pornography are in a constant state of flux simply because no adequate definition of "obscene" has yet been established.

Until very recently no scientific studies had been published which attempted to determine whether or not pornographic materials did in fact have a detrimental effect on those observing them, and thus opinions were based largely on cultural tradition and ignorance. However, at least two excellent studies are now available: The first is that of the Danish Forensic Medical Council, carried out at the request of the Minister of Justice and the Danish Parliament and published in 1966. The second is the report of the United States President's Commission on Obscenity and Pornography (Bantam Books), published in 1970. The findings of this commission had the "distinction" of being rejected by both the President and Congress before they were even published!

Both the Danish and the United States studies were in depth, and even included actual experiments carried out with human subjects. Thus their findings, which are remarkably in agreement, have at least some scientific validity as opposed to the usual opinions and conclusions. Some short direct quotations from each report are in order, as they will neatly illustrate the main findings. The first is from the report of the Danish Forensic Medical Council:

> Thus the Council have no knowledge of scientific research which can be taken as proof that the reading of the specific writings in question, either by adults or children, contributes to infringements of the Penal Code by the parties in question.
>
> Whether such reading or looking at "obscene" pictures or films can be said to influence the sexual leanings of adults, the Council can state that it is commonly known in medical science that sexual leanings are fixed at an early age, probably around 5 or 6 years old, and are in any case completely established by the end of puberty. It is, therefore, hardly likely that the reading of "obscene" writings or the sight of films, etc., will change the sexual leanings of an adult person.
>
> Most people will be sexually stimulated by explicit erotic and pornographic description, unless the pornographic description is so coarse and unaesthetic as to be immediately repulsive to sexually normal people. The writers of such works aim at influencing the emotions erotically. This kind of sexual stimulation cannot in itself have any harmful effect on the reader. It can lead to sexual activity either with others or in the form of masturbation. As far as an adult individual is concerned, there are no bases for assuming any detrimental influence therefrom, either on the development of the person's mind or on his attitude to sexual activity. It is a matter of whether this sexual stimulation arises from porno- graphic writing of the type describing normal or deviating sexual activity, or whether it arises from the sight of "obscene" films, pictures, etc., displaying normal or deviating scenes of sexual activity.
>
> Before we approach the question of the possible effect on children and young people, it must be remarked that the Council is of the opinion that those people who buy and read pornographic books and procure "obscene" pictures and films are, for the vast majority, middle-aged and elderly men who seek sexual stimulation in this way. We can leave any detrimental effect completely out as far as pre-school-age children are concerned, since the means in question here—pornographic literature, pictures and films—will hardly be understood by the child as pornography. Early childhood may be assumed to have great importance in the psycho-sexual

development of the child, but here it is emotional experiences within the family in connection with the child's role as a boy or a girl and the identification with parents and brothers and sisters which will determine this development.

School age children will apparently often show an interest in and be able to a large extent to "understand" pornography; but the sexual role of the child is by now so fixed that one can scarcely reckon with further means, such as pornography, changing the sexual leanings of the child in any essential respect. Nor is there any reason to suppose that such further influence can cause the development of neurosis or other mental suffering in the child.

At puberty sexual experience acquires such a strong and socio-psychological quality that the question of the influence of pornography becomes more relevant than during actual childhood. The personality of the young person is insecure and undefined, open to influences from different directions, and fantasy is easily stimulated in those spheres aimed at by pornography. It must be stressed that at this age also the personal influence of contemporaries, parents and teachers and so on is essential for the general mental and psychosexual development of the young person. The effect of pornography will consist above all in the stimulation of sexual inclinations in the already existing direction and it is therefore doubtful whether pornography can change the direction of sexual inclinations.

In conclusion from the above, it can be stated as far as children and young people are concerned, that the experience of child and juvenile psychiatry gives no basis for assuming that pornography has any detrimental effect of significance which may cause sickness or abnormality. It is personal impressions, relations with individual people, and not coarse, external means which determine the development of a psychosexual nature in children and young people.

To sum up, the Council will hereafter state that, as far as the Council is aware, no scientific experiments exist which can lay a basis for the assumption that pornography or "obscene" pictures and films contribute to the committing of sexual offenses by normal adults or young people. On the basis of psychiatric and child-psychiatric experience it can neither be assumed that sexual leanings, the development of personality, and the ordinary attitude to sex and to ethical-sexual norms either in children or adults, can be detrimentally affected by the means in question (pornographic literature, pictures and films). It is doubtful whether these can have a beneficial effect on sexually shy, neurotic people, but it cannot be completely ruled out. This statement holds good regardless of whether the pornographic writings, pictures, etc., are of normal or sexually perverted content.*

The United States report is much longer and more diverse, thus two separate quotations are more appropriate.

Exposure to erotic stimuli appears to have little or no effect on already established attitudinal commitments regarding either sexuality or sexual morality. A series of four studies employing a large array of indicators found practically no significant differences in such attitudes before and after single or repeated exposures to erotica. One study did find that after exposure persons became more tolerant in reference to other persons' sexual activities although their own sexual standards did not change. One study reported that some persons' attitudes toward premarital intercourse became more liberal after exposure, while other persons' attitudes became more conservative, but another study found no changes in this regard. The overall picture is almost completely a tableau of no significant change.

Several surveys suggest that there is a correlation between experience with erotic materials and general attitudes about sex: Those who have more tolerant or liberal sexual attitudes tend also to have greater experience with sexual materials. Taken together, experimental and survey studies suggest that persons who are more sexually tolerant are also less rejecting of sexual material. Several studies show that after experience with erotic material, persons became less fearful of possible detrimental effects of exposure.†

Delinquent and nondelinquent youth report generally similar experiences with explicit sexual materials. Exposure to sexual materials is widespread among both groups. The age of first exposure, the kinds of materials to which they are exposed, the amount of their exposure, the circumstances of exposure, and their reactions to erotic stimuli are essentially the same, particularly when family and neighborhood backgrounds are held constant. There is some evidence that peer group pressure accounts for both sexual

_____

*Report of the Danish Forensic Medical Council, The Council, Copenhagen, Denmark, 1966.

†Report of the President's Commission on Obscenity and Pornography, New York; Bantam Books, pp. 29-30.

experience and exposure to erotic materials among youth. A study
of a heterogeneous group of young people found that exposure to
erotica had no impact upon moral character over and above that of
a generally deviant background.

Statistical studies of the relationship between availability of
erotic materials and the rates of sex crimes in Denmark indicate that
the increased availability of explicit sexual materials has been accompanied by a decrease in the incidence of sexual crime. Analysis
of police records of the types of sex crimes in Copenhagen
during the past 12 years revealed that a dramatic decrease in reported sex crimes occurred during this period and that the decrease
coincided with changes in Danish law which permitted wider availability of explicit sexual materials. Other research showed that the
decrease in reported sexual offenses cannot be attributed to concurrent changes in the social and legal definitions of sex crimes or in
public attitudes toward reporting such crimes to the police, or in
police reporting procedures.

Statistical studies of the relationship between the availability
of erotic material and the rates of sex crimes in the United States
presents a more complex picture. During the period in which there
has been a marked increase in the availability of erotic materials,
some specific rates of arrest for sex crimes have increased (e.g.,
forcible rape) and others have declined (e.g., overall juvenile rates).
For juveniles, the overall rate of arrests for sex crimes decreased
even though arrests for nonsexual crimes increased by more than
100%. For adults, arrests for sex offenses increased slightly more
than did arrests for nonsex offenses. The conclusion is that, for
America, the relationship between the availability of erotica and
changes in sex crime rates neither proves nor disproves the possibility that availability of erotica leads to crime, but the massive
overall increases in sex crimes that have been alleged do not seem to
have occurred.

Available research indicates that sex offenders have had less
adolescent experience with erotica than other adults. They do not
differ significantly from other adults in relation to adult experience
with erotica, in relation to reported arousal or in relation to the
likelihood of engaging in sexual behavior during or following exposure. Available evidence suggests that sex offenders' early inexperience with erotic material is a reflection of their more
generally deprived sexual environment. The relative absence of
experience appears to constitute another indicator of atypical and
inadequate sexual socialization.

In sum, empirical research designed to clarify the question has found no evidence to date that exposure to explicit sexual materials plays a significant role in the causation of delinquent or criminal behavior among youth or adults. The Commission cannot conclude that exposure to erotic materials is a factor in the causation of sex crime or sex delinquency.*

As a result of their studies, the United States Commission made four recommendations so far as this country was concerned:

1. Pornography plays a significant sex educational role in the absence of formal sex education, therefore there should be formal sex education on a wide scale.
2. Pornography is not dangerous to society, and there should be no censorship for consenting adults.
3. Pornographic materials should be denied to children under 16, even though there is no evidence that it does them any harm.
4. There should be extensive research into the effects of erotica on people's lives.

It is clear from both the Danish and United States reports, and almost all psychologists will agree, that sexual mores and behavior are determined not by the sight of pornographic materials, but by intimate parental and social relations very early in childhood. There is probably not a single man, woman, or child who has not had at least some exposure to pornography. The vast majority will quickly find it very boring and consequently discard it. A sexually disturbed minority will perhaps find it fascinating, but there is no evidence that it will change their sexual behavior in any way. It is also worthwhile noting that sexual offenders are almost invariably sexually ignorant.

All the evidence we have indicates that parents and society worry quite unnecessarily about the effects of pornography, particularly on children. Perhaps this is a reaction (conscious or unconscious) to their own inadequacies in supplying a healthy sexual environment for young children. Parents in particular bear an awesome responsibility in this regard, and it is truly tragic that we know so little about it. Our aim should be to drive pornography out by good sexual education.

Variations in sexual behavior, like all behavior, are difficult and complex problems, but it is certain that only tolerance, rational study, and judgments free of ignorance and bigotry are likely to improve the situation. The cruelty humans inflict on other humans is far more shocking than any of the various forms of sexual behavior.

---

*Ibid., pp. 30-32.

STUDY TOPICS

1. Explain the meaning of each of the following: (a) transvestism, (b) bisexuality, (c) heterosexuality, (d) homosexuality, (e) lesbianism.

2. Explain the meaning of each of the following: (a) pedophilia, (b) fetishism, (c) exhibitionism, (d) sadism, (e) masochism, (f) sodomy, (g) bestiality, (h) voyeurism, (i) incest.

3. Why do you think variant sexual behavior is more common among males than females?

4. At what age are sexual behavioral patterns formed? What is the evidence for this?

5. Describe some of the factors typical in the background of homosexual behavior.

6. What kind of gratification does a transvestite seek?

7. Discuss the social problems associated with pedophilia.

8. Discuss what kinds of problems are associated with sadism and masochism.

9. Explain the conclusions of the President's Commission on Obscenity and Pornography.

10. How would you tackle the problem of pornography? Is there a problem?

FOR FURTHER READING

Brownmiller Susan, *Against Our Will*. New York: Simon and Schuster, 1975.

Caprio, Frank S., *Variations in Sexual Behavior*. New York: The Citadel Press, 1961.

Goldstein, Michael J., Harold S. Kant, and John J. Hartman, *Pornography and Sexual Deviance*. Berkeley: University of California Press, 1973.

Green, Richard, *Sexual Identity Conflict in Children and Adults*. New York: Basic Books, 1973.

Karlen, Arno, *Sexuality and Homosexuality—A New View*. New York: W.W. Norton, 1971.

Marmor, Judd (Editor), *Sexual Inversion, the Multiple Roots of Homosexuality*. New York: Basic Books, 1965.

The Report of the Commission on Obscenity and Pornography. New York: Bantam Books, 1970.

Storr, Anthony, *Sexual Deviation.* Baltimore: Penguin Books, 1964.

CHAPTER TEN

Fertilization, Pregnancy, and Childbirth

*I think, dearest Uncle, you cannot **really** wish me to be the 'Mamma d'une **nombreuse** famille'; for I think you will see with me the great inconvenience a **large** family would be to us all, . . . independent of the hardship and inconvenience to myself; men never think, at least seldom think, what a hard task it is for us women to go through this **very often.***

Letter from Queen Victoria of England to her uncle, King Leopold of the Belgians, January 5th, 1841.

Queen Victoria's admonition to her uncle, King Leopold of the Belgians, did not prevent her from having nine children! Giving birth to many children has been the lot of most women until very recent times—and childbearing has usually been a dangerous business. A little over a century ago about ten women in every 100 died shortly after childbirth from puerperal fever, an infection of the genital tract commonly called "childbed fever." Mankind owes a great debt to the Hungarian physician Ignaz Philipp Semmelweiss (1818-1865), who reduced maternal mortality from over 10% to less than 2% simply by ordering that all attendants at childbirth in his Vienna hospital wash their hands "in an aseptic" solution—in his case "chlorinated lime." It is interesting also that many historians have noted that the stage of a civilization may be judged by its attitude to the childbearing woman. All too commonly this profound process and its effect on the women concerned are not understood, nor are the women given the respect and care they so richly deserve and need.

Sexual intercourse can be seen to have several functions: the release of sexual tensions, the establishment of emotional ties with another person, the expression of deep love and partial dependency, and reproduction. Unrestricted sexual intercourse, without the use of contraceptives, will sooner or later (usually sooner) result in fertilization of an egg and the beginning of a new individual. In the human being the average time span from fertilization to birth is 267 days, or about nine months. The growth of the human fetus, like most biological processes, is extremely complex, and enormous changes take place in the mother to accommodate her baby. During the nine months or so that the fetus is within the mother she is said to be pregnant, and this condition terminates with the birth of the baby.

PRELIMINARY CONSIDERATIONS

It is pretty well agreed today by most people that the production of a new human being should be an act of the highest responsibility, undertaken only after full consideration of the potential consequences. Hopefully, such consideration will include the understanding that the world is overpopulated now, that to be responsible parents means to give up many freedoms for long periods of time, that one's whole way of life will inevitably be altered, and that the mother will go through a permanent physical transformation. It seems obvious, also, that the production of a new human being should not take place unless the parents have a reasonable chance of giving their offspring good care and opportunity, and this will be greatly facilitated if the parents are themselves in good physical and mental health. Obviously no parents can hope to be perfect, but at the same time many couples, if properly aware and advised, would not and should not, have children if the welfare of the children is of any concern. All this having been taken into account, human reproduction can nevertheless be a great emotional and very satisfying event.

FERTILIZATION

Sperm were first described in 1679 by the Dutch microscopist Anthony van Leeuwenhoek (1632-1723), and in 1827 the German zoologist Karl Ernst von Baer (1792-1876) described the human egg. It was not until 1843, however, that the English physician Martin Barry (1802-1855) observed and described the fertilization of a mammalian egg, and thus made possible our present understanding of how a new human embryo begins. This process of fertilization is an excellent example of what is known as a *tissue-specific reaction,* where sperm will enter only an egg and an egg will receive only a sperm. As might be suspected, this process is also a *species specific reaction* in that sperm will usually only enter an egg of the same species—though there are exceptions.

Under average conditions it takes about one hour for a human sperm to move from the cervical opening to the upper third of the Fallopian tube where fertilization usually takes place. Once a sperm penetrates an egg the egg is referred to as a *zygote,* and in a remarkable process the outer membrane of the zygote, called the *zona pellucida,* lifts up from the surface and goes through various chemical changes, the results of which are that no more sperm can gain access (Fig. 10.1). Normally only one sperm enters an egg, but occasionally more get in, in which case only one fertilizes the nucleus of the egg. Multiple fertilization may also result in the death of the zygote. It is estimated that at least one third of all zygotes die shortly after fertilization. When the egg is fertilized, its 23 chromosomes are combined with the 23 from the sperm, restoring the total number to 46, the diploid number for the human species. If the egg receives a male-determining sperm, the zygote will start the long process of development toward a human male, but if it receives a female-determining sperm, the child will be female. In both cases, however, many other factors enter into sexual development. (See Chapters, 3, 4, and 5.) Since both types of human sperm are produced and ejaculated in approximately equal numbers, it is interesting that far more male sperm reach and fertilize an egg than do female sperm. Exact figures are very difficult to obtain, but is is probable that there are about 150 male zygotes to 100 female zygotes. By the time of birth the figures are about 106 males to 100 females; in the late teens it is about 100 to 100; but from there on the number of females exceeds the number of males until in the eighties there are twice as many females as males. With whatever advantages nature and society may have endowed the male sex, long life certainly is not one of them! Females are simply biologically more durable than males.

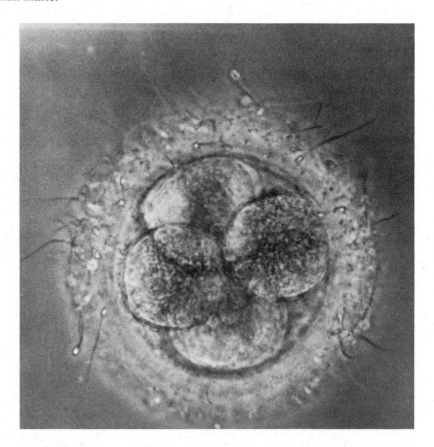

Fig. 10.1. The human zygote in the four-cell embryonic stage of development. Note the sperm in the outermost layer still trying to enter the developing embryo. (Courtesy of Dr. R.G. Edwards, Physiological Laboratory, Cambridge University, England.)

Within hours after fertilization the zygote will start to divide and the process of cleavage begins. Even at this early stage there is some differentiation within the zygote, certain parts being destined for various anatomical organs. Once cleavage is under way it is quite rapid, and within five days the zygote will have formed a hollow sphere called a *blastocyst.* This contains about 100 cells, most of which are concentrated in a tiny disk on one side of the hollow blastocyst. About four or five days after fertilization, the blastocyst emerges from the Fallopian tube and enters the uterus. By this time the zona pellucida has been lost and the blastocyst, which is only about 1/10 mm in diameter, is covered by a layer of cells called the *trophoblast.* The trophoblast is of the utmost importance, since these cells are destined to become the membranes of the placenta which will in turn produce special hormones. At this stage the blastocyst is ready to implant, and this event occurs usually within one day after the blastocyst enters the uterus.

What causes a blastocyst to implant in the wall of the uterus, while an unfertilized egg simply passes on through, has been the subject of much speculation and scientific study. Many factors are involved. The uterine lining must have reached a certain stage in the proliferative phase and the blastocyst must have developed to a certain point which includes the loss of the zona pellucida. Some scientists believe hormonal reactions are involved, while others believe that many chemical reactions are working at once. Whatever the causes, however, the blastocyst quickly becomes completely imbedded in the tissues of the uterine wall (Fig. 10.2). The implanted blastocyst is referred to as an *embryo* until the eighth week, when it is called a *fetus.* Once implantation occurs, the maternal uterine lining changes; glandular activity increases, as well as blood flow and the storage of glycogen and fat. At the same time the trophoblast cells of the embryo start to divide and produce the hormone *chorionic gonadotrophin.* The functions of this hormone are not entirely clear, but it probably acts on the maternal ovaries and pituitary gland in such a way that it stops the menstrual flow which would otherwise occur some two weeks after ovulation (in this case, fertilization). It should be noted that while menstruation usually ceases after implantation (giving the female a signal that she is pregnant), this is not inevitable. Sometimes menstruation will continue for two or three months after pregnancy begins. Conversely, as previously pointed out in Chapter 4, the cessation of menstruation is no guarantee that pregnancy has begun. Once the trophoblast of the embryo starts to produce chorionic gonadotrophin, it quickly appears in the mother's urine, and its presence in the urine is a sure sign that pregnancy has begun. There are now quick and cheap biochemical tests for detecting it, and it is unfortunate that these tests are not more easily available.

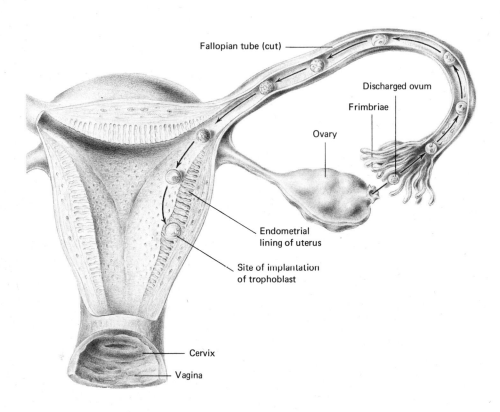

Fallopian tube (cut)

Discharged ovum

Frimbriae

Ovary

Endometrial
lining of uterus

Site of implantation
of trophoblast

Cervix

Vagina

Fig. 10.2. Cross section of the human uterus, showing implantation.

Details of the complexities of embryonic development are not meant to be part of this book, but a few words of explanation are in order. After implantation the disk of cells within the cavity of the blastocyst starts to form a cavity called the *amniotic cavity.* The enclosing membrane of this cavity is called the *amnion.* The amnion grows out and surrounds the embryo, while at the same time the cavity fills with fluid, providing a watery, marinelike cushion in which the embryo will be bathed until just before birth. On the opposite side to the amnion, there is an outgrowth called the *yolk sac.* At the same time the outer layer of cells of the trophoblast, called the *chorion,* starts to put out *villi* which invade the endometrial lining of the uterus. The chorionic villi together with the attached lining of the uterus is called the *placenta,* which is attached to

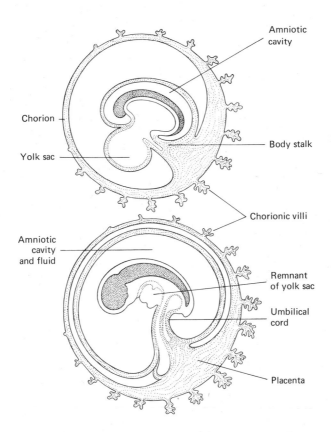

Fig. 10.3. Diagrams of the human embryo at two different stages of development, showing relationships of amniotic cavity, yolk sac, chorion, villi, umbilical cord, and placenta.

the developing embryo by the umbilical cord. This is shown diagramatically in Fig. 10.3. So rapid is the growth of the placenta that within four weeks of implantation it covers 20% of the internal surface of the uterus. It will eventually cover 50% of the uterine lining and with the villi will have a surface area of many square yards. By four weeks the embryo, while still tiny, is well differentiated and on the road to becoming a new human being (Fig. 10.4).

The growth rate of the human embryo up to eight weeks is shown diagramatically in Fig. 10.5. At three months the fetus is more or less completely formed, but still weighs less than an ounce. The fetus puts on 90% of its birth weight during the last four months, and 50% during the last two.

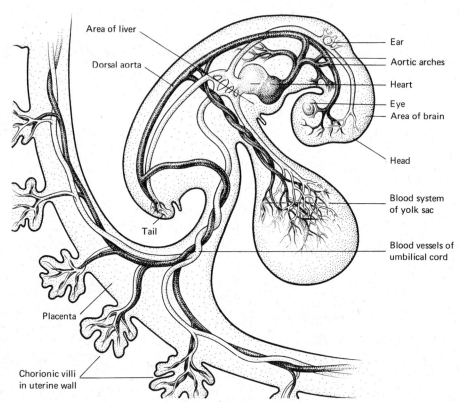

Area of liver

Dorsal aorta

Ear

Aortic arches

Heart

Eye

Area of brain

Head

Blood system
of yolk sac

Blood vessels of
umbilical cord

Tail

Placenta

Chorionic villi
in uterine wall

Fig. 10.4. Development of the human embryo at four
weeks, when it is still only one-fifth of an inch long.

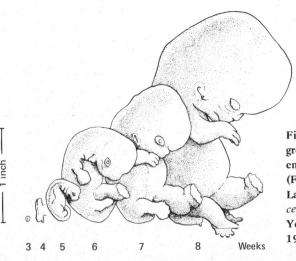

1 inch

3 4 5   6   7   8   Weeks

Fig. 10.5. Approximate
growth rate of the human
embryo up to eight weeks.
(From Roberts Rugh and
Landrum B. Shettles, *Conception to Birth.* New
York: Harper and Row,
1971. Used by permission.)

The placenta is actually an exchange organ between the mother and the developing embryo. Capillaries from the mother and the embryo intertwine within the placenta in such a way that exchange of materials across the membranes takes place without actual mixing of maternal and embryonic blood. The placenta performs five major known functions for the fetus: It acts as a respiratory organ, exchanging gases (principally oxygen and carbon dioxide) between the mother and the fetus. It acts as a feeding organ by which the fetus is fed from the mother's blood. It acts as an excretory organ, removing the fetal wastes (urea, etc.) via the mother's blood. It is also the fetus' main barrier against infection. Finally, it is an endocrine organ secreting gonadotrophins which have a profound effect on the developing fetus, and it may have an additional endocrine function in initiating the process of birth.

PREGNANCY

With initiation of implantation, profound changes start within the mother's body, the effects of which will result in accommodating the developing embryo. The first sign that pregnancy has begun is usually a missed menstrual period. However, other symptoms may also rapidly occur. The breasts become heavier and fuller, and also more tender. There may be an increase in the frequency of urination, and feelings of nausea may develop. This nausea, which often includes vomiting, occurs in over 60% of pregnant women, usually lasts about four to six weeks, and, regrettably, its cause is quite unknown. If all these symptoms occur in conjunction with a missed menstrual period, then it is highly probable that the woman is pregnant, and it is important that she should seek the advice of a competent physician as soon as possible.

After pregnancy begins, the mother's uterus starts to grow rapidly, and it will eventually extend as high as the lower ribs and fill much of the abdominal cavity. Its weight will increase to perhaps 16 times that of its normal state. Its blood vessels increase in size, as do its muscle fibres, and all through pregnancy there are some contractions of the uterine muscles. These become more marked in later pregnancy, though they are not usually felt by the mother. As pregnancy progresses the cervix becomes softer, which will help it to expand more easily during birth. There are other major changes in the mother—her pituitary gland enlarges to almost double its normal size, and the thyroid, parathyroids, and adrenals also increase in size. As might be expected, these changes greatly alter the hormonal balance, which in turn exerts its effect in many ways. These include possible changes in the skin texture and pigmentation which often persist after pregnancy is over. The breasts enlarge and undergo considerable modification to prepare them for milk production. The skin glands become more active, hair may be shed in excess of normal, and the nails commonly become more brittle. There is also usually some increase in the mother's weight in addition to the weight of the fetus. As pregnancy advances there is a general increase in metabolic rate, also in the output of blood from the heart and in total blood volume. The nervous system may respond in a variety of ways, depending on the individual and her general health and well-being. These are but a few of the major transformations taking place during pregnancy, and they may give rise to many side effects. These can, in large part, be prevented or satisfactorily controlled with the help of proper care and diet, and competent medical advice. Thus, for the sake of her own health and that of her baby, it is important for the mother to receive professional advice as soon as possible in her pregnancy.

In comparison to former times our modern knowledge of bio-chemistry and physiology is enormous. The physician of today has at his or her command a great variety of accurate tests which can be used to detect many potential problems during pregnancy, and in large measure these problems can be satisfactorily controlled. It should be realized, however, that our ignorance is also great, and no one can hope for miracles or even perfection. Regrettably, maternal, fetal, and infant death rates are high, more so in the United States than in many other countries, and birth defects and maternal illnesses also inflict a heavy toll. The United States ranks only about 14th in infant mortality, 25th in life expectancy, and 18th in doctor-patient ratio. Good care and advice for a pregnant woman are priceless assets, and it is unfortunate that—for monetary or other reasons—all too few women seek it.

The physician undertaking the care of a pregnant woman may or may not be an obstetrician, but in any case he or she should have up-to-date knowledge on the subject. As more and more women enter the medical profession it is entirely desirable that they should specialize in obstetrics, since women are more likely to understand and respond to the problems of a pregnant woman. At present, however, most doctors in the United States are men, so we will refer to the doctor as "he."

In general it may be said that the more a physician knows about the physical and mental health of an expectant mother and the expectant father, and the hereditary background of both, the better able he will be to forestall and control any problems which may arise from a pregnancy or birth. Thus the initial prenatal examination is likely to be lengthy, and the expectant mother should be patient about it, for while pregnancy and childbirth are of course normal biological processes, they are demanding ones. The physician will want to know the woman's age and whether this is her first pregnancy. If it is not, he will want to know her experiences with previous ones, as well as her mother's experiences with pregnancy. He will also take a complete history of the woman's health, and will want to know about the husband's health as well. Most important, he will ask about any tendency toward certain illnesses in her family background, such as diabetes; heart, vascular, and lung diseases; and nervous disorders. The hereditary background of the expectant mother may be important to her own well-being, and the hereditary background of both the expectant mother and father may be of extreme importance to the baby. It is now possible to predict with good accuracy the possibility of certain severe hereditary defects while the fetus is still at an early age of development within the mother. The technique, which is at present expensive and not generally available, consists of withdrawing a small sample of fluid from the amniotic cavity (Fig. 10.6). This fluid normally contains cells from the body of the fetus, and these cells can be subjected to a variety of biochemical tests and chromosome analyses. At the present time over 40 severe hereditary diseases can be detected in this way at about the sixteenth week of development. If there appears to be a serious possibility of severe genetic defect in the fetus as a result of hereditary background, it may be well to seek the tests, and if they are positive, to decide whether to terminate the pregnancy.

The initial interview with the expectant mother will continue with questions about her present health and will be followed by an extensive physical examination. The physician will be concerned to know if she is suffering from nausea, cramps, breathing problems, vaginal discharges, headaches, swelling of hands or feet, or anything else which may be disturbing her. The physical examination will include such routine things as height, weight, the relation between the two, and blood pressure. Particular attention will also be paid to the heart, lungs (including an X-ray to detect tuberculosis), teeth, breasts, legs, etc., and any area where the woman may be experiencing difficulties. Routine tests include urinalysis and blood analysis. The object of the urinalysis is to detect glucose in the urine, the presence of which may signify diabetes, and also to detect certain proteins, particularly albumin, which may signify a danger of toxic conditions, possibly due to kidney malfunction. As previously explained urinalysis will also confirm pregnancy. Proper analysis of the expectant mother's blood will determine blood type, in the event that a transfusion might be necessary. It will also determine the Rh factor, and it may be necessary to determine this in the father also. Blood tests will also be made of the hemoglobin level to guard against anemia, and for the presence of the syphilis bacteria. Syphilis can be passed from the mother to the fetus, but this can now, fortunately, be prevented.

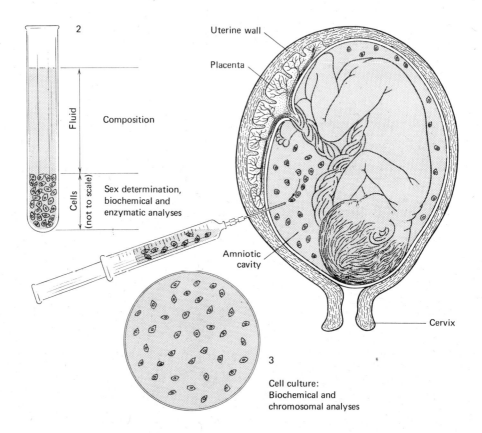

Fig. 10.6. Technique for detecting severe hereditary defects in a fetus.

Next, the physician will undertake a thorough pelvic examination, both external and internal. This is not at all painful and its purpose is simply to detect any potential problems. He will measure the pelvic girdle and calculate whether the mother is likely to have difficulty in delivering the baby. This may involve X-ray examination. If there is a danger, it may later be decided to deliver the baby by Caesarean section (i.e., by cutting through the mother's abdominal and uterine wall).

After the physician has all pertinent information he will of course advise the woman on any special treatments or precautions she should take during her pregnancy, and will at the same time arrange regular appointments, usually monthly, so that he can check that all is proceeding satisfactorily. Individual cases will vary, of course, but some generalizations regarding self care of the pregnant woman are in order. This care is designed in the best interests of both the expectant mother and her future child.

The adverse effects of overweight are too well-known to reiterate, but a certain amount of weight gain for a pregnant woman is inevitable and indeed normal. A gain of some 15-20 pounds over the 9 months is considered perfectly satisfactory. About one-half of this will be the weight of the fetus and placenta. The rest is comprised of stored fat and fluid, and the mother will want to take this off after the birth of her child. The more there is of it, the harder it will be to lose. It is also important that the weight gain should be fairly even and regular over the nine months. The gain is usually somewhat faster in the later months than in the early ones, but any sudden and rapid gain should be controlled. Closely related to weight, of course, is diet, and this is important to both the fetus and the pregnant mother. It has been remarked with some accuracy that a new human being starts off with only an egg and a sperm, "and everything else comes from the grocery store." The mother's diet should, therefore, contain everything necessary for the healthy development of the fetus, as well as for her own health. It is known beyond reasonable doubt that an inadequate diet in a pregnant woman can seriously damage fetal development, and adversely affect the health of both the mother and the newborn child. Some of this damage may be permanent. Details of recommended diet for a pregnant woman are available from many health organizations, but in general the usual well-balanced diet is advised with the daily intake of calories not increased by more than 300 over normal—and most of this only in the later months. It is particularly important that the pregnant woman get an ample supply of protein, vitamins, and minerals, and she should seek good advice as to a proper diet in her particular case.

Adequate exercise is essential to keep the human body in good condition, and the pregnant woman is no exception. Walking, bicycling, swimming, golf, tennis, etc., are all considered good methods of exercise for the pregnant woman. Special exercises may also be advised in individual cases. Since the woman's body is supplying all the physical needs of the fetus as well as her own, it is obvious that her physiological processes, such as heart function, take more energy, and therefore she may tire easily. Thus it is important that she take periodic rests between bouts of exercise and during her daily routine. Regular sleeping habits will also be helpful. In today's society many women have jobs, and it is generally felt that unless there are special reasons to the contrary the pregnant woman is well-advised to continue at her job until about a month before the birth is due. Obviously the nature of the job may be the deciding factor, but so long as the work is not too strenuous and does not involve too much standing or other undesirable aspects, there is no reason why normal work should not be continued and indeed be beneficial. Travel in moderation is perfectly safe so long as excessive fatigue is avoided. Travel during the last month or two of pregnancy, however, is not usually sanctioned by most physicians.

There are other important things to watch during pregnancy. For some reason teeth have a greater tendency to decay in the pregnant woman, and thus dental care is advised. Some women tend to become constipated during pregnancy, and this should be controlled by proper diet, not by taking laxatives which may effect the fetus. Similarly, douching is not advised; in any case nature usually has adequate means of keeping the vagina clean and in good condition. Needless to say, bodily cleanliness is important, and a daily bath or shower is recommended. Particular attention should be paid to washing the genitals and the breasts. During pregnancy the nipples of the breasts may excrete a watery fluid called *colostrum,* and unless this is washed away it may encrust and cause cracking of the nipples. When taking showers or baths, the pregnant woman must be especially aware of the danger of slipping and falling.

Normal sexual relations can be continued during pregnancy with both emotional and physical advantage to the woman and her sexual partner. Some modification of the positions customarily used by the partners may be necessary, and, as always, a considerate and cooperative male is a help. As pregnancy advances sexual intercourse will become more difficult and possibly painful to the woman, and thus it is not advised after about the seventh month. Sexual satisfaction can still be achieved, if desired, by mutual or individual masturbation.

Despite all precautions and proper care a pregnant woman may experience physical difficulties in addition to those already mentioned (morning sickness, increased urination, constipation, etc.). Such complaints as backache, heartburn, faintness, emotional upsets, shortness of breath, hemorrhoids, varicose veins in the legs, and other things may occur. However, common sense and medical advice will usually control them easily. No attempt to treat them with drugs or "home-made" remedies should ever be made without the advice of a physician.

The use of any drug by a pregnant woman poses a special problem, because while the particular drug may alleviate her physical or psychological difficulty, it is entirely possible (and often highly probable) that it will cause some harm—temporary or permanent—to the developing fetus. The use of drugs in general is something with which modern society will soon have to come to terms, for we have developed into a society of drug takers, and the local drug store is literally part of our lives. It is imperative that everyone understand that no drug yet discovered is entirely harmless. Even an aspirin tablet, perhaps one of the most widely used of all drugs, is potentially dangerous to some people. Thus the problem should always be to balance the need against the danger. If the need for the drug is great enough then the risk may be worth it, but there can be no doubt that in today's society we tend to exaggerate the need while minimizing, and commonly ignoring, the dangers.

The toll of human misery as a result of severe birth defects cannot easily be put into words, for children so born are a tragedy not only to themselves but to their parents and society in general. Somewhere between 5 and 10% of all children born have some kind of severe deformity, yet it is estimated that only 20% of such births are directly due to hereditary factors; the remaining 80% are due to an unfavorable embryonic and fetal environment. It is important to realize that the most vulnerable period is the first 12 weeks after conception, for it is then that the organs and organ systems are actually being formed. After that it is mainly a matter of increase in size. As previously pointed out, factors such as poor nutrition, general health, and habits in a pregnant woman may cause serious harm and even death to her fetus, and while it would be folly to blame all nonhereditary birth defects on the use of drugs by pregnant women, there can be no doubt that a high proportion of them are due to precisely that cause. Needless to say, the more a drug is used, the greater the danger.

While not wishing to be alarmist, we must note, some further highly pertinent facts. Such common habits as cigaret smoking and drinking alcohol, while potentially harmful to everyone, are especially dangerous for pregnant women. Unfortunately, the placental membranes are no barrier to most drugs which pass easily from the mother's blood through the placental membranes to the blood of the fetus. For example, nicotine, carbon monoxide, and carbonic acid—all found in cigaret smoke—pass readily to the fetus, and even one cigaret can cause the heartbeat of the fetus to increase and its blood vessels to contract. It has also been established beyond reasonable doubt that mothers who smoke heavily are more prone to have abortions and premature births, and their babies to convulsions and fits. Similarly, alcohol readily passes to the fetus, and there is evidence that it tends to concentrate there, particularly in the tissues of the brain and other organs. Other drugs are known to cause much more serious damage to a developing fetus, and no one should forget the terrible effects, and subsequent warning, of the drug thalidomide in the early sixties. In summary it may be said that the golden rule for any expectant mother contemplating the use of any drug is—DON'T. If the mother is in real difficulty and her need is great, she should consult a physician.

One other thing of which expectant mothers should beware is the danger of infectious diseases. Unfortunately these, like most drugs, may severely affect the developing fetus. Most bacteria are too large to cross the placental membranes, and thus the fetus is normally protected from them, but this is not true of the toxins that bacteria produce. Furthermore, most viruses can easily cross the placental membranes, and a developing fetus is highly vulnerable to diseases spread by these organisms. Among the common diseases an infected mother may pass to her fetus are smallpox, chicken pox, measles, German measles, mumps, scarlet fever, and syphilis. These and other diseases may cause havoc and even death to a developing fetus. As always, it is in the earlier embryonic stages of development that infection is likely to cause the most damage. For example, infection of the mother by German measles during the first month of pregnancy carries a 47% risk of serious and permanent damage to the fetus. The figure is reduced to 22% if the infection occurs during the second month and to 7% during the third month. In view of what is now known about the dangers to the fetus of maternal infection by German measles and other diseases during early pregnancy, the mother and other concerned persons may wish to consider a therapeutic abortion if the circumstances warrant. It seems obvious also that a pregnant woman should avoid contact with a potential source of infectious disease. Vaccines are available as protection against many diseases—including German measles—and a woman contemplating having children would be well advised to seek information on these some two to three months before she actually becomes pregnant.

CHILDBIRTH

Throughout the months of pregnancy the expectant mother should be preparing herself, physically and psychologically, both for giving birth and for the future care of her newborn baby. The process of giving birth—or parturition, as it is more technically called—is a major biological event, and it is imperative that the expectant mother approach it in good health and a good frame of mind. It is not appropriate in a book such as this to advocate any one form of preparation, and of course much will depend anyway on the advice of the particular physician. The expectant mother should, however, look into the great variety of prenatal books and classes which are available. Among those gaining great popularity today among younger women is the so-called "Pavlov-Lamaze" method of psychoprophylaxis, named after the great Russian physiologist Ivan Pavlov (1849-1936) and the French physician Fernand Lamaze (1890-1957). It is also sometimes called "childbirth without pain" or "childbirth without fear," and it consists basically of a course of prenatal exercises, particularly in breathing, combined with psychological conditioning that minimizes the fear and tensions which so commonly cause pain and distress during labor and parturition. It also stresses a basic knowledge of the physiological changes which take place during late pregnancy and parturition. This knowledge is extremely important to the woman in allaying fears and relaxing tension. (Labor, by the way, does not mean "the assumption of severe pain." It simply means "hard work," which accurately describes it.) However the expectant mother decides to prepare herself, a cooperative and understanding physician will be essential. Another essential factor will be a cooperative and understanding partner, and it is becoming more popular to have the father participate with the mother to the maximum degree. This includes his presence at labor and birth to physically and psychologically assist her in every way possible. Fathers who are willing, who have the necessary preparation, and who are permitted to participate in this process, experience deep emotional involvment with the mother, and are likely to have a special attachment to the newborn child. They were there!

It was pointed out earlier that the human fetus is more or less completely formed at about 12 weeks of development, and that the remainder of the nine months of pregnancy consists mainly of growth. This is true, though an enormous amount of complex development, particularly of the nervous system (formation of reflexes, etc.), takes place during the later part of pregnancy. By the seventh month a fetus is usually far enough advanced to survive alone, should it be born at this time; but important biological processes, such as the formation of antibodies and other defense mechanisms have still to take place. By the ninth month, however, if all has gone well, the fetus is fully ready to leave its watery "marine" environment and become a free-living, air-breathing, terrestrial mammal.

The usual position of the fetus at about one month before birth is shown in Fig. 10.7. By then it has grown to the point where it is in a very confined situation, and the mother's abdominal organs are being severely pressed and her abdominal skin stretched to the limit. Some two to three weeks before birth the blood vessels of the placenta start to degenerate, which in turn slows the growth rate of the fetus, and the mother may actually lose weight. Some 12 days or so before birth the heavily laden uterus descends into the pelvic basin, not only giving physical relief to the mother, particularly in her breathing, but also clearly indicating that the beginning of labor is not far off. By this time the expectant mother should have made full preparations to receive the best care possible during parturition.

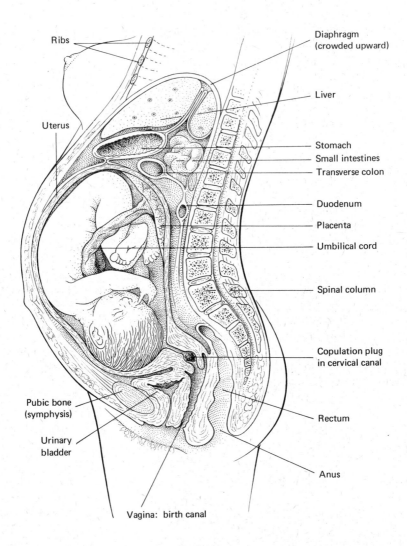

Figure 10.7. Position of the fetus within the expectant mother about one month before birth.

It is not known exactly how the whole process of labor and parturition is initiated and controlled, but it is probable that the hypothalamus of the brain is deeply involved, and certainly the posterior lobe of the pituitary gland releases a hormone, *oxytocin*, which has the effect of increasing the contractions of the uterine muscles. For each woman labor may start in a different way; the first sign may be simply strong uterine contractions, or there may be a slight bloodstained discharge from the vagina, or the amniotic membrane may rupture and release some of the amniotic fluid via the vagina sometimes in a considerable amount. This last, however, may not take place until much later in labor. When any or all of these signs occur, the expectant mother should get in touch with her physician. Quite commonly there is a condition known as "false labor," in which the uterine contractions may start to occur once or twice an hour, but instead of increasing their frequency may just stop and disappear completely. But whenever any of the other symptoms mentioned are also present, labor will probably continue with more frequent and regular contractions, birth will be imminent, and the woman should go to that hospital or clinic with which arrangements have been made. Once in the hospital she will, of course, receive various medical examinations, and will be carefully prepared for the birth of her baby. This preparation will most likely include a bath, the shaving of the pubic hair, and the administration of an enema; these are all designed as hygenic measures to protect the baby, and by emptying the rectum the enema will also assist the woman with labor. (See Fig. 10.7).

The whole process of parturition is commonly divided into three stages. The first stage consist primarily of the dilation of the cervix, which is necessary to allow the fetus to pass out of the uterus into the vaginal barrel. As dilation progresses, the lower and narrower part of the uterus and the cervix itself are merged with the main muscular walls of the uterus. At the same time the fetus is gradually pushed downward. When the cervix is fully dilated, the uterus, cervix, and vagina form the complete birth canal through which the fetus will pass, and the first stage of labor has been completed. The time span of this first stage may vary enormously, but it is almost always longer for the first pregnancy than for subsequent ones. About 16 to 20 hours is not uncommon for the firstborn, while 6 to 10 hours or less is common thereafter. It is during these long and often difficult hours that the father can be of the greatest assistance to the mother. Not only can he share the experience with her emotionally, but he can encourage her and physically help her with her body posture, relaxations, and breathing techniques which have been well worked out beforehand. It seems wholly unnatural and unnecessary that the father should be prevented from assisting the mother at this climactic event of parturition.

The second stage consists of the actual expulsion of the fetus through the birth canal (Fig. 10.8). This may last anywhere from 10 minutes to two hours depending on the particular woman and whether it is her first birth or a later one. It is during this stage that the mother will wish to use her abdominal muscles to supplement the rhythmic

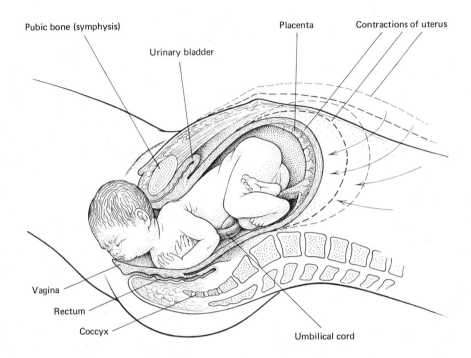

Pubic bone (symphysis)

Urinary bladder

Placenta

Contractions of uterus

Vagina

Rectum

Coccyx

Umbilical cord

Figure 10.8. Expulsion of the fetus via the birth canal during the second stage of parturition.

contractions of the uterine muscles. This is called "bearing down," and if properly carried out, together with effective breathing technique, it will greatly assist the mother in the process of birth. At any time up to and including the second stage, the attending physician may help any distress the mother is having by administering a drug or anaesthetic, but this should be left to his discretion. He may also decide during the later part of the second stage to perform an episiotomy. This consists of making a small cut at the opening of the vagina, to facilitate the passage of the baby's head and prevent possible tearing of the vaginal tissue. Between uterine contractions the baby's head may recede, only to emerge farther with subsequent contractions, but there comes a time when it is pushed fully through the vaginal opening and is exposed to the outside world. Once the head is through, the rest of the body usually follows rapidly, and the complete baby emerges still attached to the mother via the umbilical cord. At the same time that the baby actually emerges, there is a rush of the remaining amniotic fluid, which is highly bloodstained. Some few minutes after birth, but with no rush, the physician ties and severs the umbilical cord, and the physical attachment of the baby to the mother is ended.

The third stage of parturition consists simply of the explusion of the placenta. This occurs quite naturally as a result of uterine contractions, usually about 15 minutes after birth. Since the placenta actually separates from the uterine wall, it is not surprising that there is a certain amount of hemorrhage accompanying its expulsion, but clotting in the uterus soon takes place, and the bleeding stops rapidly.

The newborn baby will normally start to breathe quite naturally, but the physician may find it necessary to artifically encourage this by making the baby cry. Immediately after birth the baby will have a few drops of antibiotic placed in each eye. This is required by law almost everywhere, and is designed to protect the eyes against possible infection by the bacteria of gonorrhea. The baby will then be given a thorough physical examination and bath before it is given to the mother to hold. This is a great moment in her life as well as in that of the father, for together they have brought a new human being into the world, an act which will bring unmatched joys and inevitable sorrows—and heavy responsibilities which hopefully they are both willing and able to accept.

STUDY TOPICS

1. Explain the meaning of each of the following: (a) tissue specific reaction, (b) species specific reaction, (c) amnion, (d) chorion, (e) placenta, (f) morning sickness, (g) fetus, (h) embryo.

2. Explain the meaning of each of the following: (a) puerperal fever, (b) zygote, (c) Caesarean section, (d) colostrum, (e) parturition, (f) false labor, (g) oxytocin, (h) episiotomy.

3. Explain when, where, and by whom sperm and mammalian eggs were first described.

4. When and at what stage does the zygote become implanted in the uterine wall? What are the results of this implantation?

5. What are the major functions of the placenta?

6. What major physiological changes outside the uterus occur in a woman who becomes pregnant?

7. What changes, if any, should an expectant mother make in her normal daily life?

8. Make a list of infectious diseases that may endanger the fetus when contracted by the expectant mother.

9. Explain the dangers of an expectant mother using drugs, medicines, cigarets, alcohol, etc.

10. Describe the technique which can detect some severe hereditary defects in the fetus.

11. Give reasons for analysing an expectant mother's blood.

12. Describe the three stages of parturition.

FOR FURTHER READING

Edwards, R.G., and Ruth E. Fowler, "Human Embryos in the Laboratory," *Scientific American,* December 1970.

Friedman, Theodore, "Prenatal Diagnosis of Genetic Disease." *Scientific American,* November 1971.

Guild, Warren R., Robert E. Fuisz, and Samuel Bojar, *The Science of Health.* Englewood Cliffs, N.J.: Prentice-Hall, 1969.

Harrison, R.J., *Reproduction and Man.* New York: W.W. Norton, 1967, 1971.

Hytten, Frank E., and Isabella Leitch, *The Physiology of Human Pregnancy,* 2nd Ed. Oxford: Blackwell Scientific Publications, 1971.

Karmel, Marjorie, *Thank You, Dr. Lamaze.* Garden City, N.Y.: Dolphin Books, 1959, 1965.

Netter, Frank H., *Reproductive System,* Vol. 2, The CIBA Collection of Medical Illustrations. Summit, N.J.: The CIBA Pharmaceutical Co., 1965.

Rugh, Roberts, and Landrum B. Shettles, *From Conception to Birth—the Drama of Life's Beginnings.* New York: Harper & Row, 1971.

Film: *A Child is Born,* 16 mm, color, 22 min. New York, Holt, Rinehart & Winston.

CHAPTER ELEVEN
Contraception

Most girls just pray.

Title of an article in the *New York Times*,
October 1, 1971.

Contraception consists of any artificial means of preventing the sperm from fertilizing the egg. Its primary purpose is to permit sexual intercourse with a minimum risk of conception. Despite the historical necessity of human beings to reproduce in the face of war, pestilence, plague, and famine, people have for many centuries attempted to control their numbers by contraception, as well as by abortion and—more drastically—infanticide.

ANCIENT CONTRACEPTIVE PRACTICES

Clearly recorded references to intravaginal contraceptives date back as far as 1850 B.C., to an Egyptian medical text called the "Petri" papyrus. A more precise reference is given in the "Ebers" papyrus of about 1550 B.C. A subheading of the latter reads: "Beginning of the recipes made for women in order to cause that a woman should cease to conceive for one year, two years, or three years." There follows a description of what may quite accurately be called a lint tampon, and there are instructions for soaking it in honey or gum arabic before insertion into the vagina. Such methods, which have often included other substances like lemon juice or butter, have been used throughout the ages down to the present day. They do have some logical basis and value, for it has been well demonstrated that such substances immobilize sperm and so prevent them from gaining access to the cervix.

The literature of the ancient Hebrews, which has had such a profound influence on western civilization, contains references to the use of intravaginal sponges and to the method of coitus interruptus which is still in wide use today. The former method was used by the woman and was apparently generally permitted, while the latter method had to be carried out by the man and was considered a violation of the command to propagate. In general, the human race has always given the "divine laws" commanding propagation precedence over human welfare, an attitude which shaped the modern world and still exerts its influence today.

As might be expected, various means of preventing conception were known to such highly developed civilizations as those of the ancient Greeks and Romans. In his famous scientific work "Historia Animalium," Aristotle (384-322 B.C.) noted the fact that "some prevent conception by anointing that part of the womb where the seeds fall with oil of cedar, or with ointment of lead, or with frankincense commingled with olive oil." Another Greek, Soranos of Ephesus (98-138 A.D.), who practiced medicine in Rome and is commonly considered one of the earliest known gynecologists, discussed abortives and contraceptives at great length and agreed that it was much more advantageous not to conceive than to destroy the embryo. It seems obvious therefore, that some knowledge of contraception has always been available in western societies, and indeed there is no lack of reference to it in Chinese, Indian, Islamic, and other surviving literatures. Even in Medieval Europe something was known about it, despite the Christian church's heavy hand of condemnation.

INFLUENCES ON MODERN BIRTH-CONTROL PRACTICES—PRO AND CON

The development of modern contraceptives has unquestionably been one of the major factors that have freed women from their traditional role as "reproductive machines" and contributed immeasurably to general human welfare. The development of contraceptive devices was only half the battle, however; the other half was to gain social and political acceptance of contraception as a valuable tool for the promotion of human welfare, rather than as an invention of the devil. The battle has not been an easy one.

With the coming of modern times, and particularly the industrial revolution in the 18th and 19th centuries, new factors arose which were destined to largely break the religious and political condemnation of contraception. The two major factors were the rapid increase of appalling poverty in what became the urban slums of industrial towns, and the beginnings of preventive medicine. The latter had the effect of upsetting the longstanding balance between births and deaths; public sewers, clean water and later chlorinated water, vaccinations, and inoculations all decreased the death rate while leaving the birthrate untouched. This caused a rapid increase in the rate of population growth, which in turn compounded the urban poverty.

Robert Malthus

The English economist and clergyman, the Reverend Thomas Robert Malthus (1766-1834), while by no means understanding the causes, recognized the problem of overpopulation and in 1798 published (anonymously) his famous work *An Essay on the Principle of Population as It Affects the Future Improvement of Society.* The influence of this work, which has often been misinterpreted, has been astounding. Malthus argued that human beings tend to multiply faster than their food supply, and that human misery and its accompanying high death rate were inevitable. He argued further that it was quite useless for social reformers to attempt to change this situation by providing relief for the poor, because the poor would then rapidly increase their population, negating any rise in their standard of living and continuing the vicious circle.

Malthus was a clergyman in the Church of England, and while he found the whole thing rather sad, he nevertheless felt that it was the way

God had ordained the human lot and that it was not up to man to question or defy the law of God. He saw only three ways of adjusting the human population to the available food supply: vice, moral restraint, and misery. Malthus supported traditional morality, and to him anything that interfered with the process of conception was a vice, and abhorrent. (It is ironical that birth control should later come to be called "Malthusianism"!) By moral restraint Malthus meant that the poor should refrain from marriage and thus not have any sexual relations at all. This was the only method of population control that he advocated and could morally justify, though he was quite astute enough to know that it was not likely to work. There remained misery, an inevitable fact of life in Malthus' opinion, and one which it was useless to attempt to change.

Malthus' philosophy did have a sort of rough logic to it, and perhaps needless to say, he came to be hated by the poor and positively glorified by the rich. Landowners used his arguments as an excuse for evicting the peasants from their estates, and industrialists both in Europe and the United States found his theories an easy justification for ruthless commercial practices. Thus population, poverty, and misery continued to grow at an ever-increasing rate, and the stage was set for social reformers who would argue that contraception was no vice, and in any case was preferable to misery.

Francis Place

Though he had many predecessors, the English political and social reformer Francis Place (1771-1854) is usually referred to as the founder of the modern birth-control movement. He came from humble origins but rose to have considerable political influence. In 1822 he published *Illustrations and Proofs of the Principle of Population,* and the following year he published three handbills which were widely distributed. In these works he directly advocated contraception as a substitute for the moral restraint supported by Malthus. He further argued that the standard of living of the masses could be raised by limiting their numbers and thus making their labor in short supply. It was also his view that unrestricted births were a cause of child labor. Above all, however, Place's handbills gave direct and clear instructions on the methods of contraception then known, namely the sponge, coitus interruptus, and various kinds of tampons. The influence of Francis Place was enormous and he had many prominent helpers, but although he sought medical advice, the medical profession did not support his movement. Considering the general condemnation of Place's work by almost all the ruling classes, it is indeed remarkable that he did not find himself in jail. Subsequent advocates of contraception were not so fortunate.

Robert Owen

The birth control movement quickly spread to the United States, where in 1830 Robert Dale Owen (1801-1877) published *Moral Physiology*—the first book on birth control to be published in America. The techniques Owen offered were nothing new, but he showed remarkable foresight by pointing out that birth control was inevitable and that it would increase the rights of women.

Charles Knowlton

Two years after Owen's book, in 1832, Dr. Charles Knowlton (1800-1850), noted Massachusetts physician and free thinker, published *Fruits of Philosophy; or, the Private Companion to Young Married People.* In this work Knowlton not only discussed the moral and social aspects of contraception and the various methods then known, but added a new method which he claimed to have invented, namely douching. He designed a great variety of solutions for the purpose, and it is noteworthy that while it was by no means perfect, douching as a method of contraception proved effective enough so that it is still in use today, though not generally advocated. Knowlton also pointed out the advantage that it placed control in the hands of women—a matter of some importance. Dr. Knowlton is affectionately known as the "Father of American Birth Control," and his influence in this early period of the movement was great. In fact, so great was his influence that he got into trouble with the law—and had the dubious distinction of being the first person to be actually imprisoned for advocating birth control.

Bradlaugh, Besant, and Truelove

In the latter half of the nineteenth century some important events occurred which had profound effects on the birth-control movement. The first of these were two trials which took place in London in 1878. In the course of their efforts to spread knowledge of contraception, two English freethinkers, Charles Bradlaugh and Annie Besant, had pamphlets printed from Charles Knowlton's work and distributed them with the specific intent of testing the laws on obscenity. Similarly, one Edward Truelove had Robert Owen's book, *Moral Physiology,* reprinted and distributed. Legal action followed promptly at the instigation of the Society for the Suppression of Vice, and in the ensuing trials—which attracted much publicity—Charles Bradlaugh and Annie Besant were acquitted and their right to publish Knowlton's work upheld. Edward Truelove, however, was found guilty and sentenced to four months in prison, and the books in question were ordered destroyed. The result was electric, and a large section of the public rushed to Truelove's defense. Despite much pressure, he had to spend some time in jail, but upon release was hailed as a hero.

The social effects in England of these two trials went a long way (though not all the way) to making contraception legal. Distribution of contraceptive knowledge became widespread and contraception was practiced by all classes of society. Publication of books and pamphlets on contraception greatly increased, and general knowledge of the subject grew rapidly. Circulation of Charles Knowlton's work alone jumped from 1000 copies a year to a quarter of a million! More important still was the fact that from the time of the Bradlaugh-Besant trial the birthrate in England has progressively and continuously declined.

Anthony Comstock

In the young and rapidly expanding United States the need for contraceptive knowledge was not as great as in the more static European societies. Nevertheless, throughout the middle of the nineteenth century various efforts were made to spread such information. Some of the efforts succeeded, others were suppressed. Then, in 1873, the axe fell in the form of incredible bigotry from which this country has not yet fully emancipated itself. In that year the congress passed a bill which later became known as the "Comstock Law." This law explicitly banned the mailing, interstate transportation, or importation of "any obscene, lewd, or lascivious or any filthy book, pamphlet, picture, etc.—or other matter of indecent character, or any drug, medicine, article or thing designed, adapted, or intended for preventing conception, or producing abortion, or for any indecent or immoral use." From about the nineteen-thirties onward, this law has gradually been weakened by various court decisions, though its damage has been immense—and it is worthy of note that it has never been repealed!

Anthony Comstock (1844-1915) has a special place in the history of the birth-control movement in the United States, for he probably did it more harm than all other opponents put together. He was the secretary of the New York Society for the Suppression of Vice, and in this capacity had enough influence to get his law through congress. He then promptly arranged to have himself appointed special assistant to the post office in order to enforce the law, which he did with enthusiasm. It is said that in the years which followed, he was responsible for the imprisonment of over 300 people, the imposing of hundreds of thousands of dollars in fines, and the seizure of vast quantities of literature and contraceptive devices. He literally terrified anyone engaged in teaching contraception or using it, and regrettably his influence is still felt.

Margaret Sanger

No account of the struggle to make contraception available and acceptable in the United States can be complete without an account of the pioneer work of Margaret Sanger (1883-1966). In the early years of this century she was a public health nurse in New York, and at times her work took her to the poorer parts of that city where women lived in abject poverty and constant ill health, producing one child after the next—a classical Malthusian situation. Abortion was rife, and many women died either from self-induced abortions or from those performed by quacks. Margaret Sanger was appalled, but she quickly realized that one way of helping them would be to make contraception available. She knew virtually nothing about it herself, and being unable to get any help from the medical profession she went to Europe to gather practical information. On her return she published a periodical called *The Woman Rebel,* which was designed to test the Comstock law and to rally support for militant feminism and contraception. It was said that the paper was "as red and flaming as possible." Of course it was soon banned, but it was replaced by another paper called *Family Limitation.*

As a result of her activities, Margaret Sanger was indicted for nine federal offences, while her husband, who was also her loyal helper and supporter, was sent to jail. Under an assumed name she went into hiding in Canada and thence to Europe again, where she met such distinguished birth-control leaders as Marie Stopes and Havelock Ellis. In 1915 Comstock died, and shortly afterward Margaret Sanger returned to the United States. The federal charges were dropped, and in 1916 she and her sister, Ethel Byrne, opened the first birth-control clinic in the United States. They were quickly arrested and the clinic closed. Ethel Byrne was imprisoned, went on a hunger strike, and was forcibly fed. A courageous woman, she continued her hunger strike until she was almost dead. Finally, authority responded to her situation and she was pardoned. Margaret Sanger, released on bail, promptly reopened the clinic, was arrested again, and received a 30-day sentence. While she was still in jail her new journal, *Birth Control Review,* made its first appearance, and its circulation increased rapidly. From that time onward, and for the rest of her life, Margaret Sanger led an uphill fight to have contraception made legal and adopted as a major means of securing human welfare. At the time of her death in 1966 her work was universally recognized and she had been responsible for organizing many international birth-control organizations. Indeed, every woman in this country today owes Margaret Sanger a debt of gratitude for freeing her from the role of merely a reproductive machine.

Margaret Sanger (The Sophia Smith Collection, Smith College, Northampton, Mass.)

Churches

Throughout the modern development of contraceptives, and education in their use, a fervent and unrelenting opponent has been the official hierarchy of the Roman Catholic Church. Some other faiths, usually of fundamentalist conviction, have also opposed the use of contraceptives. However, despite such opposition, many people practicing these faiths eagerly accept contraception when it is made available to them.

Nations

There are few countries in the world today where contraceptives are actually forbidden by law, though there are many where they are still not available to much of the population—mainly for economic reasons. Some densely populated countries like India, China, and Egypt actually have official government policies aimed at reducing the birthrate by making contraception easily available. Visitors to China report that that nation currently has the best birth-control program in the world. In retrospect, the success of the birth control movement, particularly in the present century, may prove to be one of our most successful social achievements in hopefully saving us from the horrors of overpopulation and untold individual misery.

BIRTH-CONTROL TECHNIQUES

Modern contraception consists of a blend of techniques, some very old and some very new, and constant efforts are being made to develop yet newer and better ones. At present there is no ideal contraceptive for any person; all have their advantages and disadvantages. What is suitable for one person may be entirely unsuitable for the next, and what may be appropriate at certain times and under certain conditions in a person's life may not always be so. Thus there is the ever-present need to adapt what is available and best suited to the requirements of the individual. This is far from easy, but full knowledge will certainly help in the process. In the following pages we will consider the various techniques available today, their origins, method of functioning, and effectiveness, together with their advantages and disadvantages. For the sake of completeness all potentially available methods will be mentioned, though some of these are of little more than marginal interest, and of value only in an emergency.

Coitus Interruptus

This consists of withdrawal of the penis from the vagina just prior to the male orgasm, so that the semen is ejaculated outside the female genital tract. Coitus interruptus—or withdrawal, as it is sometimes called—is probably the oldest contraceptive method known and has been used throughout the ages both in and out of wedlock. Amazingly enough, this method has at times proved quite effective as a birth control measure. In France, toward the end of the eighteenth century, it became popular among married couples and reached a scale of effectiveness sufficient to cause an appreciable decline in the birthrate. The popularity of the method spread to other European countries with subsequent declines in their birthrates. It does not seem to have ever been popular in the United States, though it has been and still is used here. In many countries today it occupies first place, and is in fact probably still the most widely used method in the world. Its use is generally inversely related to socio-economic status.

The advantages of the method are simply that it requires no supplies or preparation and costs absolutely nothing. These advantages are not inconsiderable, and for many people, particularly in poorer circumstances, they may prove to be the deciding factor in the choice of a contraceptive technique. There are, however, serious disadvantages. The method makes great demands on the male's self-control, and some men simply cannot master this to the degree necessary. In addition, unless the woman should reach orgasm prior to the male withdrawal, some form of further stimulation—usually manual—will be needed for her to achieve any reasonable form of sexual satisfaction. The mere fact that the technique is entirely under male control is also a disadvantage, as it is desirable that any one method used should be under female control—though contraception in general should be a mutual responsibility of both partners. A wide variety of both biophysical and psychological problems have been attributed to the use of coitus interruptus, though real substantiation for these is generally lacking. Good studies have clearly shown that for those couples who learn to practice it, it is only slightly less effective than the more modern chemical or mechanical means. Failure may of course result from the escape of semen prior to withdrawal, or to the deposition of semen in any part of the vagina during the withdrawal process. Its effectiveness is generally underrated or even ridiculed, but there is no good cause for this, for it can certainly be of great value in the absence of other techniques.

Coitus Reservatus

This method is similar to coitus interruptus, but differs in that the male controls himself to such a degree that he does not reach orgasm. He remains in the coital position with full intromission while the female has her orgasm, then allows his erection to subside. The method is very old, though nowhere near as widely practiced as coitus interruptus, probably because only a small proportion of men are able to develop the necessary control.

The advantages and disadvantages are much the same as those of coitus interruptus, and it is only as effective as the male's self-control. Coitus reservatus and the rhythm method are the only two contraceptive techniques currently acceptable to the Roman Catholic Church.

Prolonged Lactation

It has been known since time immemorial that a woman who is breast-feeding a baby is less likely to conceive than under ordinary conditions or if she does not breast-feed it. The reason for this is that maternal lactation following birth normally causes a delay in the reestablishment of both ovulation and the menstrual cycle. This fact has often led women to prolong lactation in the hopes of postponing another pregnancy. It is interesting that in most primitive societies, prolonged lactation is the rule. This no doubt helps to reduce the birthrate.

The advantages are the same as in the two techniques already discussed: it requires no supplies or preparation and costs nothing. However, the disadvantages are rather serious. It is unfortunately very unreliable as a means of birth control for there is no way of predicting when ovulation will begin again. Worse, ovulation may start before the onset of the menstrual cycle, thus a lactating woman can—and often does—become pregnant without any obvious warning sign. A further disadvantage of prolonged lactation is that if nursing continues to the point where the baby's teeth erupt, they may cause damage to the mother's breasts. Furthermore, if the mother's milk is relied on as the main food for too long, the child may well be undernourished. It is highly desirable that no woman should become pregnant too soon after giving birth, but prolonged lactation should not be relied on to prevent it.

Postcoital Douche

Douching consists of using a syringe to inject water or various solutions into the vagina following coitus, the aim being to wash away the semen before the sperm swim through the opening of the cervix. As previously pointed out, douching was advocated as a contraceptive technique in the nineteenth century by Dr. Charles Knowlton, and it quickly became very popular and widespread. It was the principal method used in Europe and North America until about 1940, but its popularity has declined markedly since then and it is now mainly confined to the lower socioeconomic groups. A factor contributing to its widespread use in the United States was that vaginal syringes could be sold for use in "feminine hygiene," thus circumventing the Comstock Law. In the 1930s, when the birthrate in the United States fell rapidly, douching was just about the only contraceptive technique available to women, and it is a credit to the women of that generation that they were persistent enough to make it work.

Considering the biological facts, it is remarkable that douching is effective at all. It has been well demonstrated that within 90 seconds of the male's ejaculation, sperm are already in the cervical opening and therefore beyond reach, so to speak. Thus for any form of douching to be effective it must be used immediately after the male orgasm. Pharmaceutical companies do a brisk business in all kinds of products which are said to make the douche more effective than plain water. Not only is it very unlikely that they do as claimed, but persistent douching—particularly with any harsh solution—may damage vaginal tissues. Certainly it reduces the numbers of the normal bacterial flora which are in part nature's way of keeping the vagina clean and healthy. If douching is used, it is important that it be done properly, otherwise its limited effectiveness will be even further reduced. Proper douching requires that the water be given sufficient pressure to distend the vagina, thus reaching the sperm within the crevices and washing it all away. This may be done by holding the labia majora together while the syringe is flowing, temporarily preventing the water from flowing out. If a bulb syringe is used, it can be squeezed hard enough to create the necessary pressure inside the vagina. This procedure should be repeated several times.

The advantages of douching as a contraceptive technique are very limited; however it is relatively cheap—the only cost being for the syringe, which requires no medical prescription—and it is under the female's control. In modern industrial societies it can certainly be of value in an emergency, such as when a condom breaks. The main disadvantages are that it is very inconvenient and requires privacy and the immediate use of bathroom facilities. It also requires great self-control on the part of the woman, who must remove herself from the arms of her lover immediately after his orgasm—and perhaps before hers—in order to carry out the rather unaesthetic procedure of douching. Even then it may fail, for it is the least effective of modern techniques. Whatever the disadvantages, however, it is certainly much better than nothing—and, as previously mentioned, it may have emergency value where another technique has failed or is temporarily unavailable.

Rhythm Method

As fully explained in Chapter 4, all normal adult human females have an ovarian cycle of approximately a month's duration (closely associated with the menstrual cycle) during which an egg is shed from the ovary. For a period of some 24 hours only, this egg is in a state in which it can be fertilized. Quite simply then, the rhythm method of birth control consists of trying to determine when ovulation occurs, then avoiding sexual intercourse for that period of time before and after ovulation which constitutes the period of maximum fertility, or the "unsafe period." This method has a checkered history, for in the nineteenth century it was thought that the human menstrual cycle was the same as the estrous cycle in many other mammals, and that menstruation itself corresponded to the period of another mammal's "heat." It has long been known that it is during heat that most mammals are likely to become pregnant, and it was assumed that the same would be true for the human female, i.e., during or just after her menstrual period.

It was not until the 1920s that this theory was shown to be almost wholly wrong, and that the most likely time for the human female to conceive is approximately halfway between menstrual periods. Techniques have been worked out by which some women can calculate when ovulation—and hence their unsafe period—is likely to occur. But these calculations are based on the assumption that the woman has a reasonably regular cycle, and since the great majority of women do *not*, such techniques are by no means guaranteed. Furthermore, while the egg can only be fertilized for some 24 hours after it is shed from the ovary, sperm are capable of remaining fully active in the female's genital tract and fertilizing an egg for some 72 hours after they have been deposited by the male. Thus it is recommended that the unsafe period be extended at least three days prior to ovulation and two days after it.

According to the best evidence we have, ovulation is most likely to occur some 14 to 16 days prior to the onset of the next menstrual period. Of course, the time of the beginning of the next menstrual period is never known for certain, but supposing a woman has a completely regular cycle of 28 days, with the onset of the menstrual period counted as day 1, then it is a reasonable guess that ovulation will take place between day 13 and day 15. Allowing three days prior to day 13 and two days after day 15, we determine the unsafe period to be from day 10 to day 17. In this case, then, it would be "safe" to have intercourse on days 1 to 9 and 18 to 28. This would be ideal timing, but the reality is otherwise and it is in fact necessary to make allowance for the inevitable irregularities.

The most reliable method consists of the following steps.

1. Keep an accurate record of each menstrual period for at least a year, and at the end of this time determine the shortest and longest cycles.
2. Subtract 18 from the number of days in the shortest cycle, which will give the first unsafe day of the period.

3. Subtract 11 from the number of days in the longest cycle, which will give the day on which the unsafe period ends.

An example will clarify this method. Suppose that over the period of a year the cycles ranged from 26 days to 30 days. Then the unsafe period would be from the eighth day (26 minus 18) to the nineteenth day (30 minus 11). Wording it another way and again counting the onset of menstruation as day 1, it would be "safe" to have intercourse until day 8 and after day 19. For a second example, assume that the shortest period was 28 days and the longest 32 days. Then the unsafe period would be from the tenth day (28 minus 18) to the twenty-first day (32 minus 11).

Another method of determining the unsafe period is based on the recent discovery that there are slight, but usually detectable, changes in the female's body temperature during her menstrual cycle which are associated with the actual event of ovulation. A typical example of this is shown in Fig. 11.1. This shows that at the time of ovulation there is a drop in body temperature of about 0.3°F, followed by a rise of between 0.5°F and 0.9°F. Thus for the second half of the menstrual cycle the woman's body temperature is slightly higher than for the first half. This can be a fairly accurate means of determining when ovulation *has* taken place, but not when it *is going* to take place, so when using this method alone sexual intercourse should be restricted to the post-ovulatory part of the cycle. However, in conjunction with the menstrual cycle records, the temperature method can help determine the unsafe period somewhat more accurately.

To use the temperature method, it is necessary to have a special thermometer which accurately records changes in temperature of only 0.1°F. These can be obtained at most drugstores, which also supply charts for keeping the temperature records. The temperature (preferably the rectal temperature, which is more accurate than the oral) must be taken every day immediately on awakening—before undertaking any activity or drinking or eating anything—and the temperature should be recorded at once. Unfortunately, the temperature pattern can be upset by emotional problems, or even a minor illness, and these must be watched for and recorded. Nevertheless, if the woman has a reasonably regular pattern and if she is patient and persevering, her body-temperature charts can be a valuable aid in determining her unsafe period.

The advantages of the rhythm method are not very great but it is relatively cheap in that it requires only the cost of the charts (they can also be homemade) and possibly the special thermometer. Its control is in the hands of the woman, and there are no physical side effects. Its special advantage is that it is acceptable to those people who feel morally bound

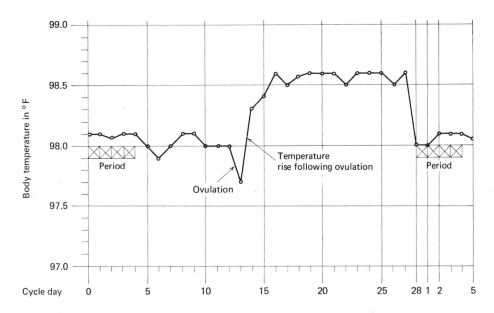

Fig. 11.1. An example of changes in the
female body temperature during a menstrual cycle, showing a detectable change
at the time of ovulation and after ovulation.

to follow their religious convictions in such matters. The disadvantages, on
the other hand, are that the woman must keep constant and accurate
records of her menstrual cycle over long periods of time, and this requires
great perseverance and correct interpretation of the charts. The latter may
require medical help and advice, which is a further disadvantage. There is
also the ever-present fear that something may upset her cycle and thus
alter the time of ovulation. It is only suitable for women with very regular
cycles, who are a minority, and the opportunity for coitus is greatly
reduced, thus putting what may be undue, or even unbearable, strain on
the woman and her male partner.

The effectiveness of the rhythm method has been the subject of
much controversy. However, it appears that if correctly taught, correctly
understood, and consistently practiced by women with regular cycles, it
can be quite an effective method of birth control. In reality it is used
mostly by Roman Catholics, and even then mainly by the lower
socioeconomic groups.

Spermicides

These are substances which exert a contraceptive effect by immobilizing and eventually killing sperm. They are normally inserted into the vagina by hand or by a small applicator (consisting of cylinder and plunger) some time before sexual intercourse, and thus are present when ejaculation takes place. As pointed out previously, spermicides have a long history going back to ancient civilizations, but with the development of modern chemistry in the nineteenth century, systematic .efforts were made— particularly in Germany, Sweden and England—to develop highly effective spermicides which were also harmless. In the twentieth century the search has been intensified, and there are now many different kinds of spermicides sold under a vast variety of trade names. (Fig. 11.2)

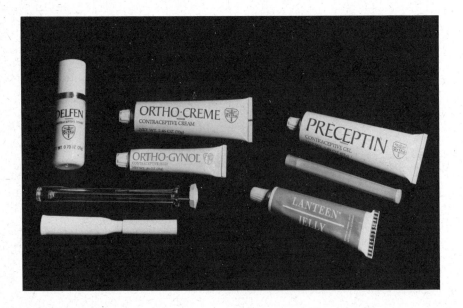

Fig. 11.2. Various kinds of spermicides.

There are at present spermicidal jellies, creams, and foams, there are suppositories or wafers that melt inside the vagina, and there are tablets that dissolve on contact with the moisture of the vagina to produce a dense foam. All these are designed for use without a diaphragm and most require a waiting period of a few minutes after insertion and prior to coitus to allow them to fully dissolve and spread throughout the upper part of the vagina—particularly over the cervix. Jellies, creams, and foams are inserted by simple plastic applicators, and it is most important that they be deposited well into the vagina and as near the cervix as possible. Suppositories and tablets can be inserted by hand, but again should be placed near the cervix.

Spermicides have the advantages that control is in the hands of the woman, they are relatively simple to use, and they do not require any pelvic examination or doctor's prescription. The disadvantages are that many women using them complain of vaginal leakage, and in rare cases they have caused irritation and inflammation of the vagina and cervix. Forethought is necessary for insertion prior to intercourse, and there should be a short waiting period after insertion. Regrettably, they are not cheap. A tube of cream or foam currently costs from four to six dollars, and a sexually active woman may use up one of these in a month or even less.

The effectiveness of spermicides by themselves is a matter of some disagreement, compounded by the fact that manufacturers certainly make exaggerated claims for their products. They are certainly more effective than postcoital douching or the rhythm method, but less effective than a vaginal diaphragm or an oral contraceptive. Of all the different types of spermicides, vaginal foams seem to have a slight edge in effectiveness. In summary, spermicides are reasonably convenient and safe and are fairly effective contraceptives when properly and consistently used.

Vaginal Diaphragm

This contraceptive device, invented before 1882 by the German physician, Wilhelm Mensinga (1836-1910), consists of a rubber dome with a spring rim. It is placed inside the vagina in such a way that it covers the cervix and forms a tight seal around it. At the back the rim fits into the posterior fornix, a small pocket behind the cervix, and at the front it fits behind the pubic bone (Fig. 11.3) Before insertion some spermicidal jelly or cream is spread around the rim and over the outer and inner curved surfaces of the dome. So applied, the diaphragm is a very effective block to entering sperm. Initially some women find this task aesthetically troublesome, but this feeling can be quickly overcome and application can easily be made a routine matter. Similar to the diaphragm are rubber cervical caps which fit directly over the tip of the cervix. Though not extensively used, they are as effective as the diaphragm and are applied the same way.

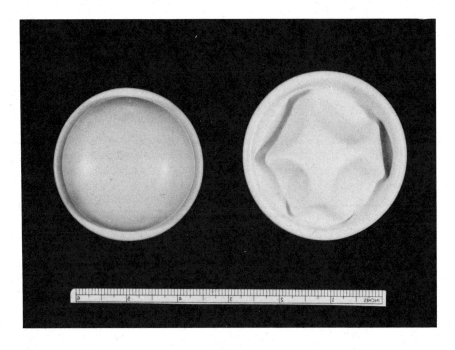

(a)

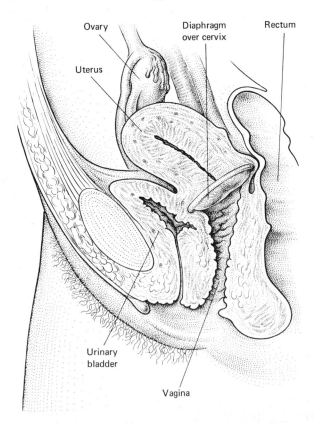

Some precautions are important. Every woman using a diaphragm should be individually fitted for it, and periodically refitted if there has been any major change in her anatomy. A virgin woman can be fitted for a diaphragm, for example, but she should be refitted after experiencing sexual intercourse as intercourse will stretch the vagina somewhat. She should also be refitted after childbirth, miscarriage, or anything else which might affect the vagina. All this requires the services of a doctor and a prescription for the diaphragm.

It is important that the diaphragm should not be inserted more than two hours before intercourse. If more than two hours should elapse, an applicator of spermicide should be inserted into the vagina. After intercourse the diaphragm should be left in place for six hours. Vaginal douching is not necessary after the diaphragm is removed, but some women prefer to do it. Before any diaphragm is inserted it should be checked for possible leaks by holding it before a strong light, and after use it should be washed with soap and water, dried, and powdered.

A woman can carry on any normal activity with a diaphragm inserted, though it is always well to check that it is in place as immediately before intercourse as possible. Usually, neither the woman nor her sexual partner can feel a properly placed diaphragm during intercourse.

A vaginal diaphragm has the major advantage of being a much more effective birth-control device than spermacides alone, though slightly less effective than an oral contraceptive. Also it is in the hands of the woman and is virtually without any side effects. The disadvantages are that it requires a pelvic examination to determine the right size, and a prescription to purchase it. Subsequent refittings may be necessary. All this makes it a relatively costly procedure, particularly if the women goes to a private doctor rather than a birth-control clinic. Privacy and forethought are both necessary, and if the diaphragm is not properly applied it may slip (remember that the inner two thirds of the vagina expands during the plateau and orgasmic phases of the sexual response cycle).

Throughout the 20 years from 1940 to 1960, the diaphragm was probably the most widely used female contraceptive in this country. But with the introduction of oral contraceptives and intrauterine devices in the 1960s, the popularity of the diaphragm gave way to these two methods. However, it is now enjoying a comeback, due primarily to the often serious side effects of oral contraceptives and intrauterine devices.

Fig. 11.3. (a) Vaginal diaphragm. (b)
◄ Cross section of female pelvis showing
vaginal diaphragm in place.

This seems wholly desirable as the diaphragm is a very effective contraceptive when used properly and has no side effects of any significance. It is particularly suitable for women in the upper socioeconomic groups who have the motivation, the money, and the private facilities to make its use convenient. It may be noted here also that if pregnancy would be a very serious matter to the woman's health (either physical or psychological), or if she is too old to have children, or if none are wanted, then even additional precautions should be taken (i.e., the male should wear a condom). It is said commonly that in our society most couples do not take sufficient care with contraceptives until the unwanted child is already there! In other words if a couple plans only one child, they will commonly end up with two, and if they plan two they will end up with three. This can be a major disaster for many people, but with knowledge, care, and concern it is avoidable.

Intrauterine Devices — (IUDs)

It has been known for thousands of years that any object placed in the uterus of a mammal tends to prevent pregnancy. This fact led to experiments on humans with IUDs in the nineteenth century, but these experiments and the idea were generally condemned by the medical profession. It is only in the last decade or so that experiments on humans have been revived (and with some success), mainly as a result of the efforts of the Population Council in New York.

The way in which an IUD works is by no means understood. In experiments on mammals, it has been found that IUDs cause the cells of the uterine lining to be altered in such a way that the fluids they secrete into the uterus create a hostile environment for both sperm and fertilized eggs. Whether this is true in the human female, only further research will determine.

IUDs are usually made of the plastic polyethylene, but some are made of copper or stainless steel with a coating of plastic. Some common IUDs include the Lippes loop, the copper 7 and copper T, the relatively new Progestasert, and there may well be others on their way. The Lippes loop consists of a spiral which can be straightened by pulling into a plunger (Fig. 11.4), making it easy to insert through the cervix into the uterus. Once the tip of the plunger is in the uterus the loop is pushed out and will return to its spiral shape. The plunger is then withdrawn and the attached thread cut so that it is left projecting into the vagina. (All IUDs are inserted in much the same way.) The presence of this thread in the vagina is the woman's own guarantee that the IUD is there and in place, and it is important that she should frequently check this. The device may be removed by gently pulling the thread, but under no circumstances should the woman do this herself. It must be done by a physician or other trained health worker.

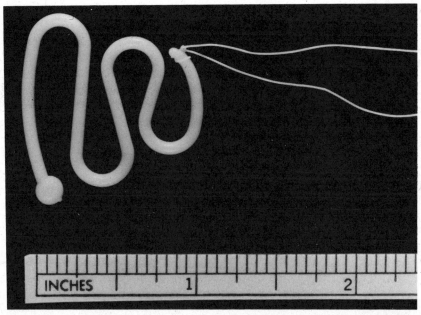

(a)

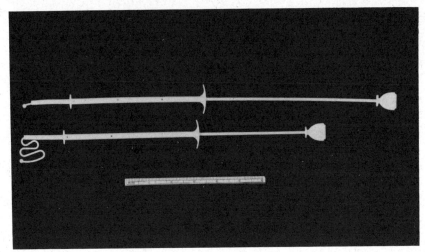

(b)

Fig. 11.4. (a) Lippes loop. (b) Loop attached to plunger (bottom) and (top) drawn into plunger.

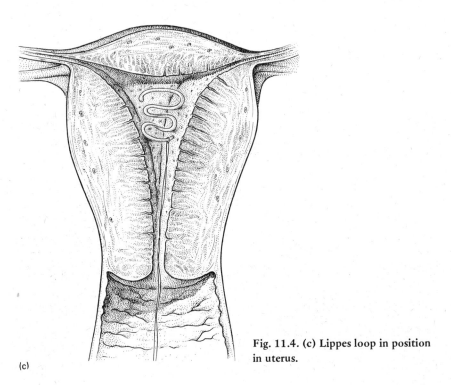

Fig. 11.4. (c) Lippes loop in position in uterus.

(c)

The copper 7 and copper T (Fig. 11.5 a, b) work on a slightly different principle, in that in addition to the mere presence of the device in the uterus they also release copper in very small amounts into the uterus, and it is thought that this also helps to alter the uterine lining in such a way that it rejects fertilized eggs and/or sperm even more. The Progestasert (Fig. 11.5 c) is a relatively new device, referred to as a biologically active IUD. There will probably be others available before long. The principle on which this works is that in addition to the presence of the IUD in the uterus, it also releases progesterone into the uterine cavity on a continuous basis but at a very low rate (average 65 μg/day), and it is thought again that this alters the uterine lining so that it is a more hostile environment to sperm and/or fertilized eggs. Each device contains enough progesterone for about a year, after which it must be replaced. Theoretically a biologically active IUD releasing progesterone, or a combination of other hormones, directly into the uterus would have enormous advantages over oral contraceptives. The latter of course raise considerably the level of hormones within the bloodstream, with all the inevitable complications and side effects. The biologically active IUD, however, bypasses the whole systemic system and exerts its hormonal effect (and in much smaller amounts) directly on the uterine lining. It would be very nice if it were as simple as that, and while research in this direction will undoubtedly continue, the biologically active IUD is certainly no panacea, and all the problems commonly associated with IUDs (to be discussed presently) have already been reported. Furthermore, large and long-term studies have not yet been carried out.

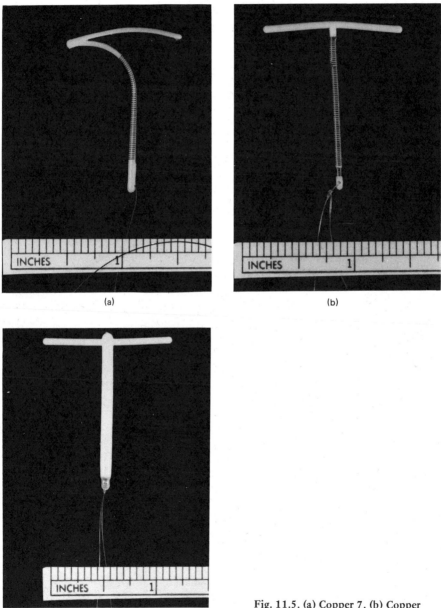

Fig. 11.5. (a) Copper 7. (b) Copper T. (c) Progestasert.

All IUDs must be inserted by a physician or other trained health worker because this procedure requires sterile or aseptic conditions to avoid infection. IUDs are usually inserted only during the menstrual period, partly because this is reasonable guarantee that the woman is not already pregnant and partly because the cervix is softer and more pliable at this time, allowing easier insertion of the device. Insertion of an IUD may involve some discomfort, particularly in women who have not been through childbirth at least once.

Opinions differ, but at present IUDs are not usually recommended for women who have never been pregnant. The pain of insertion may be greater for them than for women who have been pregnant, and they may experience severe pain following insertion. Also they are much more likely to expel the device than women who have been pregnant. Some 10 to 12% of all women spontaneously expel an IUD within the first year—most of them in the first three months—and about 10% more have side effects unpleasant enough to make removal of the IUD necessary. These side effects can include pain, cramps, backache, bleeding from the uterus, and extra heavy menstrual flows. More serious however, are cases of pelvic inflammatory disease, perforation of the uterus, inflammation of the vagina, spontaneous abortion, ectopic pregnancy, anemia, and many others. These usually occur soon after insertion, and a woman with a new IUD should be particularly watchful for side effects so that they can be treated quickly. The development of new IUDs is an active area of research, and the technology is likely to change rapidly, but because of the dangers attached some IUDs have already been withdrawn from use, and no one can predict the future. However, biology being what it is, it is unlikely that there will be any magical IUD with no side effects. Furthermore, one must always be on guard against the promotion campaigns of companies, with exaggerated claims of effectiveness and minimal dangers. Once again everyone has to weigh the need versus the risk.

As with other contraceptives, the effectiveness of the IUD is controversial. However, providing the woman does not spontaneously expel it, it is certainly more effective than spermicides, and probably equal to the diaphragm. However, contrary to initial hopes and the exaggerated claims of their manufacturers, IUDs are not perfect contraceptive protection and pregnancy can occur with the device in place. In fact it is a common joke in the obstetrical wards of hospitals that "the baby was born clasping the IUD in its hand!"

The advantages of IUDs are that they are good contraceptive protection for those women able to use them. The technique requires low motivation, because insertion is not associated directly with coitus, and all that is necessary is for the woman to check that the nylon thread is in the vagina. For this reason IUDs are particularly suited to large-scale birth-control programs. But a well-educated couple with high motivation will not find that IUDs give any greater protection than the diaphragm, oral contraceptives, or the condom. The contraceptive effect is completely reversible, once the IUD is removed the woman quickly becomes fertile again.

The disadvantages are that while IUDs are cheap, they must be inserted by a physician or other trained health worker. This usually increases the cost considerably, but it does not recur very frequently. They are more suitable for women who have had at least one child than for those who have not had any. Unfortunately they are not without potential and serious side effects, and it is not known whether there are any long-term effects. There is an apparent slight increase in spontaneous abortion among women wearing IUDs, but apart from this there is no extra danger to babies born to a woman wearing an IUD.

Oral Contraceptives ("The Pill")

Attempts to control fertility by swallowing various substances are as old as recorded history, but until very recent times such attempts have had little scientific basis and even less effect. But as knowledge of the human female's ovulatory cycle increased, it became feasible to control the cycle in such a way that ovulation itself could be prevented, thus preventing fertilization and conception. The pioneer work on modern oral contraceptives was done in the 1950s—primarily by the Americans Dr. John Rock and Dr. Gregory Pincus (1903-1963)—and by 1960 they were available for general use.

At present oral contraceptives consist of synthetic hormones which closely resemble estrogen and progesterone and are thought to exert their contraceptive effect in the following manner. Taken orally as prescribed they raise the level of estrogen and progesterone in the blood, which in turn causes the hypothalamus to inhibit the release of FSH and LH from the anterior pituitary. It will be recalled (from Chapter 4) that these two hormones normally govern the maturation of the Graafian follicle and the eventual shedding of its egg. Thus with the daily pills keeping estrogen and progesterone at a high level in the blood stream, the follicle does not mature and ovulation does not take place.

There are currently two methods for taking oral contraceptives—the combined and the sequential. In the combined method the pills contain a combination of both estrogen and progesterone, and these are taken usually from the fifth to the twenty-fifth day of the cycle. In the sequential method the first 15 or so pills contain estrogen only and the next five contain both estrogen and progesterone. Within a few days after the last pill is taken menstruation will begin, and then the sequence should be started again on day 5. Another form of the sequential procedure consists of three weeks on the pill and one week off. Actually, pills are taken for the whole four weeks, but those for the fourth week are inert. The inert pills are included so that the woman using this system can take a pill every day of the cycle, making it unnecessary for her to remember when to begin again.

All users of oral contraceptives must have a doctor's prescription. This seems very necessary when it is recalled (from Chapter 4) that no hormone is independent of any other, and that their effects on the human body are widespread and by no means fully understood. For example, it is known that carbohydrate metabolism and liver and thyroid functions all deviate from normal in many women who take the pill. This is bound to be cause for concern even though there may be no immediate adverse effects. Similarly, the short-term side effects which may occur on starting the pill are also cause for concern. These include nausea, headaches, dizziness, weight gain, discoloration of the skin, tenderness of the breasts, and others, and may be so severe that some women are forced to abandon the pill in favor of other methods of contraception. It is most important that oral contraceptives should not be used by women who have any history of or tendency toward liver problems, kidney disorders, high blood pressure, blood congestion, or who are over 40.

The long-term side effects of oral contraceptives are sometimes serious and of grave concern, to say the least. Furthermore we learn more of these almost every day. One of the first long-term side effects to be discovered was thromboembolic disease, which is a disease involving clotting of the blood and which can have a fatal outcome. While this risk cannot be overlooked, it should not be overestimated, for it is less than the risk of death due to various complications of childbirth, at least in advanced industrial societies. Nevertheless it is about five times higher in pill users than in nonusers, and the risk of the disease is three times higher for those women with blood groups A, B, or AB than for those with O. These facts have been determined by at least three independent studies in England and one in the United States. In recent (1975-1976) studies, by reliable authorities, both in this country and in England it has been determined that there is also an increased risk of coronary thrombosis (both fatal and nonfatal) in users of oral contraceptives. Generally this rate is increased by a factor of three for users, but in women over the age of forty it is ten times as high. It has also been determined that the risks are considerably increased if the woman smokes. Other long-term side effects which have been clearly demonstrated include a higher risk of certain kinds of stroke and blood pressure rise, benign liver tumors, gall bladder disease, faster blood clotting time (10%) and firmer clots, changes in blood sugar and in the composition of mother's milk, anemia, headaches (three times higher risk), migraine headaches (two times higher risk), and many others. There is also one birth defect (congenital limb reduction), an increased risk of which has been linked to oral contraceptives. In addition, weight gain in users is often a serious and ongoing problem with all its inevitable complications. In fact, it seems highly probable that at least some of the appalling obesity in young women (particularly in the United States) is pill-related. Considering all the foregoing it is pleasant to report that despite popular opinion to the contrary, there is at this time (1977) no evidence to implicate oral contraceptives in the production of malignant tumors.

The advantages of oral contraceptives are that they are very effective (almost 100% when taken as prescribed), that their use is not related to sexual intercourse, that they are in the hands of the woman, are aesthetically acceptable to almost everyone, and do not require high motivation. Another advantage is that they regularize the woman's menstrual period, which is most convenient for her.

The disadvantages are that this method requires a doctor's prescription, the pills are not cheap, and there may be considerable side effects, both short- and long-term, as already mentioned.

It would be very easy for me, as the author of this book, to leave the matter there and let every person be his or her own judge. However I do not think this would be a worthwhile service to the readers. It would be well at the outset if every reader would review Chapter 4 (particularly the section on hormonal control of ovarian and menstrual cycles) regarding hormonal function, their enormous complexity, what we know and above all what we don't know. Then consider what oral contraceptives consist of and how they are thought to work. Finally the question must arise if the risks are really worth it. Some authorities argue that the advantages outweigh the disadvantages, while others argue exactly the opposite. Yet again the question is often posed, if there are all these serious side effects, why is it permitted that oral contraceptives are sold? The answer is not easy. On the one hand authorities are reluctant to remove from the market such an effective and convenient contraceptive device, and they have behind them a powerful lobby of the pharmaceutical industry, and at present also various groups (including women's groups) concerned with population control in general. Also, we should not overlook women themselves, who are under strong peer pressure to conform in this regard. On the other hand there are many organizations concerned with public health who are much opposed to oral contraceptives. It is worthwhile pointing out that the British Royal College of

General Practitioners first commissioned the studies on the long-term side effects of oral contraceptives and thus sounded the initial alarm. Of course it is possible that ongoing research may solve some of the problems, but in view of their very basic biological nature we cannot look for any magical breakthrough. I am fully aware how convenient oral contraceptives are for women, but for me "the writing is clearly on the wall" and the risks are far too great in most cases, particularly when other effective methods are available, such as the diaphragm and the condom.

Research into various modifications of oral contraceptives is very active, and also into their various side effects. No doubt by the time this book gets into print much new information will be available, but the basic problems will still remain. About all the average person can do is to try to keep up to date with reliable sources of information (see reading list at the end of this chapter) and to beware of promotional campaigns and special interest groups. Every woman should ask herself the question if "the pill" is really necessary for her, and if she is willing to take the serious risks involved in its use.

In writing this section on oral contraceptives, I have tried to be understanding and yet objective, but no doubt many will disagree with me.

The Condom

The condom consists of a cylinder-like sheath, open at one end (Fig. 11.6), which is rolled on over the erect male penis prior to intercourse and thus prevents the deposition of semen in the vagina.

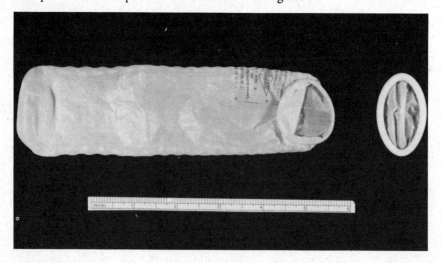

Fig. 11.6. Condoms, unrolled and rolled.

The condom has a long and interesting history. The first known reference to it dates from the sixteenth century and the work of the great Italian anatomist Gabrielo Fallopius (Chapter 4), who claimed to have invented it. He did not intend it as a contraceptive, however, but as a protection (for males!) against syphilis, for which it is still effective. Fallopius said that his condoms were tried on 1100 men, none of whom contracted syphilis—somewhat of an exaggeration, no doubt. They were made of linen, and this type persisted for many years, though animal membranes were also used extensively. Then in 1844 Charles Goodyear invented the process of vulcanization, making it possible to make condoms of rubber and, eventually, of latex. Unfortunately, throughout their history condoms have always been associated with prostitution, and have been thought of primarily as a prophylactic (see Chapter 12). This has tended to make people belittle their usefulness as contraceptives, but it is gradually being realized that condoms are one of the most effective contraceptive techniques available.

Although skin condoms are still used, the vast majority today are made of latex. Their manufacture in the United States is under the control of the U.S. Food and Drug Administration, and high standards have to be met. Modern condoms are strong, almost completely free of defects, and are usually packaged under sterile conditions in paper envelopes or aluminum foil. They are also very thin and transmit heat and physical sensations well. Some men claim that using a condom cuts down significantly on their sensations, but this is in fact unlikely. Such men may have inhibitions about the condom, or may be trying to avoid their share of responsibility for contraception.

Latex condoms are of one size only—about seven inches long—and are normally pre-rolled. They can also be bought dry or prelubricated, and plain- or teat-ended.

Condoms should be put on the erect penis properly and before there is any intromission. If they do not have a teat end, they should be unrolled about one-half inch and this portion at the closed end held tight while the rest is unrolled up the shaft of the penis. This will prevent air from being trapped in the closed end and will allow space for the semen when ejaculated. If a man is not circumcised, he should pull back the foreskin before unrolling the condom. It is important also that it be unrolled over the entire length of the penis.

Perhaps the greatest cause of failure when using the condom is incorrect withdrawal following the male orgasm. At this time there is always some loss of erection and it may be enough for the condom to become loose on the penis, allowing semen to escape through the upper end. Or the male will perhaps wait too long before withdrawing and the condom may slip right off into the vagina, allowing the semen to escape. In order to avoid any such possibility the male should not wait too long after orgasm before withdrawing, and should always hold the upper part of the condom tight against the base of the penis as he withdraws, and before it is taken off. With this simple precaution it is most unlikely that the condom will fail in any other way, though there is always an outside chance that it will be defective and tear. If it should fail for any reason, the woman should at once insert an applicator full of spermicide in her vagina or take a douche. This may not guarantee the desired result, but it will certainly help.

The advantages of condoms are that they are very effective, rating about equal with—though some authorities claim better than—the dia-phragm and the IUD, and only slightly behind oral contraceptives. Also the presence of an intact barrier after coitus adds reassurance. They are easy to use and do not require any special facilities and are virtually without any side effects. They also have the outstanding advantage that they are the only contraceptive that gives any protection against venereal diseases (see Chapter 12). This protection is considerable though not 100%, and in this respect it is just as efficient for the female as for the male. The use of a condom also gives the female protection against poor penile hygiene on the part of the male, a most important and often over-looked aspect of sexual intercourse. Condoms may be bought by anyone without prescription in almost any drug store in most states and countries.

The disadvantages of the technique are that it requires forethought and some slight interruption of foreplay while the male puts the condom on. It is also in the hands of the male, though of course the female can insist that the male use it. They are relatively expensive at present (1977), costing two to four dollars a dozen. This cost can be reduced by washing and rerolling them after use, so they can be used again, but they are commonly used only once.

About one billion condoms are used in this country every year, and while this figure may seem enormous it is really not that great. Surveys indicate that there is still much opposition to its use, particularly on the part of males who do not seem able to disassociate it from prostitution. Hopefully, better education will overcome this opposition and the many advantages of condoms will be fully recognized.

Surgical Sterilization

In the male this procedure consists of "vasectomy," or the removal of a small piece of the vas deferens (see Figures. 3.3 and 3.4) leading out of the testes. The two ends are then tied and sometimes buried in the surrounding tissues. It is important that a piece of the tube is actually removed rather than the tube being simply tied, for in the latter case it may join up again. The operation is performed on both vasa deferentia, which prevents sperm from the testes from reaching the penis and being ejaculated. In the female the procedure consists of removing a small piece of each Fallopian tube (see Fig. 4.1) and tying the ends, which prevents sperm from reaching an egg in the tube or an egg from reaching the uterus.

Sterilization in the modern sense has nothing in common with the very ancient practice of castration. The procedures for the male and female which have just been outlined were first suggested in 1823 by the English physician Dr. James Blundell (1790-1877), but it was not until the latter part of the nineteenth century—with the coming of anesthesia and aseptic surgery—that effective techniques were developed. Now, however, the operations are relatively simple and when properly done are 100% effective.

In the male the operation may be done under local anesthesia in about 20 minutes by a surgeon trained in the technique. A small incision on either side of the upper part of the scrotum is necessary, but the person may walk immediately after the operation and complete recovery is only a matter of days. The contraceptive effect of vasectomy cannot be depended on for the first three months after the operation, because sperm produced before the operation may be present in the semen. After that time it is advisable to have a specimen of semen examined under the microscope for the complete absence of sperm. There are no known side effects—except possibly emotional ones—and the man's sexual desires as well as his response cycle continue as normal. The operation is sometimes reversible, but this should not be counted on.

In the female the operation is a little more difficult and a general anesthetic is usually necessary. It is best done within a day after the woman has been delivered of a child, for at that time the Fallopian tubes are easily reached. However, the operation may also be quite satisfactorily performed on a woman who has not recently had a child, though recovery may take a few days. In a new technique a very small abdominal incision is made, and with special sophisticated instruments the surgeon can actually cut the Fallopian tubes by use of a weak electric current. This is called laparoscopic sterilization, it is easy to perform, and the woman can usually go home the same day. No waiting period is necessary for the contraceptive effect, and as with the male there are no side effects. No guarantee of reversibility can be given, though it has been accomplished on occasion.

The advantages of surgical sterilization are that it is a one-time-only affair and provides maximum contraceptive protection without further thought, action, or side effects. To many couples this gives an enormous feeling of relief and consequent increased pleasure in sexual relations.

The disadvantages are that it requires a surgical operation, with its inevitable expense, and since it is not likely to be reversible, those who have the operation should not expect to be able to change their minds and have more children. As with all surgery, there is a small risk of infection or other problems, but in competent hands the risk is very small.

Sterilization should not be undertaken lightly by any man or woman, but where more children might cause serious harm or even death to a woman, or where they are not desirable for economic, psychological, hereditary, age, or other reasons, sterilization has much to commend it, particularly for the male. (As an alternative to sterilization in such cases, both the male and female should use a contraceptive for coitus.) Large-scale government sponsored programs of vasectomy as a method of population control are currently in use of India and other countries, while in the United States the popularity of vasectomy is increasing rapidly, and about half a million men now voluntarily undergo the operation annually.

Abortion

Although artificially induced abortion is not a contraceptive, the end result is the same in that it prevents children from being born. Unfortunately, many women are so desperate not to have children that they will attempt self-induced abortions or put themselves in the hands of amateurs and quacks operating illegally, usually with disastrous results. This situation is never likely to get better until societies change their attitudes and ways in relation to sexual education (contraception is certainly preferable to abortion), the delivery of medical advice, and care and general concern for human welfare.

As a result of extreme pressures the laws governing abortion have recently been liberalized in some countries and states. In this country as a result of the recent (1973) Supreme Court ruling, it is now not difficult for a woman to receive a safe, medically performed abortion—provided she knows where to go and has the money. All offices of the Planned Parenthood Federation and some Public Health Departments will now give free advice on this subject, and there is no longer any good reason why a woman seeking an abortion has to be hacked about by some incompetent person rather than having the operation performed under aseptic conditions by a trained physician. This assumes of course that the woman seeking the abortion considers it to be morally acceptable. It is not pertinent here to discuss the moral problem, except to say that the laws should be known and the decision left to the individual (or individuals) concerned. It may be noted, however, that there are still many who oppose abortion. Some opponents advocate a constitutional amendment to outlaw it.

Until very recently the medical technique used for induced abortions was dilation of the cervix and curettage (D and C), i.e., the scraping out of the uterus by means of a sharp, spoonlike instrument. However, there is now a very simple and safe method which was first developed in China. Called "vacuum curettage" or "uterine aspiration," it is almost universally used for abortions performed up to the twelfth week of pregnancy—certainly the best time period in which to have it done. The procedure, which must be done under aseptic conditions, can be carried out with a local anesthetic in somewhat less than 10 minutes, and most women are fully recovered in a matter of hours except for some menstrual-like bleeding which may last up to a week. The operation itself consists of dilating the cervix and passing a plastic tube into the uterus. The other end of the tube has a vacuum pump attached and the contents of the uterus are simply sucked out. This may be followed by a quick and final slight scraping of the uterine wall. There are other methods of performing abortions, but any abortion should be in professional hands and performed only after it is determined that there is no special danger to the woman having it.

Medication does exist that sometimes makes it possible to have an abortion immediately after fertilization but before implantation, i.e., within a time span of some five days (see Chapter 10). It is referred to as "the morning-after-pill," and it consists of prescribed doses of a synthetic estrogen called diethylstilbestrol (DES). This is a very potent drug, sometimes with severe side effects, and cannot be administered without extreme caution, but may occasionally have its uses—as in cases of rape or other serious circumstances. However, it does not always produce the desired result.

Potential New Contraceptives

It is clear that a contraceptive can be effective only if it is used, and all professionals in the field are agreed that a contraceptive is likely to be used only if it has certain properties. First, it should be simple, easily applied, and cheap. Second, it should be aesthetically and morally acceptable. Third, it should be in the hands of the woman—though this is in no way meant to absolve the male from his responsibility. And fourth, it should have no side effects. Obviously no such contraceptive exists today and thus constant efforts are being made to improve those that do. Much work is being done at the Population Council in New York, the International Planned Parenthood Federation in London, and other such institutions. The problems are very complex and difficult, and no one should expect miracles or quick results. However, a summary of just a few

of the research projects under way in this field may prove interesting.
There is no guarantee that they will come to fruition, of course, for most
scientific experiments fail!

For Use by the Female

1. Once-a-month antiovulant pills or injections. The steroids so administered would be stored in the fatty tissues and gradually released
   over a month. This could possibly be extended to a year.
2. A subdermal implant of progesterone-estrogen which, when gradually released, could inhibit ovulation over a long period.
3. Improved biologically active IUDs.
4. The use of prostaglandins. These are a whole new group of recently
   discovered hormones, and they have enormous potential.
5. Immunization with sperm antigens. The aim is to prevent sperm
   which are deposited in the vagina from achieving fertilizing capacity
   in the Fallopian tubes.
6. A better and safer "morning-after pill."
7. Many others, including improvement of present methods.

For Use by the Male

1. Subdermal implants or periodic injections of long lasting androgens,
   which can suppress the production of FSH and thus prevent
   spermatogenesis.
2. A subdermal implant of progesterone which, when gradually
   released, might prevent sperm maturation in the epididymis. This
   has worked in some other mammals.
3. Oral tablets which might alter the seminal fluid in such a way that it
   would be hostile to sperm.
4. Immunization against sperm production by certain sperm antigens.
5. Attempts to make vasectomy easily and completely reversible.

In concluding this chapter on contraception it will be well to realize
that despite all technical advances and the gradual but incomplete victory
of making contraception acceptable and available, no one has cause for
complacency. Ignorance, embarrassment, inhibitions, and lack of any
formal education on the subject inevitably result in millions of unwanted
pregnancies with the disastrous consequences of unwanted children.
Furthermore, the alarming rate of abortions and the ever-increasing
numbers of human beings are all clear evidence of people's failure, for one
reason or another, to use contraceptives or to accept their use as a primary
mutual responsibility.

It is an unfortunate fact that most couples simply do not take proper contraceptive precautions until the unwanted child is already there, and most initial experiences of sexual intercourse, particularly in the very young, are without any protection at all. It is rather depressing that still, in this day and age, "most girls just pray."

STUDY TOPICS

1. Explain the significance of the following in the history of the birth-control movement: (a) Robert Malthus, (b) Francis Place, (c) Charles Knowlton, (d) Charles Bradlaw, (e) Annie Besant, (f) Edward Truelove, (g) Anthony Comstock, (h) Margaret Sanger, (i) Ethyl Byrne.

2. Explain what is meant by coitus interruptus and coitus reservatus. What are the advantages and disadvantages of each?

3. Explain how the postcoital vaginal douche functions. What are some of the problems associated with its use?

4. Explain the rhythm method. What are its advantages and disadvantages?

5. Discuss the advantages and disadvantages of spermicides.

6. Discuss the history, the advantages, and disadvantages of the vaginal diaphragm.

7. Discuss the history, the advantages, and disadvantages of intrauterine devices. How are they thought to function?

8. How are oral contraceptives thought to function? Discuss their history, their advantages, and disadvantages.

9. Discuss the history, the advantages, and disadvantages of the condom.

10. Explain what is meant by surgical sterilization in both men and women. What are the advantages and disadvantages of this?

11. Explain the modern technique of abortion. What are the social and moral problems associated with abortion?

12. What are some potential new methods of contraception for both men and women?

FOR FURTHER READING

"Abortion: The Continuing Controversy." *Population Bulletin,* (August 1972), The Population Reference Bureau, Washington, D.C.

Collaborative Group for the Study of Stroke in Young Women, Oral Contraceptives and Stroke in Young Women: Associated Risk Factors. *Journal of the American Medical Association* 231: 718, 1975.

Family Planning Digest, Rockville, Maryland: National Center for Family Planning Services, Health Services and Mental Health Administration, Dept. of Health, Education, and Welfare.

Faulkner, William L., and Howard W. Ory, Intrauterine Devices and Acute Pelvic Inflammatory Disease. *Journal of the American Medical Association* 235 (17): 1851-1853, 1976.

Frejka, Tomas, The Prospects for a Stationary World Population. *Scientific American,* March, 1973.

Hafez, E.S.E., and T.N. Evans (ed.), *Human Reproduction — Conception and Contraception.* Hagerstown, Maryland: Harper & Row, 1973.

Hardin, Garrett, *Birth Control.* New York: Pegasus, 1970.

Himes, Norman E., *Medical History of Contraception.* New York: Schocken Books. 1936, 1970.

Huber, Sally Craig *et al.,* IUDs Reassessed — A Decade of Experience. *Population Reports,* Series B(2): B21-B48, Jan. 1976.

Karim, Sultan M.M. (Editor), *The Prostaglandins—Progress in Research.* New York: Wiley Interscience, John Wiley & Sons, 1972.

Kennedy, David M., *Birth Control in America—The Career of Margaret Sanger.* New Haven: Yale University Press, 1970.

Langer, William L., Checks on Population Growth: 1750-1850. *Scientific American,* February, 1972.

Mann, J.I., and W.H.W. Inman, Oral Contraceptives and Death from Myocardial Infarction. *British Medical Journal* 2: 245, 1975.

Mann, J.I., *et al.,* Myocardial Infarction in Young Women with Special Reference to Oral Contraceptive Practice. *British Medical Journal* 2: 241, 1975.

Oliver, M.F., Ischaemic Heart Disease in Young Women. *British Medical Journal* 4: 253, 1974.

Potts, Malcolm, *et al.,* Advantages of Orals Outweigh Disadvantages. *Population Reports,* Series A(2): p A29-A52, 1975.

Royal College of General Practitioners, *Oral Contraceptives and Health.* London: Pitman, 1974.

Segal, Sheldon J., and Christopher Tietze., *Contraceptive Technology: Current and Prospective Methods.* The Population Council, July 1971.

Shapiro, S., Oral Contraceptives and Myocardial Infarction. *New England Journal of Medicine* 293: 195, 1975.

Tietze, Christopher, and Sarah Lewit, "Abortion." *Scientific American,* January, 1969.

Vessey, Martin, *et al.,* A Long-Term Follow-Up Study of Women Using Different Methods of Contraception—An Interim Report. *Journal of Biosocial Science* 8: 373-427, 1976.

Westoff, Leslie Aldrige, and Charles F. Westoff, *From Now to Zero—Fertility, Contraception and Abortion in America.* Boston: Little, Brown, 1971.

Wood, Clive, and Beryl Suitters, *The Fight for Acceptance—A History of Contraception.* Aylesbury, England: Medical and Technical Pub. Co. Ltd., 1970.

Film: *Contraception,* 16 mm, color, 17 min. New York, John Wiley & Sons.

RELIABLE SOURCES OF UP-TO-DATE INFORMATION

United States Food and Drug Administration, Department of Health Education and Welfare, Silver Spring, Maryland 20910.

Department of Medical and Public Affairs, The George Washington University Medical Center, 2001 S. Street, N.W., Washington, D.C. 20009.

Planned Parenthood Federation of America, Inc., The Alan Guttmacher Institute, 515 Madison Avenue, New York, N.Y. 10022. (They publish a useful bimonthly journal entitled "Perspectives.")

International Planned Parenthood Federation, 18-20 Lower Regent Street, London SW1Y 4PW, England.

CHAPTER TWELVE

Venereal Diseases

*News have I that my Nell is dead i' th'
spital Of Malady of France;*

William Shakespeare
Henry V, Act V, Sc. 1.

Despite the taboos and the hushed horrified tones of voice with which veneral diseases are commonly mentioned, they are in fact, nothing out of the ordinary compared to many other bacterial diseases. What puts them in the "forbidden" category is simply that they are contracted almost invariably by direct sexual intercourse, and consequently have been looked on as just retribution for illicit sexual relations. This despite the fact that they may be contracted by licit sexual intercourse, as well, and may even be congenital!

The word venereal is said to be derived from Venus, the Roman goddess of love, and it has been known throughout recorded history that certain human ailments were contracted by sexual relations. Unfortunately, the different types of venereal diseases were often confused with each other, and it is only within the last century or so that they have been clearly defined and their various symptoms recognized.

HISTORICAL BACKGROUND

Venereal diseases have certainly played a large part in man's history, and at times have undoubtedly altered its course. There are many references to the spread of these diseases throughout the ancient empires of the Mediterranean area, as armies moved back and forth. It is interesting that syphilis was generally believed to have been brought to Europe by the men returning from Christopher Columbus's expedition to the New World, particularly to the island of Hispaniola, toward the end of the fifteenth century. This theory seems most unlikely from a biological point of view, and it is far more probable that the disease has always been with the human species and simply confused with other diseases.

What is certain, however, is that from about the end of the fifteenth century onward, syphilis (in perhaps a very virulent new form) spread rapidly throughout Europe and became its scourge — so much so that people named it after their enemies. To the French it was "le mal de l'anglais," or "le mal de Naples," while to the English it was the "malady of France," or "the Spanish disease." Syphilis and other venereal diseases have always been prevalent in times of war and other social upheavals, when armies of men have been on the move from their home ground. Recent wars have all too clearly shown that modern armies are no different.

It is important to realize that throughout history the sexual urges and prowess of human beings have never been, nor are they ever likely to be, inhibited by the threat of the severe pain, complete disability, and even death which so commonly result from venereal infection. It is interesting also that venereal diseases are no respecter of persons, famous or infamous, for among the many historically important people who suffered from syphilis or gonorrhea or both are: the painters van Gogh and Goya; the composers Beethoven and Schubert; men of letters Keats, Thackery, Molière, Boswell, Oscar Wilde, Dean Swift, Dostoievski, Strindberg, and Walt Whitman; philosophers Nietzsche and Schopenhauer; churchmen Cardinal Wolsey and Cardinal Richelieu; the religious leaders Pope Alexander VI and Pope Leo X; rulers Napoleon Bonaparte of France, Frederick the Great of Prussia, Ivan the Terrible of Russia, Louis XIV of France, Henry VIII of England, and Mary I of England ("Bloody Mary"), who in all probability was congenitally syphilitic, having contracted it from her mother, Catherine of Aragon, who in turn got it from her husband Henry VIII. Finally, and one may justly say "of course," Casanova!

The historical attempts of society and the medical profession to master, cure, and eradicate venereal diseases are of equal interest. It is always dangerous to make any exact interpretation of ancient writings, Biblical or otherwise, but it would seem highly probable that there is direct reference to some form of venereal disease in Chapter 31 of the Book of Numbers. The Israelites, who have successfully conquered the Midianites, are ordered by Moses to "kill every woman that hath known man by lying with him." The text makes it plain that the purpose of this was to protect the Israelites against potential infection, and the soldiers were also ordered to remain in quarantine outside their own camp for seven days. Moses, in addition to being a priest, can be classed as an early public health official as well.

Throughout the early history of Europe there are frequent references to what must have been the venereal diseases gonorrhea and/or syphilis, but it is not until the end of the 15th century that they seem to have spread widely and to have become a major problem. From that time onward many attempts were made to prevent and treat the disease. As previously noted in Chapter 11, the Italian anatomist Gabrielo Fallopius "invented" the condom as a prophylactic against syphilis in the 16th century when the disease was rampant. Until the invention of vulcanization in the 19th century, condoms had to be handmade and were expensive. Thus they were mainly used by the upper classes, though there were no inhibitions about advertising or using them. An interesting document in support of this point survives from about 1776 in the form of a handbill. It was widely distributed in London by one Mrs. Phillips, who kept a shop near the Strand where she sold linen condoms ("implements of safety") and other articles for the prevention of disease.

The handbill was addressed to captains of ships and gentlemen going abroad, and part of it was in the form of a poem:

> To guard yourself from shame or fear,
> Votaries to Venus, hasten here;
> None in my wares e'er found a flaw,
> Self preservation's nature's law.

The condom, now much improved, is still the most effective preventive measure today, as discussed in Chapter 11.

By the 18th century, medicine was far enough advanced that there was lively controversy as to whether syphilis and gonorrhea were in fact the same disease. In 1767 the most famous doctor of his day, John Hunter (Chapter 2) performed an experiment which he hoped would settle the matter once and for all. He believed the diseases were one and the same, and in order to prove it he obtained pus direct from the urethra of a patient with gonorrhea and inoculated himself. He got gonorrhea, but unfortunately the patient was also infected with syphilis, and John Hunter contracted both diseases. Despite his own treatments he died of syphilitic heart disease some 30 years later, convinced to the last that gonorrhea and syphilis were the same disease. In 1793 a Scottish physician, Benjamin Bell (1749–1806), clearly distinguished between the two diseases by inoculating his students! This was confirmed in 1838 in similar experiments by the French physician Philippe Ricord (1800–1889). It was not until the beginning of the 20th century, however, that the causative bacterial agents of syphilis and gonorrhea were actually identified.

For centuries the only treatment for syphilis and/or gonorrhea was mercury. Sometimes it cured, sometimes it did not. This was succeeded in the 19th century by potassium iodide, which in turn was replaced by arsphenamine or Salvarsan in the early part of this century. At this time also serological tests for syphilis were developed. It was not until about 1943, however, with the discovery of the antibacterial properties of penicillin by Sir Alexander Fleming (1881–1955), that there was any easy or certain cure, particularly for syphilis. The discovery of these properties of penicillin was undoubtedly the greatest therapeutic advance in all the history of medicine. Because of it the effective treatment of most venereal diseases is now simple, short, cheap, and painless, with complete cure virtually guaranteed. There is one proviso, and that is that treatment is given in the early stages before permanent damage has resulted.

Sir Alexander Fleming (Reproduced by courtesy of St. Mary's
Hospital Medical School, London.)

PRINCIPAL VENEREAL DISEASES

There are many venereal diseases, of which some six are of significance in the United States. These are syphilis, gonorrhea, chancroid, lympho-granuloma venereum, granuloma inguinale, and herpes, and they will be discussed in turn.

Syphilis

The organism which causes syphilis is a spirochaete, classed as a bacterium, known as *Treponema pallidum* (Fig. 12.1). It is closely related to the bacterium which causes yaws, a widely distributed tropical disease. It is highly probable that at times syphilis and yaws have been confused. Although *Treponema pallidum* can, by special techniques, be transferred to some monkeys and to rabbits, it cannot, normally, live outside the human body for more than two or three seconds. Thus infection is virtually impossible except by direct physical contact of one person with another. During the physical contact spirochaetes from an infected person pass through an intact mucous membrane of a noninfected person, or through an abraded point in the skin (usually far too small to be seen by the human eye), where there is virtually a blood-to-blood contact. Once inside the body of a new person they quickly multiply and spread to all parts of the body via the lymphatic system and blood vessels.

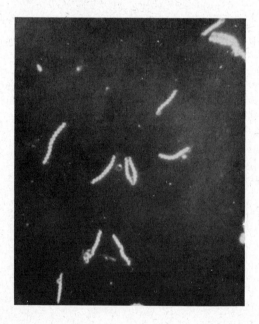

Fig. 12.1. *Treponema pallidum,* the spirochete which causes syphilis (×4200). (Courtesy of Dr. James M. Miller, School of Medicine, UCLA.)

Syphilis is primarily a disease of blood vessels. It is these that the organism ultimately attacks and damages, and thus any part of the body may be adversely affected. As a result, syphilis may "mimic" many other diseases, and even doctors are often confused by it. This fact led one of the most famous physicians of the last century, Sir William Osler (1849—1919), to tell his medical students, "He who knows syphilis, knows medicine."

By far the most common points of infection are the genital organs and surrounding areas; particularly the penis of the male and the general vulval area of the female, including the cervix. Infection is possible also via the anal area. In addition it should be clearly understood that the disease can be contracted by means of sexual play which does not necessarily involve sexual intercourse. This includes petting and kissing. Thus infection may take place via the lips, tongue, tonsils, nipples, or in rare cases via a small cut in the finger. (For reasons unknown, the latter type of infection commonly remains local and does not spread.) Syphilis can also be transmitted by blood transfusions, and by an infected pregnant woman to her embryonic child (congenital syphilis).

Some preventive measures against the possibility of contracting syphilis are helpful. The use of a condom by the male in sexual intercourse supplies good (though not perfect) protection equally to both male and female. Washing with soap and water after sexual intercourse also is helpful, though it, too, carries no guarantee. It is surely obvious as well, that no one should have sexual relations with a person who has any obvious chancre or other suspicious lesion. This would simply be begging for trouble.

Usually in men the symptoms are easily recognized, but because of the female's anatomy and the fact that the point of infection is usually inside the vagina, women are commonly unaware for many months, and even years, that they have the disease at all. It is doubly important, therefore, that a male who contracts syphilis should inform his female partner so that she can seek professional help. In addition, a woman should protect herself not only by insisting that her partner wear a condom, but by requesting her doctor to do a blood test for syphilis periodically. This test is not usually done in normal medical check ups, except at a time such as the initiation of pregnancy. Unfortunately, there is no immune reaction to syphilis, and it can be contracted more than once.

The course of the disease, if untreated, may vary considerably, but there is what may be termed a generalized pattern, which has for convenience been divided into three steps; primary, secondary, and tertiary.

Primary stage. After infection there is an incubation period of from 10 to 90 days. At some time during this period, but typically at three weeks after contact, a rather characteristic chancre—a Hunterian chancre— usually appears at the point of infection. (Black and white photographs do not show this well, but see the colored photographs in "Syphilis," US-PHSP No. 1660.) It must be stressed, however, that the appearance of this chancre is not inevitable, and there may in fact be no primary symptoms at all! In the male the chancre is usually on the penis or the immediate surrounding area, while in the female it may be anywhere on the vulval area, but more commonly inside the vagina or on the cervix. This presents a special problem for women, in that they may be completely unaware of the chancre and thus not realize they may have contracted the disease. In both sexes the chancre may also be on the lips, tongue, or anal area, depending on the circumstances. Although there are inevitable variations, the chancre is typically single, round, and with a greyish base surrounded by a pinkish rim. It may be quite small or quite large, but it is almost always painless. At this time there may be some additional symptoms, such as headache, mild nausea, enlargement of the lymph glands and pain in the joints—particularly in women, for some reason.

The chancre usually persists for weeks, during which time it is highly infectious. The spirochaetes are found teeming right within the tissue of the chancre, and their presence there is used as a diagnostic test. At this stage blood tests are usually negative and do not normally give a positive result until from about one to three weeks after the first appearance of the chancre or four to six weeks after infection.

In due course the chancre will spontaneously heal, and the infected person may unfortunately think that he or she is naturally cured. Nothing could be more false, and it is of the utmost importance that the infected person should receive professional treatment as soon as the first symptoms occur. The earlier the treatment, the quicker and easier the cure. By no means are all chancres of syphilitic origin, and they may easily be confused with many other diseases, so careful diagnosis is very important. The least suspicion should warrant professional help. Patent ointments, creams, etc., or homemade remedies are useless as cures, only clinical therapy in the form of antibiotic treatment (usually by penicillin) is of any value.

Secondary stage. After the primary chancre has spontaneously healed there are no further symptoms for some weeks or months, when a localized or generalized rash appears over the body. It may even occur before the chancre is fully healed, though this is rare. The rash or skin lesions are of great variety, and there may also be lesions in areas where there are moist mucous membranes, such as the ano-genital region, the cervix, the lips, the mouth, and the throat. Other symptoms sometimes are loss of hair (ie., a "moth-eaten" scalp), or loss of eyelashes and part of the eyebrows. There is nearly always general enlargement of the lymph glands and less commonly fever and a feeling of malaise.

Like the primary stage, the secondary stage is highly infectious, and live spirochaetes may be found in any of the skin lesions, but particularly in the moist lesions of the mucous membranes. Blood tests are usually positive at this stage.

Just as the primary chancre may be confused with other diseases, so also are the skin lesions of the secondary stage easily mistaken for many other diseases, and once again professional help must be obtained for proper diagnosis and cure. No homemade cures are possible. As with the primary stage, however, there is spontaneous healing of the rashes and lesions associated with the secondary stage, and this occurs within two to six weeks of their appearance. In about 25% of cases there is a relapse of the skin lesions some weeks or months after they have healed, but in most cases the disease enters a latent stage where there are no outward symptoms at all, though it may still be detected by blood tests. Once again the infected person is in danger of thinking he or she is cured.

Tertiary stage. Up to the secondary stage of syphilis, no serious or permanent damage to the body tissues results, and complete cure is possible by antibiotic treatment. Since syphilis is primarily a disease of blood vessels, however, once these become damaged, serious and permanent complications occur which may well lead to death. After the secondary stage is healed, it is common for the disease to lie dormant for months, but more commonly for years (even up to 50!), when it errupts again without warning in a variety of far more serious forms. In fact almost any part of the body may be seriously damaged, primarily due to damage of the blood vessels. Typically there may be breakdown of the skin in the form of gummy ulcerations called gummas. This may involve the degeneration of an organ like the nose, but may also be within the mouth and on the tongue. There is often permanent damage to joints and bones, including the skull. The disease also manifests itself at this stage in a form known as neurosyphilis. This may result in many neurological disorders including paralysis and death. Cardiovascular syphilis may involve damage to any blood vessel but especially to the aorta and heart, sometimes leading to death. Damage to the eyes may lead to blindness. Tertiary syphilis, in short, may damage almost any organ of the body.

Needless to say, once the tissues have been seriously damaged by tertiary syphilis, any repair is virtually impossible, though in some cases the course of destruction can be arrested. All of these symptoms of tertiary syphilis, however, may easily be confused with other diseases having nothing to do with syphilis. Once again, professional diagnosis and treatment are essential.

Congenital Syphilis

An embryonic fetus may become syphilitic by passage of *Treponema pallidum* across the placenta from the mother's blood to that of the fetus. This does not usually occur, however, until after the eighteenth week of pregnancy. If pregnancy occurs while the mother is in the primary or secondary stages of syphilis, a stillbirth is a common result. If she is in some part of the latent or tertiary stage, however, then a whole variety of ailments may manifest themselves in the infant. It is important to note that adequate treatment of the mother before the eighteenth week of pregnancy prevents infection of the fetus, while adequate treatment *after* the eighteenth week will also cure the infected fetus.

Congenital syphilis is divided into stages just as is acquired syphilis. Since the organism is introduced directly into the fetal blood stream, however, there is no primary stage; only what are referred to as the early and late stages.

Early stage. This stage is characterized by lesions which occur before the age of two. They include:

1. Skin lesions which may occur shortly after birth or in later weeks.
2. Mucous membrane lesions, particularly of the nose and pharynx, causing heavy mucoid discharges which often contain blood as well. (The spirochaetes abound in both the skin and mucous membrane lesions at this time, thus the lesions are highly infectious.)
3. Bone lesions, such as inflammation of both bones and cartilage.
4. Anemia.
5. Enlargement of the liver and spleen.
6. Damage to the central nervous system, including abnormal cerebrospinal fluid.

Late stage. (The late stage exists after two years of age, but commonly the symptoms do not occur until puberty or later.)

1. Damage to the eyes including the cornea, often leading to blindness.
2. Poor development and deformities of the teeth.
3. Damage to the eighth cranial (auditory) nerve, leading to deafness.
4. Neurosyphilis with symptoms similar to those of the acquired condition.
5. Bone lesions, particularly the nose and hard palate.
6. Skin lesions including gummas, as in the acquired disease.
7. Cardiovascular lesions.

8. Deformities of the joints, particularly the knees.
9. Facial disfigurement (rhagades) in the form of fissures or cracks in the skin. This condition is obvious in portraits of Mary I of England.

Gonorrhea

In contrast to syphilis, gonorrhea (sometimes called "clap") is primarily a disease of the urinogenital tracts and associated glands, though sometimes it spreads via the bloodstream to other parts of the body. Its causative agent is a bacterium called *Neisseria gonorrhea* (Fig. 12.2), which is a kidney-shaped diplococcus easily visible under the microscope.

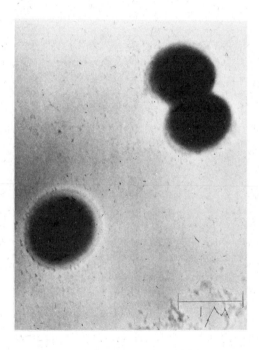

Fig. 12.2. *Neisseria gonorrhoeae*, the bacterium which causes gonorrhea (x 30,000). (Reproduced with permission of Technical Information Services, State and Community Services Division, Center for Disease Control, Health Services and Mental Health Administration, Department of Health, Education and Welfare.)

In virtually all cases the disease is contracted by direct sexual intercourse with an infected person. "Accidental" infection, while theoretically possible, is extremely rare. The organism is passed directly from one moist mucous membrane to another. For an understanding of how this disease is contracted and spread, a knowledge of the internal male and female sexual anatomy is essential (Chapters 3 and 4). In men the primary site of infection is the internal epithelial lining of the urethra, while in women it may be the urethra but is more commonly the cervix. In men the incubation period is only four to seven days. In women it may be the same, but more commonly the symptoms are trivial or there may be none. Thus most women who contract the disease are unaware of it, though they can easily transmit it.

In men the first symptom which commonly occurs is some form of painful urination. This may be only a slight itching or burning initially, but the pain commonly and quickly becomes intense, and may be accompanied by prolonged and abnormal erection of the penis. This is followed rapidly by discharges of pus from the urethra, which has a characteristic smell. There also may be enlargement of the lymph glands. If the disease is untreated at this stage, it may spread rapidly with serious complications. Typically, infection and inflammation, commonly accompanied by abscesses, will spread up the urinogenital tract, and any or all of the following may be affected: the penis in general, Cowper's ducts and glands, the prostate gland, the seminal vesicles, the bladder, the ejaculatory ducts, the vasa deferentia, and the epididymis. Naturally this is usually accompanied by intense pain, and may lead to permanent sterility.

In women the symptoms and course of the untreated disease vary greatly. There may be, as previously pointed out, no symptoms for long periods. The urinary opening may become infected, however, and discharges may result with accompanying vulvitis (i.e., swelling and reddening of the labia). If the cervix is infected, it may become inflamed, and there may be a secretion from the opening which contains pus. Just as in the case of the male, if the disease is untreated, it may spread to other urino-genital organs and affect any of the following: Bartholin's glands and ducts, the bladder, the uterus (with accompanying menstrual dysfunction), and the Fallopian tubes. There is a great deal of pain, and there may be nausea and a rise in body temperature. Just as in the male, permanent sterility may also result.

In both men and women the untreated disease may accidentally be spread from the genital region to the anal area, and particularly to the eye as well. These secondary infections cause discomfort and pain and perhaps serious damage. The eye of a baby can be infected by the mother during the act of birth; hence an antibiotic is always put in the eyes of newborn babies as a protection. It is rare for gonorrhea to spread beyond the urino-genital tract into the general blood stream, but if it does, it may affect the joints, causing arthritis.

The symptoms of gonorrhea are easily confused with other diseases, and early and proper diagnosis is vital for effective treatment. Treatment is mainly by antibiotic therapy. If the disease is recognized early and treated promptly, it can be completely cured without any permanent damage. Any suspicion of its presence should cause the person to seek professional help at once.

Use of a condom by the male during sexual intercourse supplies excellent protection (better than for syphilis), and once again the protection is about equal for both male and female.

Gonorrhea is usually diagnosed by taking a smear from the infected part, and then by laboratory procedures identifying the bacterium under the microscope. Men usually seek treatment rapidly simply because of the intense pain which accompanies infection. However, when women have the infection in the cervix, which is commonly the case, they may be unaware of it. Thus when a male contracts it, he will perform a great service to his sexual partner if he so informs her, so that she can be examined and treated if necessary. Women can also protect themselves against infection by insisting that the male wear a condom. Just as is the case with syphilis, there is no immune reaction, and there are many cases where the disease is contracted several times in a person's life.

Chancroid

This is a venereal disease, sometimes called "soft chancre," which is common in tropical countries, and although relatively uncommon in more temperate climates, it does, nevertheless, occur. It is caused by a bacterium, *Hemophilus ducreyi*, which is transmitted usually during sexual intercourse through a small skin abrasion. It seems quite probable, however, that it can be transmitted by close physical contact other than actual sexual intercourse. This is certainly more likely in hot, humid climates where the human skin is likely to be moist.

For some reason not at all clearly understood, the symptoms are very much more common in men than in women, and indeed, women may be carriers for long periods of time without the slightest suggestion that they are infected. The incubation period is rapid, the first symptom appearing in about one to nine days with an average of three days. In men this is the appearance on the penis of one or more small sores. These are typically at the junction of the glans and the penile shaft, but may also appear at the opening of the urethra. They rapidly become pustules that burst and spread, forming open ulcers with ragged red edges which are usually very painful. Secondary infection to adjacent areas may result. In women the sores and ulcers spread in much the same way as in men, except that they normally start on the vulva, in the vagina, or on the cervix. If the disease remains untreated at this stage, further complications commonly occur. These involve the lymph glands of the groin which, when infected, become large and hard, forming a huge, intensely painful, pus-filled bubo. This in turn may burst, leaving an open sore, and there may be severe damage to the tissues of the genital organs themselves.

Unfortunately, correct diagnosis of chancroid is not simple, though usually the symptoms themselves are sufficient. Sometimes the bacteria can be detected by taking smears from the sores, but not always. There is no effective blood test known at present. Fortunately, the disease is fairly easily cured if diagnosed and treated before it spreads too far. Treatment must be professionally administered, and usually consists of a drug called tetracycline hydrochloride administered orally. Sometimes the disease is not completely eradicated and there is a relapse. Thus careful watch should be kept for at least a year after treatment.

Lymphogranuloma Venereum

Like chancroid, lymphogranuloma venereum is a disease more common in the tropics, but its incidence in the United States is increasing due apparently to importation by Americans returning from Southeast Asia. The disease has the same name as the organism which causes it. This is apparently a large virus rather than a bacterium, though its exact nature is not known.

It is transmitted during sexual intercourse, but perhaps it may also be transmitted by close physical contact which is nonsexual. The incubation period is from a few days to three weeks, and the first symptom (which does not always occur) is a small pimple-like sore. In the male this is usually on the glans penis, and in the female on the vulval area or within the vagina. Since it is small and painless, it is very commonly not noticed by the infected person, and in a few days it will disappear without any treatment. The virus, however, far from disappearing, invades the lymphatic system, and within two or three weeks severe symptoms may be present. In men large bubos occur in one or both groins with much accompanying destruction of the lymph glands. The bubo may or may not burst. In women, since infection is often within the vagina, the organism invades the deeper lymph glands, but there is commonly no bubo. In both sexes, however, there may be considerable pain throughout the body, with fever and a general feeling of malaise.

If the disease is still left untreated it may spread to the anal-rectal area, causing severe damage. Another complication is blockage of the lymph vessels of the penis or vagina, causing enlargement of these organs and a condition known as genital elephantiasis. For some reason this is more common in women than in men.

Lymphogranuloma venereum can be confused with other venereal diseases, but there are fairly accurate blood tests for it. As always, early and correct diagnosis is important. It is difficult to treat, unfortunately, but it usually responds slowly to proper doses of tetracycline hydro-chloride. To be sure that the disease is fully cured, follow-up examinations, including blood tests, are necessary for at least a year.

Granuloma Inguinale

This is another disease mainly found in the tropics, but sometimes occuring in more temperate climates. It is caused by an organism called *Donovania granulomatis*, but whether this is a bacterium or a protozoan is still open to question. It seems to be transmitted by direct sexual intercourse, but possibly also by other means, such as the human louse.

The incubation period is uncertain, but is probably about one to six weeks, when the first symptom appears in the form of a blister on or near the sexual organs. It is painless, but quickly breaks into an open sore with a red granular base that spreads across the skin. It bleeds easily, and gradually becomes painful as the ulcerations spread over the genital areas, to the groins, or even further. The whole area may be raw and, consequently, easily infected by other bacteria. If untreated, these raw areas may remain so for years, but the infected person is so weakened that he or she easily succumbs to other illnesses.

Diagnosis of this disease is fairly easy simply by identification of the infecting organism in smears taken from the raw open area of the skin. Fortunately it responds well to treatment with tetracycline hydrochloride and other antibiotics. After the initial treatment, follow-up examinations for at least a year are advisable to be sure the cure is complete.

Herpes

The virus *Herpes simplex,* the causative agent of the common cold sore, may also be spread by sexual relations, and infection by this means is becoming increasingly common in this country. Following infection by coitus the incubation period is only about a week and, after this, small grouped skin lesions occur on or near the genital organs. In men they are typically on the glans penis, the penile shaft, and surrounding area. In women they may be over the whole vulval area and also the cervix. They rapidly ulcerate and develop a bright red ring. At this stage there is severe itching followed by pain, and the lymph nodes are often enlarged. The disease is not as serious as the others previously discussed, and the lesions will usually heal in about two to three weeks. But there is danger of spreading and secondary infection, and thus it is imperative that professional advice should be sought as soon as possible.

The six venereal diseases which have been discussed here are by no means the only ones, though perhaps they are the most serious. Nevertheless, there are all kinds of other possible infections of the genitals which may not all be of venereal origin. Any suspicious sore, bump, wart, or other lesion on any part of the genital organs should receive prompt professional attention.

The object of these accounts of veneral diseases is not to frighten anyone with their horrific nature. (Scare tactics have never worked as a preventive measure.) Rather it is meant simply to inform correctly, so that the individual can have a venereal disease treated like any other disease—while giving thanks that effective treatment is now available.

Although there are over 2,000,000 new cases of gonorrhea each year in North America alone, and perhaps 100,000 new cases of syphilis (with 1,000 deaths from it per month), the problem is never likely to be solved until there is a change of public attitude toward these diseases. So long as disgrace is attached to contracting venereal diseases, and so long as embarrassment and fear are part of reporting it and seeking help, then they are likely to remain in epidemic proportions, and perhaps increase even further. It is imperative for the public good that there should be mass education at every level on the subject of venereal diseases. This must include their causes, how they are contracted, their symptoms, preventive measures, and the fact that they can be cured. All this is particularly important for the very young and ideally should be part of formal sexual education.

Finally, it is vital to realize that almost everywhere there are public health clinics which give free, confidential advice and treatment to anyone seeking it. Since they are specialists in the diseases, they are often much better equipped to handle them than private physicians. Thus anyone with the slightest suspicion of infection would do well to use them.

STUDY TOPICS

1. Write a short historical account of venereal diseases, and people's attempts to control their spread and to cure them.

2. Give an account of syphilis under the headings (a) cause, (b) methods of contraction, (c) symptoms in both male and female, (d) course of the untreated disease, (e) methods of prevention, (f) method of cure.

3. Explain what is meant by congenital syphilis. What steps can be taken to prevent it? What are the results if it is not treated?

4. Give an account of gonorrhea under the headings (a) cause, (b) methods of contraction, (c) symptoms in both male and female, (d) course of the untreated disease, (e) methods of prevention, (f) method of cure.

5. Explain the means of contraction of chancroid, and the course of the untreated disease.

6. Explain the means of contraction of lymphogranuloma venereum, and the course of the untreated disease.

7. Explain the means of contraction of granuloma inguinale, and the course of the untreated disease.

8. Explain what is meant by herpes, and what are its symptoms.

9. Venereal diseases are on the increase in our society; how would you tackle this problem?

10. Do you think venereal diseases could ever be eliminated? What steps would be necessary to do this?

FOR FURTHER READING

Brown, William J., and James B. Lucas, *Gonorrhea*. Washington, D.C.: U.S. Department of Health, Education and Welfare, Public Health Service, 1970.

Grimble, A.S., *McLachlan's Handbook of Diagnosis and Treatment of Venereal Diseases*, 5th Ed., Edinburgh: E. & S. Livingstone, Ltd., 1969.

Management of Chancroid, Granuloma Inguinale, Lymphogranuloma Venereum in General Practice. Public Health Service Publication No. 255. Washington, D.C.: U.S. Department of Health, Education and Welfare, 1972.

Morton, R.S., *Venereal Diseases*. London: Penguin Books, 1970.

Netter, Frank H. *Reproductive System*, Vol. 2, The CIBA Collection of Medical Illustrations, Summit, N.J.: The CIBA Pharmaceutical Co., 1965.

Rosebury, Theodor, *Microbes and Morals*. New York: The Viking Press, 1971.

Syphilis—A Synopsis, Public Health Service Publication No. 1660. Washington, D.C.: U.S. Department of Health, Education and Welfare, 1968.

Wright, A. Dickson, "Venereal Disease and the Great." *British Journal Venereal Diseases* **47**, 295, 1971.

Film: *Venereal Diseases*, 16 mm, color, 17 min. New York, John Wiley & Sons.

CHAPTER THIRTEEN

Some Psychological and Social Aspects of Sexuality

Let Me Live!

Title of a book by William Lyon
Christopher Publishing House, 1970.

Throughout this book various psychological and social aspects of sex have been touched upon, but in this chapter we will discuss these in a somewhat broader context. The biological basis of sex as a mechanism of reproduction in all mammals cannot be disputed, but in addition biologists make the observation that as one goes up the evolutionary scale, the sexual behavior of animals is less and less at the mercy of hormones, and more and more under the control of the central nervous system, that is, humans have more choice. Humans are very highly evolved animals and the central nervous system is capable of exerting an enormous influence on sexual behavior. At the same time this massive central nervous system is very complex, and gives rise to the various mental processes, feelings, desires, conflicts, etc., (so characteristic of humans) and which collectively we term the science of psychology. (The word is derived from the Greek "psycho" which literally meant spirit or soul, but today is translated as mind). Before embarking on the psychology of sex, we should note that psychology as a science is still very much in the theoretical stage, the various theories are difficult to test, and there is much disagreement amongst psychologists themselves. Above all, we should not forget that humans vary greatly from individual to individual psychologically as well as biologically.

PSYCHOSEXUAL THEORY OF FREUD

Sigmund Freud's theory of the psychosexual development of humans still dominates this aspect of psychology, though as we shall point out there is healthy criticism of it, and there are alternate theories. For our purposes there are two important concepts associated with Freud, unconscious sexuality and infantile sexuality, and we will consider the former first.

We have all heard the popular phrase that "what he doesn't know won't hurt him," but, according to Freudian psychosexual theory, this is not realistic. Within the human psyche, the unconscious (which is part of the mental process) while beyond voluntary control, nevertheless plays a major role in how we think, feel, and behave. While we are normally unaware of the unconscious, it surfaces at times in dreams and may be uncovered by various methods of psychoanalysis.

Mental Processes

In order to explain the mental processes of the mind, Freud divided them into three categories — the id, the ego, and the superego. The id, according to Freud's theory, is composed of the basic biological drives, which includes the libido (Latin for lust) or sex drive, and all its contents are entirely unconscious. The drives of the id express themselves through pleasure. Pleasure is their goal regardless of the circumstances. At the other end of the scale is the superego which comprises the conscious (though not entirely), and is made up of the realities of the world in the form of learned moral codes and socially acceptable behavioral patterns. These tend to block the pleasure-seeking drives of the id and consequently there is mental conflict. It is the function of the ego (partly conscious and partly unconscious) to mediate between the id and the superego, and the success of this interaction will depend on the general psychosexual adjustment of the individual, and whether he or she experiences frustration, guilt, and all the consequences thereof.

Infantile Sexuality

The second of Freud's concepts, infantile sexuality, aroused intense emotions, and gave rise to hot debate. There has been much modification of Freud's original ideas. In its basic form the concept divides the psychosexual development of the young child into three main stages based on physiological events. These are the oral, anal, and phallic stages, and these represent the different successive areas of the body in which the libido expresses itself. Furthermore the vicissitudes, or "ups and downs," of the libido during childhood determine in large measure future sexual functioning and indeed the whole personality and psychological makeup of the individual.

Oral Stage. This stage extends from before birth to about eighteen months (though it may last much longer) and represents the period when the child explores the world through its mouth. Sucking of course is essential to the child for nourishment, but psychoanalysts see in it much more than that. To the child sucking is a pleasurable process and is also erotic. To some extent this oral stage probably remains into adult life, though its relative importance diminishes. Thus while thumb sucking usually ends in childhood, this may not necessarily be the case. Kissing is certainly an oral manifestation of erotic pleasure, and there are many other ways (eating, drinking, etc.) in which oral pleasure is obtained.

Anal Stage. This stage consists of the period during which the child is greatly concerned with defecation and its own anus. It begins when the child is about two years of age, and may be quite short, but its end is difficult to determine and it may well persist into adulthood with intense erotic sensations associated with the anus. In addition there are certain childhood characteristics which seem to go hand in hand with the onset of the anal stage. These include willfulness, stubbornness, etc. with rapid alternations between expressions of love, anger, and hate.

Phallic Stage. This stage extends from about the ages of three to six, during which the child becomes intensely aware of its genitals and enjoys the pleasure of manipulating them. Whenever possible, children of this age will also make sexual explorations of the opposite sex. It is also a period of great importance psychologically, for it is here that children develop an erotic attachment to the parent of the opposite sex (the famous Oedipus Complex) and feelings of hostility towards the parent of the same sex. Boys may develop a "castration anxiety," that is a fear of reprisal from the father because of the child's erotic love of the mother. Girls on the other hand may develop "penis envy" with their realization that they do not have such a prominent organ and, according to psychoanalytic theory, these oedipal complexes may give rise to serious psychological problems if not satisfactorily resolved. If, however, development continues without major difficulty, the child will give up the hope of obtaining erotic love from the opposite sexed parent and identify with the parent of the same sex, and eventually the whole conflict will be buried in the unconscious.

Following the phallic stage, there is generally a period of latency, during which there is little sexual interest and/or activity, though much intellectual growth and social learning. However puberty begins a new period of sexual awakening and behavior, which continues through most of adult life. This has already been discussed in Chapter 5.

CRITICISMS AND MODIFICATIONS OF FREUDIAN THEORY

During the last century Freudian theory has dominated the psychoanalysis of sexual development, and on rational as well as observational grounds one is forced to conclude that there seems to be a great deal of truth in it. However, it has not been without its critics.

The principal criticisms have been that because most of the psychosexual changes take place at the unconscious level, they are very difficult to verify. Furthermore, generalizations from Freud's theories have been too broadly and universally applied with little empirical evidence to support them. Freud also unquestionably developed his theories from a male perspective and viewed the female as simply a defective male (a male castrate). As a result, Freud never explored the data on female psychosexual development. It is also said that Freud tended to ignore the influence of physiological development (particularly hormonal aspects) on psychosexual development, and that he did not allow for the inevitable and enormous biological variations. Also most modern psychiatrists would not now view some sexual behavior patterns (such as homosexuality) in the psychosexual disaster area which Freud did.

Sigmund Freud (Sigmund Freud Copyrights, Ltd.)

The all-pervading sexual aspects of Freudian theory have been modified to include social learning as a major factor in psychosexual development. Also the relationship of the mother to the child plays an enormous influence, and through this the child learns what is satisfying and unsatisfying to it and learns to reject the latter. The influence of siblings and peers is also of undoubted importance and is receiving much attention. In addition, as Ford and Beach (see Chapter 14) so admirably demonstrated, the particular culture into which a child is born will play an enormous role in the formation of its psychosexual structure.

PROBLEMS OF PSYCHOSEXUAL DEVELOPMENT

It would be a very different world from the one in which we live if humans developed smoothly, resolved their conflicts, interacted easily both sexually and socially, and also had a trouble-free physiological constitution. As we all know, this is not often true, and to use a very old saying, "Life is not a bed of roses." Thus, much of our efforts are devoted to trying to understand the basic nature of our problems, and then attempting to resolve them in some satisfactory way. This is all we can hope for, and the task is not easy.

As the child grows, its psychosexual growth may not coincide with its physiological growth. In consequence the time sequence of the libido may vary considerably. In addition, the child's needs at a particular stage may be either inadequately satisfied or excessively satisfied. When either occurs the child is said to become fixated at a particular stage, psychosexual development is impeded, and may even become disrupted. Some manifestations of fixation in adulthood include various forms of homosexuality, buggery, exhibitionism, and fetishism. Thus some of these sexual behavioral patterns are looked upon as the persistence of childhood sexual behavior into adulthood. If the child's psychosexual needs are repressed, then psychoanalytic theory holds that the entire personality of the individual will be affected, and that he or she will become orally or anally fixated in a variety of ways not necessarily obviously sexual, and may also show behavioral traits reminiscent of the childhood traits exhibited at the various psychosexual stages.

Oedipal Conflicts

What evidence there is seems to support the view that it is best for a child's future psychosexual development to become involved in an oedipal situation and then resolve it as previously explained. If this resolution does not take place, then it seems that a variety of future problems may occur. Parents may vie for their children's love and attentions, or they may be punitive. They may also be hostile to each other, whether openly or in a clandestine manner, the child is seldom fooled. Yet again the presence of siblings and the particular child's situation amongst them, learned moral concepts, sex roles, and behavior will all play a part in the oedipal situation. Considering the vulnerability of a young child to all these and other influences, it seems remarkable that the majority of children resolve the situation so well. Nevertheless problems do occur, though we should be very careful what we ascribe to what.

Males who have not satisfactorily resolved the oedipal conflicts are said sometimes to become shy and sexually inhibited. They may also tend to shun women in general. Females on the other hand with unresolved oedipal conflicts may tend towards typical masculine behavior patterns or may become retiring and passive depending on their particular psychosexual problem. The variety of possible potential behavioral and psychosexual problems are enormous, and psychologists seem convinced that most of these have their origins in childhood. No doubt there is much truth in their theories, and one must respect the therapeutic results they sometimes achieve, not forgetting the difficulties and inevitable misinterpretations. We should also always be aware of the awesome responsibilities of parents, who quite unknowingly, and at a very early age in their children's lives, will profoundly affect their whole psychosexual development.

ADULT PSYCHOSEXUAL RELATIONSHIPS

As young persons grow up sexually in the adolescent years, they will usually go through some or all of the behavorial learning processes described in Chapter 5, and while some of these may involve intense emotions and difficult psychosexual conflicts, nevertheless it is usually only in the later teenage years (or at a greater age) that deep emotional attachments are established including love, intimacy, and dependence, and these are in all probability going to be closely integrated with sexual relationships. In addition these are not likely to be easily or satisfactorily established unless the person has had good psychosexual learning experiences in the childhood years.

Learning to Love

Since we cannot perform controlled experiments on humans involving such a complex phenomenon as love, we can only infer indirectly and cautiously from such things as experiments and observations on our fellow primates. Such experiments have indeed been done recently, principally under the leadership of Dr. H. F. Harlow, and the results are pertinent. Principally they point clearly to the fact that the ability of monkeys to copulate successfully is dependent upon a long sequence of juvenile interactions with adults and with their peers, and while it may be stretching the point to refer to love relationships in monkeys, nevertheless these interactions are only one step removed at most.

As a result of this work, psychologists refer to five basic kinds of human love. These are maternal love, infant-mother love, paternal love, peer love, and heterosexual love. It is not intended to infer that each of these is mutually exclusive but rather that each one, in a loose time sequence, prepares the individual for the succeeding one, and difficulties in one are likely to be reflected in the next. Some people who have experienced unpleasantness in these interactions have great difficulty establishing love relationships, others, who have reinforcing experiences with the various forms of love, do this much more easily.

The love of the mother for the infant is certainly the most basic of all forms of loving. It is a particularly mammalian characteristic with obvious biological value. Mothers show greater general interest and have closer relationships with their infants than do fathers. That this fact may be culturally imposed appears unlikely. Its cause is probably mainly biological. Maternal love appears in the overt forms of feeding, care, protection, and most important, actual physical contact (usually in the form of cuddling). This latter overt expression of love can hardly be overstressed if the infant is going to grow up with a good emotional psyche. These very close emotional relationships of the mother to the infant must of course be severed in due course, and this is not always easy.

Although difficult to study, infant-mother love is undoubtedly a major aspect in the psychosexual development of a child. It is no doubt at first primarily biological in that the infant quickly learns that the mother supplies food and care, but the love becomes more overtly intense when the child learns that the mother also supplies protection and security, and it seems essential for the child to feel protected and secure if it is gradually to achieve independence.

It is very difficult to be objective about paternal love. Where it has been properly studied in monkeys and apes, it would appear to play a minor role. However in humans we all know this is not necessarily the case, and intense love relations can and do develop between father and children. Paternal love is unquestionably greatly influenced by the cultural background, much more than maternal love is, but in reality we know very little about paternal love from an objective point of view. Nevertheless, this source of love is assumed to be of some importance in the child's psychosexual development.

Observations of both infant monkeys and infant humans have led psychologists to believe that peer love is probably one of the most important aspects in the psychosexual development of the child. The beginnings of the overt expression of peer love undoubtedly start in the form of play. And this in turn is usually dependent on the child having established in itself enough security to leave the protection of the mother long enough to establish such peer relationships. In humans peer relationships usually begin about age three and continue on with increasing intensity until about the age of ten. After puberty, and during adolescence, they gradually decline as heterosexual love develops. It seems important for the child's psychosexual development that two basic things are accomplished during this peer love phase; first, that the child transfer to the peers a major part of the reliance, confidence, and security which has been established with the mother and, second, that actual physical contacts are established. These also are probably a transfer of the earlier, but very essential, physical contacts with the mother. These bodily contacts are not necessarily (indeed rarely) of any obvious sexual nature, but it appears essential that they be of a pleasurable nature if the child is to develop a satisfactory psychological attitude towards future heterosexual relations. Once again the importance of the establishment of peer love can hardly be overemphasized.

Heterosexual love is of prime importance in the lives of most individuals, but as the history and literature of all peoples and all ages tell us, and as we know for ourselves, it is fraught with dangers and disasters—though of course its rewards can be enormous. The development of heterosexual love apparently has three basic requirements as theorized by Herant Katchadourian and Donald Lunde. These are mechanical, hormonal, and romantic. The mechanical requirements consist largely of a properly differentiated and functioning genital system, and the appropriate sexual behavior, in the form of posture, pelvic thrusting, etc., which lead to successful coitus. The hormonal requirements have already been discussed (Chapters 3 and 4), and while these are certainly biologically necessary in humans, the influence of the central nervous system is more important than in other primates. There remains the romantic element, and this is the most difficult to describe and come to terms with, yet its importance for humans in the psychology of sex is enormous.

It would be anthropomorphic to refer to romance in nonhuman primates, but they certainly do exhibit what can be referred to as emotional attachments in heterosexual pairs and, unlike most other mammals, they are not indiscriminately promiscuous. What is even more important is the findings of Harlow and others that if monkeys are isolated and deprived as infants so that they do not have the usual bodily contacts and social relationships with mother and peers, they seem quite incapable of forming emotional attachments as adults. Some primates, if so deprived, are quite incapable of coitus. Thus, we can feel confident that in humans this romantic element can be established successfully only if the mechanical and hormonal elements are adequate, and the individual's social upbringing is also adequate. Thus, the origins of heterosexual love have a long biological and psychological history, and profound effects on the individual's attitude, abilities, and behavior.

SEXUALITY AND LOVE

Sexuality and love are not one and the same, but before we discuss the relationship further, it will be well to make as clear as possible what we mean by each. Sexuality is an interest in or concern with sex, and usually the biological need for actual sexual experiences and outlets. It is of course perfectly possible for two heterosexual individuals, who are not in love, to have sexual intercourse which will give physical satisfaction and release to both parties, but such events are relatively rare. Love on the other hand is difficult to define, but it consists of a strong, usually passionate, affection for another person, and it can become intense and all-pervasive. Love between a man and woman will involve an increasing emotional ability to give and receive, and to establish a meaningful and very basic trust in each other. Yet again emotional interdependence seems essential, and this allows for the free exchange of the individual's deepest and sometimes inhibitory emotions, which in turn will lead to heightened communication and mutual support in a whole variety of ways. The antithesis and ever-present dangers of a love relationship are guilt feelings, fear, jealousy, selfishness, lack of confidence and truthfulness, to name but a few. These are all in us to some degree, but must be gradually overcome and reduced to a minimum as a love relationship develops. This is not easy to do, and is inevitably an ongoing process throughout life. Unfortunately too many people rush into marriage (usually from social pressures) thinking that they have established all this, when in reality their relationship, while perhaps intense, is actually very superficial, heavily weighted on sexuality, and will not stand the test of time.

Sensuousness

For those in the process of establishing a love relationship there is invariably an intense desire for both physical (with sexual overtones) and psychological intimacy, and it seems that the kingpin between love and sexuality is sensuousness. This can be defined briefly as enjoying the pleasures of the senses. However, while the biological aspect of this is of prime importance, nevertheless what we may term psychological pleasure is also prominent. There are of course many human senses and to some extent all of these no doubt play a role in helping to establish intimacy, pleasurable responses, and psychological satisfaction. However, in a heterosexual relationship by far the most dominant sense is the sense of touch which leads to caressing and the establishment of such psychological aspects as warmth of feeling, caring, gentleness, and concern. As has been pointed out earlier, nonhuman primates, such as monkeys, deprived of bodily contacts (touching) and cuddling in infancy are unable to establish normal social relationships in adulthood, and psychologists are firmly convinced that much the same is true in humans. Furthermore, they believe that children psychologically deprived of emotional warmth, care, and concern have much greater difficulty in establishing meaningful heterosexual relationships in adult life. They tend to be guilt- and anxiety-ridden, cold, insecure and to suffer from various inferiority complexes. If individuals are unable to satisfy or resolve the basic sensual needs, primarily touching, it is not unlikely that they may withdraw, and develop such feelings as hostility and aggression.

It is through sensuousness in a heterosexual relationship that physiology and psychology become closely interwoven in establishing all those intense emotional experiences known only to those who love. It is through sensuousness also that the biological desires of sexuality will be channeled towards sexual intercourse. Some people clearly prefer to have some form of love, or at least affectionate relationship, present before they proceed to sexual involvements, others find this unnecessary. Traditionally women have been said to fall into the former category, and men into the latter. However this "typing" may be largely socially conditioned, though it is difficult to tell. Be that as it may, any lasting and truly satisfying heterosexual relationship will be a blend of love and sex, and the establishment of an intimacy, both physiological and psychological, which will enrich the individuals' lives to a degree unknown in any other way. It is vitally important also to realize that this relationship can never be static, but must develop throughout life as the needs of the individuals change.

In conclusion, we must never forget that psychology is still a very tenuous science and its theories very fragile. For more detailed studies of the psychology of sex, consult the references at the end of this chapter.

SOCIOLOGY OF SEX

While sex is fundamentally a biological phenomenon in humans, as in other animals, nevertheless the human situation is such that sex pervades virtually every aspect of our lives. It is intertwined with psychology, anthropology, medicine, history, politics, religion, ethics, morality, culture, and, of course, sociology. All that can be attempted here is to touch upon some of the more obvious social aspects, with the hope that the reader will explore much further.

It is a fact well known to sociologists that people, either as whole cultures or subcultures, are very reluctant to change (let alone give up) their traditional beliefs, ways of thought and behavior, even in the face of a drastically altered social environment. Thus, our sexual attitudes and behaviors tend to be the product of how we are brought up, and these will be modified only very slowly as the generations come and go. However, because of the greatly altered environment which has engulfed advanced nations largely during the last century, our attitudes, values, and consequent behavior are changing more rapidly than at any time during our history. There are many forces that have brought this situation about, such as industrialization and urbanization, preventive medicine and the prolongation of life, enormously increased means of mass communication, ease of travel, and an ever-increasing population which makes excessive demands on the environment and finite resources of the earth. All this, and more, has not been easy for us to cope with and has given rise to intense conflicts; nowhere have these been more apparent than in sexual attitudes and behavior.

A Time of Conflict and Change

Everyone is aware of the so-called sexual revolution which is supposed to be taking place today and which apparently began a few years ago. Reliable figures on the sexual revolution are difficult to obtain because many people are unwilling to give accurate accounts of their sexual lives. Nevertheless, it seems a safe bet that today young people are having more sexual relations earlier in their lives than did the young people of a generation ago, and there is generally more sexual permissiveness throughout our society. This applies particularly to women just as it did in the last sexual revolution which occurred in the early 1920s after World War I. The 1920s revolution was a direct result of the fact that during that war women demonstrated they could work efficiently in the war factories alongside men, and could also, if need be, die beside them. Women demanded and, in due course, got the vote and other social rights, including sexual emancipation.

The generally increased premarital sexual activity of today was of course initiated by the young (this is natural, since the majority of sexual activity takes place among the young!), but it appears unlikely that this sexual activity would have occurred if parental and societal attitudes had not changed somewhat during the upbringing of today's youth. There is every evidence that this is indeed the case. As far back as the Kinsey reports, it was quite clear that there was a growing freedom with which sexual matters were discussed in various printed media, schools, churches and in common social "get togethers." But in addition visual media such as television and films have recently shown sexual behavior in a most remarkably free and realistic manner, and this has aroused heated opposition. As Dr. Garrett Hardin points out in his foreword to this book, just a mere decade ago the book could not (or at least would not) have been printed for college students. Now the market is flooded with books about human sexuality. There is still however enough opposition to the teaching of sex in primary and secondary schools (where it is greatly needed) to keep sex education out of most curriculums. Furthermore some churches and other social institutions are literally being torn apart by such problems as the ordination of women priests, sex education, premarital and extramarital sex, tolerating abortion, advocating contraception, and the acceptance of homosexuality, to name but a few problems. Indeed there is a sexual revolution (or, more accurately, a rapid evolution) going on, and society cannot easily come to terms with it. In my opinion the most far-reaching aspect is the demand of women for freedom, and equality of opportunity with men, in all matters as well as sexual. No longer will women accept the traditional double standard, or inferiority. It should be noted in passing that this "rebellion" in the status of women is largely a phenomenon of the English-speaking world, and is spreading only very slowly to other countries and societies.

Sexual Attitudes

Observers of American society during the past ten years or so cannot help but be struck by the "generation gap" in which the young are tending more and more to reject the values and advice of their parents, and "elders and betters" generally. On the other hand the establishment generation looks upon the youth as morally and socially degenerate and despairs for the future. Nowhere is the conflict greater than in sexual behavior. Of course, "generation gaps" have occurred often in the past, a fact well known to historians. Indeed, some of the oldest known clay tablets from the Middle East contain such phrases as "Alas, alas! All is lost. The youth are degenerate." Just as the cry of all students throughout the ages has been "I'm overworked!" so also has the cry of older people been "The youth are degenerate." What is new today is simply the intensity of the conflict, an intensity due primarily to the rapidity of change.

Unfortunately, most Americans usually think of morality purely in terms of sex. Moral behavior, be it sexual or otherwise, is of concern to every member of society and, indeed, no one can behave simply as he or she wishes and yet have the society survive adequately. As the 19th-century English scientist and philosopher, Thomas Henry Huxley (1825-1895), noted, "Everything that makes life worthwhile on this earth depends upon the restrictions of other people's freedom." Freedom is not the right to do as we please, (that is anarchy) but the liberty to do as we ought. The problem facing society is to find the happy medium between restraint and freedom.

The establishment generation of today can, if it wishes, teach young people a traditional sexual morality (largely based upon religious tenets) of abstinence (and usually ignorance) before marriage. But there are many reasons why young people of today are not likely to follow this teaching. For example, the young are under severe pressure from their peers and from highly sophisticated commercial advertising campaigns to be sexy and to attract a sexual partner. They are not at all sure that traditional sexual morality has any meaning in an advanced urban society, nor even that their parents observe the rules! On the other hand, young people do neither themselves nor society a service when they mistake sexual freedom for sexual license. The greatest danger in having indiscriminate sexual relations is that a young girl may become pregnant long before she is psychologically, socially, or financially able to cope adequately with the enormous responsibilities of becoming a mother. (Venereal disease also used to be a major problem, but modern drugs have diminished this problem somewhat.) Even if the young father accepts the responsibility (and many young fathers don't), he is in little better position than the mother to fulfill these responsibilities. There are few sadder social situations than that of a young girl in junior high school facing the problems of giving birth to an unwanted baby. She must either place the child for adoption or inflict its care and upbringing upon her own parents. Thus the irresponsible act of having an unwanted child leads to another, the abdication of parental duties. It seems to me that parents of sexually mature children have the responsibility not only to recognize the fact that their children necessarily have biological desires but also to equip them with the information and the means of coping with their desires. On their part, the sexually mature children have a responsibility of their own toward themselves and their parents. They must recognize the potential long-term consequences of sexual involvement and act with appropriate discretion.

Moral Sexual Behavior

Morality guides the way in which we live up to our ethic, whatever that may be. Morality is difficult to define and to prescribe. Nevertheless, there are some guidelines for today's society with which few people can have any major disagreement. For example, one guideline is that no human being on this earth can be free to act or behave solely for his or her own best interests without regard for the effects of those acts and behaviors upon others. We all must assume a responsibility to ourselves, our immediate family, our peers, our society at large, and to other peoples and nations throughout the world. Our problem is to meet those responsibilities to the best of our ability. Meeting these responsibilities will inevitably involve compromises.

Young people in particular should be taught that before they engage in sexual relations, they should consider the consequences to other people in their society and then ask themselves if their activities are morally justified. This is easier said than done! But in the kind of society in which we live, an assumption of personal responsibility for possible consequences is more likely to have meaningful results than any stringent rules imposed by parents or institutions on the one hand, or the disasters of laissez-faire on the other.

The potential consequences of sexual activity are far more serious for girls or young women than they are for boys or young men, but the responsibility for those consequences rest equally with both sexes. Some of the questions young people might be asked to consider are: Am I psychologically or socially mature enough to engage in the profound emotional aspects of sexual intercourse? Would it not be better to seek other channels for sexual release? Do I really care enough for my sexual partner to engage in sexual intercourse? If I do, how will this affect my relationship with my parents and what will be the consequences of that? If I do decide to go ahead with sexual intercourse, should I or should I not use appropriate contraceptives? If I don't, what will be the consequences if I become the mother (or father) of a child? Will that child be illegitimate and what are the consequences for the child? Who will care for the child, (which is a full-time job), and who will support it or bring it up in this expensive and complex society? What about the responsibility to the child? Will the female partner have to seek an abortion? Or will she be more or less forced to marry her sexual partner?

Parents have responsibilities to teach by example and to see that their children are properly informed on all aspects of sex. Knowledge is better than ignorance in sexual matters and imparting this knowledge is basically a parental responsibility. When to impart this knowledge is determined by the child's needs and ability to comprehend. Parental teaching should be supplemented as soon as possible with formalized instruction in school.

What do parents do when their children become sexually mature and seem likely to engage in sexual intercourse? Should parents inform sexually mature children about contraceptives and make the contraceptives accessible to the children? It is argued that if the children are kept in ignorance of or denied access to contraceptives, they will be less likely to have sexual relations. Experience shows that this isn't true. Consequently, full information of contraceptives and access to them is preferable to no knowledge of them. Once again, knowledge is better than ignorance, though knowledge in itself is no guarantee against undesirable consequences. The vicissitudes of sex are unpredictable.

SEX AND THE LAW

Chapters 9, 11, and 12 discussed some major aspects of sexual behavior as they relate to the law, and it is necessary here to mention only a few other areas of legal importance. There is a move in many states to put sexual acts between consenting adults outside the province of the law. This is a welcome innovation. Problems remain in such areas as sexual relations between young adolescents, as well as between adults and adolescents, prostitution, illegitimacy, public health (because of the spread of venereal diseases), population policies, and others. All these problems have the potential of being of social concern, and are therefore likely to have legal consequences. In this country these vary enormously from state to state, and are sufficient in themselves for another book. No survey will therefore be attempted here, but rather a few brief ideas concerning specific aspects.

Sexual Relations between Nonadults

Apart from any individual psychological damage either to those directly involved or their parents, sexual intercourse between adolescents can have serious social consequences in the form of unwanted children. These consequences have already been discussed, but it is worthwhile noting that society has not yet evolved any means or laws adequate to cope with the problem. It does no one any good to legally punish a 15- or 16-year-old mother or father because they have produced a child. The only hope of solution (and it will only be partial at best) that I see to this problem is to try to do a better job of teaching responsibility to young people, and to impress upon them the importance of contraception. Sexual intercourse between an adult (usually male) and an adolescent (usually female) is covered by laws which again vary from state to state. These commonly are written around the concept of the "age of consent," which (whatever that age may be) means that if the girl is below the age and has sexual relations with a man, he is guilty of a crime whether she gave her consent or not. If she is above the age of consent, the legal consequences usually revolve around the problem of whether she knew what she was doing and did in fact give her consent. If not, then the adult male is possibly guilty of statutory rape. This is of course a serious crime in our society, and seems to be on the increase both between adult and adolescent, as well as between adults. It will never be an easy problem to solve.

Prostitution

Prostitution, both female and male, is said to be the oldest profession in the world. It has certainly played a role in the history of every culture known to anthropologists. In some countries it is legalized, in others it is illegal but tolerated openly, in others it is ruthlessly suppressed. In the United States it is officially illegal everywhere except Nevada in which a thriving and luxuriant trade is carried on which caters mostly to clients visiting Nevada! The arguments in favor of legalized prostitution usually make the point that prostitution is inevitable anyway. Legalizing prostitution would ensure that inmates of brothels would be licensed, taxed, and also very importantly, would receive proper and regular health inspections to prevent the spread of venereal diseases. Those opposed to prostitution usually look upon it as the ultimate moral degeneracy and are determined to stamp it out. Opponents also argue that antiprostitution laws are most discriminatory because it is always the prostitutes who are prosecuted and not their clients. In some places compromises are made. Prosecution of prostitutes seldom takes place unless they make a public nuisance of themselves by soliciting. Once again, no easy solution to the problem is at hand or in the foreseeable future.

Illegitimacy

Illegitimacy is widespread in this country today, and is apparently on the increase. It is more prevalent among the lower socioeconomic groups, but occurs widely throughout society. Although the law applies no legal penalty in such cases to either the father or mother of an illegitimate child, society still adopts the traditional condemnation of the parents, but with the usual double standard of holding the mother mainly responsible. The options open to a young pregnant unmarried woman are rather limited. She may get married before the baby's birth, and risk the possibility of an unhappy marriage, she may have an abortion, legal or otherwise, or she may remain unmarried and have an illegitimate child. If she takes the latter option, her child is not only treated as a second-class citizen by society, but is also legally disadvantaged. In many states of this country the birth certificate of an illegitimate child indicates in one way or another that the child is illegitimate. Worse, the inheritance rights of the child may differ from those of legitimate children. In fact in most states an illegitimate child does not have the right to inherit automatically from his father, nor from relatives. However nearly all states now require the father to support the illegitimate child, though this is easier said than done. Israel was one of the first countries in the world to make all children legitimate, (without any indication of illegitimacy on the birth certificate) and in this country two states (Arizona and North Dakota) have followed suit. We can only hope that all others will shortly do so. Any such legal change however, though certainly a first step, will not abolish the prejudices of society towards illegitimacy. This will only come with more tolerance and understanding. We can hope also that better education both sexual and otherwise will cut down on the rate of illegitimacy, as there are certainly very few people who actually want an illegitimate child.

Human Population

The United States has no government policy regulating the size of our population. Population size is governed only by general biological, economic, and social forces. The late Walter Lippmann (1889-1974) once remarked that the world has more to fear from sexual energy than from atomic energy. There can be little doubt that we in this country would be better off materially, and be under less social and economic pressures, if there were fewer of us. Throughout the world, there are just too many people for the natural resources of this earth to support at a reasonable standard. There seems little doubt that by the end of this century societies will be forced to come to terms with these facts in order to avoid disasters of enormous magnitude.

Some "social scientists" tell us that we in this country are headed for a unisexual society. From a biological point of view, this is most unlikely. How unbiological, how absurd, how dull. I personally agree with the French, "Vive la différence!"

STUDY TOPICS

1. Explain what is meant by the following mental processes: (a) id, (b) ego, (c) superego.

2. Explain what is meant by "infantile sexuality."

3. What are the arguments against Freudian psychosexual theory and how has it been modified?

4. Explain what is meant by "Oedipal conflicts" and their importance in child development.

5. Discuss some of the problems in adult psychosexual relationships.

6. Explain the various links between sexuality and love.

7. Do you think the "generation gap" is a valid concept? Is the gap wider now than it was between generations in the past?

8. Discuss some of the moral problems of sexual behavior in a modern industrial society.

9. Explain the problems of sexual relations between nonadults.

10. What problems are posed by professional prostitution?

11. Explain the various problems of illegitimacy. Have you any solutions?

12. Do you think this country should have an official population policy? How might it be enforced?

FOR FURTHER READING

Broderick, Carlfred B., and Jessie Bernard, (eds.), *The Individual, Sex, and Society*. Baltimore: Johns Hopkins, 1969.

Harlow, H. F., J. L. McGaugh, and R. F. Thompson, *Psychology*. San Francisco: Albion, 1971.

Hutt, Corinne, *Sex Differences in Human Development*. Human Development 15: 153-170; 1972.

Katchadourian, Herant A., and Donald T. Lunde, *Fundamentals of Human Sexuality*. New York: Holt, Rinehart and Winston, 1972.

Kirkendall, Lester A., and Robert N. Whitehurst, (eds.), *The New Sexual Revolution*. New York: Donald W. Brown, 1971.

Lyon, William, *Let Me Live*. North Quincy, Mass.: Christopher, 1970.

McCary, James Leslie, *Human Sexuality*. New York: D. Van Nostrand, 1973.

Rutter, Michael, *Normal Psychosexual Development*. Journal of Child Psychology and Psychiatry 11: 259-283; 1971.

Shope, David F., *Interpersonal Sexuality*. Philadelphia: W. B. Saunders, 1975.

White, Robert W., *The Enterprise of Living*, (2nd ed.) New York: Holt, Rinehart and Winston, 1976.

CHAPTER FOURTEEN

Cross-Cultural and Historical Aspects of Sexual Behavior

When women can cherish the vulnerability of men as much as men can exult in the strength of women, a new breed can lift a ruinous yoke from us both. We could both breathe free.

Marya Mannes, *Out of My Time*, Garden City, N.Y., Doubleday, 1971.

The human species, like all other living things, has arrived at its present state by the process of organic evolution by natural selection. Inevitably, therefore, it is anything but perfect, and is in fact simply a combination of what we may term "biological compromises." Like other species, humans have special features about them, some of which are their upright posture, sparse body hair, a long thumb (which in part enables them to be so dexterous), and above all a huge development of the cerebral cortex.

THE LEARNING ANIMAL

As a result of this large and complex cortical expansion, humans far exceed other animals in their ability to learn, and consequently to modify and vary their behavior. This applies to sexual behavior no less than any other kind. Because of this fact human sexual behavior is influenced relatively less by hormonal control than is that of other animals, and relatively more by cerebral control. Thus, in contrast to other animals, humans can successfully modify their sexual behavior in a great variety of ways, depending on their background and the particular circumstances.

Humans may accurately be described as learning animals, and in the case of sexual behavior they learn to seek specific sexual partners rather than being sexually indiscriminate. Furthermore, different kinds of sexual stimulation and the circumstances which bring about sexual excitement are largely learned, and the various possible responses to these stimulations and situations depend on the individual's past experience. These learning procedures may be, and often are, purely trial and error, but by far the greater part are learned from other people and within the general social context in which the individual is brought up and lives. Thus, in addition to being learning animals, humans are also social animals, and as a result their sexual behavior is inevitably channeled into certain patterns consistent with their particular cultural background. From the culture the individual will learn right from wrong, various codes of conduct, and how, when, and where to behave in certain ways. These codes and behaviors may of course be quite different for males and females, and even between social strata within the same society. But whatever the differences, every individual will be subject to strong pressures to conform to the traditional sexual behavior patterns accumulated through hundreds, and perhaps thousands, of years of cultural heritage.

Human sexual behavior then, must be viewed with these three things in mind; the purely biological factors, the learning processes, and the social-cultural environment. Since large cultural variations exist between different groups of people throughout the world, it is not surprising to find, as anthropologists have amply demonstrated, that there are also large variations in sexual behavior.

A CROSS-CULTURAL SURVEY

In their classic work, *Patterns of Sexual Behavior,* (1951), Dr. Clellan Ford and Dr. Frank Beach made a survey and comparison of the sexual behavior of 190 different societies on a world-wide basis. While the survey was inevitably not complete in its scope, it was certainly extensive enough to be fully representative of the modern human species, and despite the passage of time it is still the best one available. Doctors Ford and Beach also compared human sexual behavior with that of other animals, particularly primates, in the hope of understanding its evolutionary origins and to help distinguish the biological aspects from the cultural ones. In their survey they reported on some societies which have been studied in detail and others which have been studied much less. And subsequent workers have investigated yet other societies at great length.

It would be quite futile to attempt any detailed description here of cross-cultural forms of sexual behavior. Only generalizations are possible, and perhaps the best way of making them will be to describe the main findings of Doctors Ford and Beach, then compare in somewhat more detail the sexual behavior of two societies with very different cultural backgrounds. This short description, however, is no substitute for the original works which truly interested readers will wish to consult.

In all the 190 societies of their sample, Ford and Beach generalize that heterosexual coitus is the major form of sexual behavior, but that rarely, if ever, is it the sole form of sexual activity. Likewise the face-to-face coital position (as opposed to rear entry by the male, as in most animals) is by far the most common position in all known societies. However, variations of the face-to-face position are numerous, and preferences for these variations differ from one society to another. For example, coitus with the woman on her back and the male lying on top is the most common position in many societies, including our own, but the side-by-side position is preferred in some societies with such diverse backgrounds as the Kwakiutl of North America and the Masai of Africa. A variation which is predominantly Oceanic consists of the woman lying on her back and the male kneeling before her. The male then draws her toward him, so that her legs straddle his thighs, and at the same time he pulls her body up so that they embrace in a semi-erect squatting position. Although a certain position may be the dominant one within a particular society, other positions are commonly used, including rear entry on certain occasions.

There are variations also in the attitudes societies take on whether the female should play an active or passive role during coitus. In our own society she was traditionally supposed to play a passive role, though this is rapidly changing. We are not the only society, however, where the woman plays a passive role, for this is also true of Colorado Indians. However, in many other societies, such as the Hopi and Trobrianders, female passivity is far from the rule, and indeed both partners are equally active. Similarly, different societies vary widely in their attitude on whether the female is supposed to reach orgasm during coitus. In general, western societies have not paid much attention to this, and as a result many women seldom or never reach orgasm. In the Oceanic societies the woman is expected to reach orgasm as a result of coitus, and men learn to delay their orgasm for considerable periods of time. Whether all the women do in fact reach orgasm is difficult to ascertain.

Sexual foreplay in humans prior to actual coitus is subject to vast variations, from virtually none to extensive stimulations over a period of several hours. The two most common forms are kissing and female breast stimulation, but even these are not universal and some societies do not employ them at all even though they may have no cultural prohibition. Mutual stimulation of the genitals of the opposite sex (either manual or oral) is very common, but cultural prohibitions may forbid this type of foreplay. For example, males of the Tikopia of Oceania are forbidden to touch their own or the woman's genitals. The infliction of pain is also commonly a part of sexual foreplay and may include biting, scratching, and hair pulling, but it is by no means universal.

In contrast to many other animals, humans almost always seek privacy for coitus, and this is usually at night. However, any generalization about prohibitions on when coitus may take place is impossible. Almost every society has different rules on this, though it is perhaps of interest that western societies, including our own, are among the most lenient in this respect—providing, of course, that it takes place within marriage. The differences in the frequency of coitus are wide, and range all the way from the Keraki of Oceania, who copulate about once a week, to the Thonga of Africa, who are said to copulate several times a night.

The physical features which societies find sexually attractive and the behavior patterns employed to attract a sexual partner are of extra-ordinary diversity. One or two examples will suffice, and these are for females, since there is not much information of similar nature for males. Many societies find a plump female body sexually desirable, while others prefer a medium or slim body. Small ankles are important to some societies, and elongated labia majora to others. The shape of the breasts is often most important, long pendulous ones being sometimes desirable in some societies, while other societies prefer small upright ones.

Direct and intentional exposure of the female's genitals as a form of sexual invitation, as in most mammals, does occur in a few societies, such as the Dahomeans of Africa and the Kurtatchi of Oceania, but this is relatively rare. The usual situation is that the female's genital area is kept covered with clothing, and this is far more common than in the case of males. Other means of attracting a sexual partner are by the appropriate use of clothes, decorations, charms, etc., gifts, special words, songs, musical instruments, and vocal intonations.

It is of special interest also that, unlike our own society, there are some in which the initiative in sexual advances is always taken by the female. These include the Kwoma of Oceania and the Mataco of South America. In this connection Ford and Beach state, "From the cross-cultural evidence it seems clear that unless specific pressures are brought to bear against such behavior (as in our society), women initiate sexual advances as often as do men."*

In cross-cultural perspective it seems quite clear that stable sexual mateships are virtually universal. The most prevalent pattern of mateship is one in which two or more females are attached to one male, but in which at any given time a majority of males have but a single mate. In Ford and Beach's sample of 185 groups for which information was available, restriction to a single mate occurred in less than 16%, and less than one third of these wholly disapproved of both premarital and extramarital liaisons. Thus our society, with its legal and moral codes, is very much in the minority. While most men in most societies are in fact monogamous, most societies nevertheless permit a man to support more than one sex partner if he can do so.

As previously pointed out, heterosexual behavior is the predominant form in all known societies, but it is probable that homosexual behavior also occurs in most if not all. In a sample of 76 societies, 36% strongly condemned any form of homosexuality, and its incidence was said to be very rare. However, 64% of the societies considered various forms of homosexual activity normal and acceptable, including anal intercourse. In fact in some societies (e.g., the Siwans of Africa and others) all men and boys engage in anal intercourse, and are indeed considered peculiar if they do not indulge in homosexual activities. Little is known about the cross-cultural aspects of female homosexuality, except that it appears to be much less common than male homosexuality. Good information on sexual relations between men and animals (bestiality) is sparse, but it certainly does occur. It is generally condemned or ridiculed, but in a few societies it seems to be fairly common.

---

*Clellan S. Ford and Frank A. Beach, *Patterns of Sexual Behavior*, New York, Harper and Row, 1951, p.105.

Since masturbation is generally frowned on, particularly in adults, good information on the incidence of masturbation in different societies is very difficult to obtain. However, regardless of the cultural mores, it seems to be universally practiced by at least some members of every society. As in our own society, it is also generally much more common among males than females.

One other form of sexual activity about which humanity seems to share the same attitude is incest. All known human societies forbid sexual intercourse between parent and offspring, and almost all forbid it between siblings.

A COMPARISON OF TWO SOCIETIES

The foregoing cross-cultural survey of sexual behavior is based on the work of Ford and Beach. We will now elaborate on it a bit by a more detailed comparison of what may be termed a "sexually permissive" society and a "sexually restrictive" one.

A Sexually Permissive Society

For an example of a sexually permissive society we will use the people of Mangaia, one of the islands of Central Polynesia. The sexual behavior of this society has been well studied by Dr. Donald S. Marshall, and this account is taken from his work, "Sexual Behavior on Mangaia".*

Young Mangaian girls and boys live and play together until they are about four years old, but between four and five they are segregated sexually in a social sense, and for the rest of their lives male and female pairs will rarely mix together in public, despite close private relationships. Although there is no formal sex education of children by parents, and sex is not even talked about in private, young boys and girls commonly live in a single hut with perhaps as many as 15 family members. Some of the family members have sexual relationships, of course, and young women frequently have young male lovers. All this appears to go unnoticed, but in reality the young boy and girl must learn much about sex from this atmosphere. They also learn sexual knowledge outside the home from boys or girls their own age, but also from a public which is acutely aware of sexual matters in the form of sexual observations, stories, and jokes, as well as folktales with detailed descriptions of sexual acts and organs. There are also highly sensuous dances performed in public.

*Dr. Donald S. Marshall, "Sexual Behavior on Mangaia," in *Human Sexual Behavior—Variations in Ethnographic Spectrum*, Donald S. Marshall and Robert C. Suggs (Eds.), New York, Basic Books, 1971.

Young Magaian boys learn "where babies come from" between seven and ten, and at about the same age they learn about and experiment with masturbation, and are said to masturbate two or three times a week at this age. Girls also masturbate, but there is little good information on this, and although parents who are aware of masturbating children may try to stop them, their efforts are not very great. At around the age of 12 or 13 some boys may experiment in sexual intercourse with older women, but not girls of their own age, who are of course, reaching sexual maturity.

At the age of 13 or 14 Mangaian boys undergo a surgical operation which is a major event in their lives, and marks the transition from boyhood to manhood. The boys are subject to extreme social pressure to undergo this operation, and in the end almost all submit to it. This is the operation of "superincision" of the penis.

The operation may be done on a single boy or on a group of boys at one time, but it is always done by an expert who specializes in the procedure. Usually performed without any anesthetic, the operation consists of pulling back the foreskin of the penis from the glans, inserting an "anvil" over the glans, and pulling the foreskin back over the anvil. A dorsal incision is then made over the entire length of the penis through the skin and through the white underlayer. As might be expected, the operation is very painful and is often accompanied by much bleeding, and the youth runs directly into the sea or a stream for relief—but at the same time proclaiming, "Now I am really a man." The organ is then dressed with various poultices, etc., and the expert is particularly careful to see that as the cut heals, the glans remains exposed on a permanent basis. During the days that follow the operation the youth is supposed to eat only certain foods, the wound is frequently bathed in the sea, and the dressings are attended to by the expert.

However, more important than the actual healing of the wound, during this post-operative period, is the fact that the youth receives detailed training in sexual behavior from the expert. He is taught techniques of coitus, various means of attracting a girl, details of sexual stimulation, ways of achieving simultaneous orgasm, and how to have his partner reach several orgasms before he reaches his. This period of formal instruction is then followed by actual coital practice with an experienced woman, the main object of which is to have the scab on the penis removed by the act of sexual intercourse. At the same time the experienced woman gives the youth practical lessons in various coital positions, timing in coitus, and delaying orgasm, as well as how to achieve orgasm in unison. This whole procedure is often carried out on the seashore.

From a social point of view the youth is now sexually acceptable, and from a psychological point of view he believes that his penis is more beautiful and that he is a much more competent and vigorous sexual partner. There is a feast in his honor, and from then on he actively seeks sexual intercourse with a variety of girls (who have also been instructed by an older woman). Mangaian custom is such that there is no dating or courtship, but rather very indirect and subdued "invitations," the object of which is clearly understood to be sexual intercourse. When the boy and girl actually meet (usually in the girl's house) there is little sexual foreplay; they tend to proceed directly to coitus. The overall result is that virtually all Mangaian boys and girls have extensive sexual experience before marriage. It is of great interest also that sexual intercourse is not the result of mutual affection. Affection may or may not result from sexual intimacy, but unlike the usual situation in western societies, sexual intimacy precedes affection. For the teenage boys and girls this period is one of sexual experimentation and adventure.

Needless to say, with all this premarital sexual activity there are many children conceived and born out of wedlock, despite the local belief that it is continued coitus with the same man which is the cause of pregnancy. Prior to the encroachment of western ideas there was no social stigmatization of an illegitimate child. Commonly, however, the mother and father subsequently marry, or the child may simply be adopted by the girl's family.

Marriage customs in Mangaian society are changing rapidly, and marriages are arranged for a variety of reasons: e.g., the woman may have become pregnant, or love may be a primary reason and sexual compatibility a secondary one. Marriages are also arranged for financial reasons or to bring together landowning families, or other material reasons.

With marriage however, the sexual relations of the man and woman change. The Mangaians believe that sexual intercourse is the main reason for marriage, and in fact there are few if any outward signs of emotional attachment between man and wife. The male also believes that he requires more sexual relations than the female, and that he has the right to keep at her until she gives in. The emphasis on coitus also shifts from the number of times each night the male can bring the female to orgasm, to whether he can have coitus each night with his wife. In any case a very active sexual life is continued.

On Mangaia both husband and wife are supposed to be faithful to each other, but the historical record and present-day reality tell a different story. Extramarital relations do in fact take place. This is particularly the case with girls who have a tendency to go back to the first man with whom they enjoyed sexual intercourse, and with men who are travelling away from home. However, just as with other societies, sexual activity tends to decline as the individuals age.

Finally, it may be pointed out that there appears to be no homosexuality in either sex on Mangaia. There is, however, quite a bit of transvestite behavior, and the individuals concerned are not condemned or discriminated against in any economic or social way.

The relatively free sexual behavior of Mangaians has its roots in their ancestral "warrior" religion, which has long since given way to Christianity.

A Sexually Restrictive Society

What may be termed a sexually restrictive society is one found on Inis Beag, a small island off the coast of Ireland. The sexual behavior of this society has been studied and reported on by Dr. John C. Messenger, of Indiana University, and the description which follows is derived from his article, "Sex and Repression in an Irish Folk Community."*

The island has maintained its stability for at least 200 years, and there are at present some 350 people living on it. Their livelihood is mainly from subsistence farming, with some fishing, and the standard of living is low. There is an informal political system dominated by a few influential individuals, but the inhabitants are subject to the laws of the mainland. Almost all householders own land, and there are about 59 families. As might be expected, there is much relatively close inbreeding, and the 59 families have only 13 surnames. Marriages are arranged almost entirely for economic reasons, with any aspect of love not being seriously considered. Late marriage is the rule, the average age for women being 25 and for men 36, while 29% of those eligible for marriage are single. Despite the protests of the women, the average family has seven children, and the functions of marriage are generally considered to be economic and reproductive. Both before and after marriage the sexes do not normally intermingle. Men associate with men, and women with women, while men in general are by far the most active socially. Some women in fact seldom leave their cottages.

Roman Catholicism is the main religion, though there are many pagan beliefs, mainly of Druidic origin. These include an array of spirits, demons, witches, and ghosts. The islanders of Inis Beag are devout Catholics, and although they are critical of their priests, their outward behavior is a near model of Christian morality. This results mainly from the social control of the priests and a genuine fear of damnation.

As Dr. Messenger points out, the society on Inis Beag is sexually one of the most naive and repressed in the world. Children are brought up in

---

*Dr. John C. Messenger, "Sex and Repression in an Irish Folk Community," Marshall and Suggs, *op.cit.*

total ignorance, and adults avoid any mention of sex when children are present. Women are unaware of the biological significance of menstruation or menopause; in fact, menopause is commonly thought to be the harbinger of madness. Men, on the other hand, believe sexual intercourse is debilitating, and that women are dangerous to the male at certain times, such as at menstruation and for months after childbirth. There is also fairly good evidence that female orgasm is virtually unknown. Courting and/or premarital coitus are also unknown, and marital coitus is carried out with a minimum of foreplay, usually with underclothing still on. Sexual advances are entirely the male's prerogative, and the superior male position is the only one used.

In the home, children are sexually segregated at an early age, and this segregation is carried on in school, church, and other aspects of daily life. Nudity, and even partial nudity, is horrifying to the society. Only very young infants have their whole bodies washed, while older children and adults wash only their faces, necks, arms, and legs. They do not learn to swim, apparently because they would have to bare their bodies in order to do so, and even seriously ill men will avoid medical treatment if it involves exposing their bodies to a nurse. Bodily contact of any kind between the sexes is shunned, and their form of dancing (i.e., "set patterns") is such that the partners are separated most of the time. However, even that is not enough for some girls, who refuse to dance because it would involve touching a boy!

The overall sexual repression of Inis Beag society is enforced by sermons from the pulpit and lectures in the classroom, so that church and school go hand-in-hand. There is also extensive use of informers, refusal of sacraments, the confessional, and other means to keep priests advised of every detail of a person's life, so that effective pressure can be brought to bear where necessary.

Children become sexually repressed in the home early in childhood, simply by parental disapproval and/or severe punishment for any sexual expression such as masturbation, mutual bodily exploration, open urination or defecation, or the use of any words relating to sex. Infants' and childrens' bodies are always covered in the presence of their brothers or sisters. Although mothers are affectionate to their children, the direct physical expression of love is replaced by verbal expression early in childhood. Sexual morality is also indoctrinated through religious journals, which are found in most homes.

The roots (and there are many) of the present sexual behavior of the people of Inis Beag reach deep into their history—an area that is beyond the scope of this book. However, the reader is referred to the original article by Dr. Messenger for many interesting theories.

A SUMMARY OF WESTERN SEXUAL ATTITUDES IN THE CHRISTIAN ERA

Whether the current sexual behavior and morality of a society is permissive or restrictive, (which are of course merely relative words of convenience) depends on a host of factors going far back into their general historical-cultural background. Needless to say, western society is no exception, and we will now consider a few historical aspects which have helped to shape our present sexual mores, attitudes, and behavior.

Western civilization derives its cultural background from many sources, including ancient Greece, Rome, Islam, Egypt, Persia, China, and others. Without a doubt the most influential element has been the Middle East, with its Judeo-Christian concepts and the eventual triumph of the Christian religion in western Europe.

However the Hebraic attitudes toward the relationship between men and women may have changed during the passage of time, originally they were very simple. The male was the dominant partner with almost absolute rights over his wife and children. The purpose of marriage was reproduction, and if it did not fulfill this purpose it could be dissolved. Anything that interfered with reproduction was wrong and in addition was defying the command of God—"Be fruitful, and multiply, and replenish the earth, and subdue it." (Genesis I, 28). This male and nationalistic orientated philosophy was probably universal in all the societies of the Near East, and certainly suited the Jewish state which was surrounded (then as now) by hostile neighbors. However, this philosophy did not save the Jews from successive slavery under the Persians, Egyptians, Syrians, and Romans.

In the centuries immediately following Christ's death, two new fundamental concepts evolved which were to have profound effects on later western civilization. The first of these was the Christian dogma of marriage, namely that it was for life even if childless. Since such a marriage might easily interfere with the laws of inheritance, this is no doubt one reason why the new religion was unpopular with the rich. But at the same time it is probably why it was initially popular with women. And since such a marriage gave women legal and financial security, this is no doubt one reason why the new religion was popular with them. The second concept, which evolved later, was far from beneficial for women, for it placed them for centuries to come in a very inferior position to men. This was the concept of "original sin," which is usually associated with St. Augustine (354-430) but whose roots go much further back to St. Paul (who was certainly not tolerant of women), and indeed to the gospels themselves. Without attempting to explain the reasoning which led to this strange doctrine, suffice it to say that St. Augustine arrived at the conclusion that there was no essential difference between "copula carnalis" (man and wife) and "copula fornicatoria" (man and prostitute). Both were sinful. Pope Gregory the Great (590-604) endorsed this doctrine on behalf of the church, and declared that the lust of the flesh itself was sinful. Men could avoid sin by a life of celibacy, and thus woman became an evil. She was the temptress (Eve) and she was the more sensual and more evil. One early father of the church, Clement of Alexandria (circa 150-206), went so far as to declare that every woman should blush at the thought that she was a woman, and the lines "Behold, I was conceived in inquity and in sin hath my mother conceived me" still form part of some church services. With this unhappy background of sexual morality, and the complete triumph of the church, European culture was shaped for hundreds of years.

With the coming of the Renaissance, the Reformation, and the Great age of Discoveries, there was certainly the beginning of change in western attitudes to sexual behavior and morality. Artists began to discover, paint, and draw the human body in the nude, writers described sexual behavior, particularly prowess, and the new Protestant church ceased to cherish celibacy as the most virtuous way of life. Even divorce again became possible. Frequent attempts were made to stop these reforms, but by and large more liberal sexual behavior became widespread. This can be seen in the plays of Shakespeare, the court behavior of the Stuart Kings of England, the French nobility, and in many other places. The trend generally continued right through the seventeenth and eighteenth centuries, though European societies were still male dominated. Women did exercise considerable influence—though always "from the bedroom"—and that influence reached its zenith in eighteenth-century France, which from a sexual point of view was extremely permissive.

While the French Revolution of 1789 was anti-old regime, which included being anticlerical, it was unfortunately also essentially antifeminist. This was due primarily to the fact that under the old regime women had been virtually deified, and there were positive arrays of court mistresses, etc., who had wrought havoc. Thus while women marched alongside their men as the Bastille was stormed, the new revolutionary regime did not even accord them the franchise, and they were excluded from all high office. Childbearing was still to be their lot in the Republic, particularly as it was soon under attack from its neighbors and in fact quickly became a military state. However, with the revolution came civil marriage and easy divorce, and unlike most military states there was little interference with private morality and behavior. Napoleon Bonaparte himself led an exceptionally open and varied sex life. He was not very different from his regal predecessors in some respects, for while at times he treated women with contempt (and on his military campaigns was said to have slept with a different one every night), at other times he idolized them. He also fell victim to one of the errors of the Kings of France before him—letting his political and military judgments be influenced by court mistresses.

At the beginning of the nineteenth century a counterrevolution began, with the tendency to return to the ways of the old regime. But more important was the fact that in 1837 the young Queen Victoria ascended the throne of England. Partly no doubt in reaction to the French Revolution (a reaction which had long since set in), and partly as a result of England's imperialistic ambitions, as well as other factors, a long period of sexual repression started. This was not confined to England, for she was by far the most powerful nation on earth, and unfortunately power is all too commonly taken as a model. Wherever the English language was spoken, and wherever English influence was felt, there too went English ideas, ways, and morals, including sexual ones.

This transformation took place gradually in the earlier part of the nineteenth century, and although there were no sudden draconian laws passed, the pressures exerted by the church, the court, and the upper-class (as well as the new and immensely wealthy merchant class, which aspired to respectability), were more effective than any laws. Sex very quickly became unmentionable and was regarded as a sort of "necessary evil" for reproduction—and Victorians were extraordinarily prolific. Whatever private lives people led, their outer appearance and behavior were of the utmost propriety, "gentility," naivety, and prudery.

Children were brought up in utter sexual ignorance, washing their bodies was avoided, and any sexual expression met with severe disapproval and punishment. Lovers were carefully chaperoned, and kissing was not permitted except when engagement actually took place. Marriage was supposed to be strictly monogamous and also male dominated. Women's dress was designed to cover up the biological fact that they had anything below the waist. Exposure of the legs became unthinkable, and later in the century when sea-bathing became popular, women's bathing attire was such that their legs were always covered—and even then the sexes were segregated. No woman was permitted to be examined by a doctor without her husband or mother being actually present.

Prudery reached incredible heights, and all literature, past and present, was subject to careful scrutiny to be sure that it was free of anything suggestive of sex. One Thomas Bowdler, who was a medical doctor, produced what he called his "Family Shakespeare." This consisted of all the works of Shakespeare which the good doctor found time to edit so as to make them "suitable" for reading aloud to a family! Even *Robinson Crusoe* and Gibbon's *History of the Decline and Fall of the*

Roman Empire were expurgated in the same manner. Presiding over all morality was a powerful Church of England with its teaching of eternal damnation for those who broke the code.

Other western societies did not go to such extremes, and as pointed out in Chapter 11, the English moral codes were already under attack toward the end of the century. However, it was the Victorian sexual ethic which led directly to the philosophy—and the legal and social power—of Anthony Comstock and others in the United States. Hopefully we are in the process of emerging from these extremely restrictive attitudes.

CONCLUSION

Historical interpretations are naturally open to question and challenge, and no doubt the explanations I have attempted here will not be agreed to by all. Nevertheless it seems to me that sexual morality and behavior in our society have been traditionally determined by strong patriarchal attitudes, with emphasis on reproduction, going far back into history. Superimposed on this have been the severe inhibitory influences exerted by Roman Catholic and Protestant churches alike, including some newer "home grown" ones. In addition, this country has a strong Puritan background in both sexual and other matters, as well as the immediate background of Victorian repression.

It is obvious to even the most casual observer that the youth of today are rejecting this background of sexual behavior and morality and are struggling to find new approaches. Tolerance, patience, and understanding for their efforts are in order. Reproduction is certainly no longer a primary goal of sexual relations, the status of women is changing, and even the institution of marriage is being questioned—and with much justification. It would be a rash person who would choose to predict where it will all lead.

One thing, however, stands out clearly to me, and that is the incredibly rapid change in men's attitude toward women and in women's aspirations for themselves. Throughout history women have been worshipped and idolized, ignored and humiliated, despised and bullied, but never accorded equal and free status beside men. They may finally be reaching that point. Society will undoubtedly be the better for it, as it will be a humanizing process that will help human beings to understand one another better. For all humans "are kin in sharing much the same interests, lusts, frustrations, loves, sorrows, and joys that are part of human sexuality."*

---

*Paul H. Gebhard, in Marshall and Suggs, *op. cit.*

STUDY TOPICS

1. What are some factors which influence human sexual behavior, and how do these affect each individual?

2. What forms of sexual behavior are more or less universal in the cross-cultural context? Describe some of the more prominent variations in sexual behavior in the cross-cultural context.

3. What historical events have influenced sexual behavior in Western Europe in the last 1000 years?

4. What forms of sexual morality would you advocate today? in the future?

5. "The world has more to fear from sexual energy than from atomic energy." Discuss.

6. Write a short note on the historical importance of each of the following.

Karl Ernst von Baer	Charles Knowlton
Martin Barry	Fernand Lamaze
Frank Beach	Anthony van Leeuwenhoek
Benjamin Bell	Thomas Robert Malthus
Annie Besant	William H. Masters
Charles Bradlaugh	Margaret Mead
Ethel Byrne	William Mensinga
Mary S. Calderone	Ivan Pavlov
Anthony Comstock	Gregory Pincus
Marquis de Sade	Francis Place
Regnier de Graaf	Philippe Ricord
Gabrielo Fallopius	John Rock
Sir Alexander Fleming	Leopold von Sacher-Masoch
Clellan S. Ford	Margaret Sanger
Sigmund Freud	Sappho
John Hunter	Marie Stopes
Virginia Johnson	Edward Truelove
Alfred Charles Kinsey	

FOR FURTHER READING

Bullough, Vern L., *Sex, Society, and History*. New York: Science History, 1976.

Ford, Clellan S., and Frank A. Beach, *Patterns of Sexual Behavior*. New York:

Harper & Brothers, Pub. and Paul B. Hoeber, Inc., Medical Books, 1951.

Kronhausen, Phyllis, and Eberhard Kronhausen, *Erotic Art—A Survey of Erotic Fact and Fancy in the Fine Arts.* New York: Grove Press, 1968.

Lewinsohn, Richard, *A History of Sexual Customs.* London: Longmans, Green, 1958.

Malfetti, James L., and Elizabeth M. Eidlitz, *Perspectives on Sexuality.* New York: Holt, Rinehart and Winston, 1972.

Marshall, Donald S., and Robert C. Suggs (eds.), *Human Sexual Behavior—Variations in the Ethnographic Spectrum.* New York: Basic Books, 1971.

Taylor, G. Rattray, *Sex in History.* New York: Ballantine Books, 1954.

Turner, E.S., *A History of Courting.* London: Pan Books Ltd., 1958.

Glossary

abdomen   The portion of the body that lies between the thorax and the pelvis.

abortion   Premature expulsion from the uterus of a fertilized egg, embryo, or nonviable fetus.

adipose   Of a fatty nature.

adolescent   A young person, usually between the age of puberty and about 18 or 19.

adrenocorticotrophic hormone (ACTH)   A hormone secreted by the anterior pituitary gland which has a stimulating effect on the cortex of the adrenal gland.

albumin   A protein found in the human body.

alkaline solution   A solution which is basic and capable of neutralizing acids.

amniotic cavity   A hollow sphere formed within the disc of the blastocyst in the developing embryo.

amniotic membrane   A thin layer of tissue surrounding the amniotic cavity.

anatomical   Referring to the structure of the body and the relation of its parts.

androgens   Hormones which possess masculinizing properties.

androsterone   A hormone found in the urine of both men and women.

anovular   Not accompanied by the discharge of an ovum.

anterior   Situated in front, or the forward part of the body.

antibody   A substance produced in the body as a reaction to the presence of an antigen.

antigen   A substance which, when introduced into the blood or tissues, causes the formation of antibodies.

anus   The opening of the lower end of the digestive tract to the exterior.

areola   The colored ring of tissue surrounding the nipple of the breast.

artery   A blood vessel that carries blood away from the heart to the various parts of the body.

atrophy   A defect or failure manifested by the wasting away of a part of the body.

bacterial flora   The entire content of bacteria for a certain region.

bacterium   A microorganism within a group of which there are many kinds.

Bartholin's gland   A paired gland in the walls of the vagina at its opening.

bilateral   Having two sides approximately the same.

biologically active IUD   An intrauterine contraceptive device which gradually releases hormones into the uterus.

biology   The science of life or living phenomena.

biophysical   Referring to living and its physical aspects.

bisexual   Having gonads of both sexes; having sexual interest in both sexes.

bladder   A sac located in the pelvis of both male and female which serves as a reservoir for urine.

blastocyst   A hollow sphere formed by the developing zygote.

breast   The mammary gland of male or female—much larger in the female.

bubo   The swelling of a lymphatic gland, particularly in the groin.

buggery   Sodomy, usually sexual intercourse via the anus.

capillary   A minute blood vessel that connects an arteriole with a venule.

carbohydrate   A compound of carbon, hydrogen, and oxygen, in which the three elements are bonded in a special way. Usually the ratio is 1:2:1. Sugars, glycogen, and starches are examples.

castration   Removal of the gonads.

cell   The basic unit of life, surrounded by a membrane.

cerebrospinal   Pertaining to the brain and spinal cord.

cervix   The neck or narrow part of the uterus that projects into the vagina.

chancre   An ulcer which is the primary lesion of syphilis.

chancroid   A venereal disease.

chorion   The outer cells of the trophoblast in the developing embryo.

chorionic gonadotrophin   A hormone secreted by the chorion in the embryo which has a stimulating effect on the testes in the developing male embryo.

chromosomes   Rod-shaped bodies found in the nucleus of most cells.

cilia   Cellular processes which commonly beat in a rhythmic manner.

circumcision   Removal of the foreskin from the penis.

clitoral hood   A small fold of skin formed by the labia minora which covers the clitoris.

clitoris   A small organ in the female, located at the upper end of the fold of tissue between the labia minora. It is the principal organ of sexual excitement in the female.

coitus   Sexual intercourse, during which the erect penis of the male enters the vagina of the female.

coitus interruptus   Sexual intercourse during which the penis is withdrawn from the vagina before ejaculation.

colostrum   A watery fluid secreted from the breast.

conception   The fertilization of an egg by a sperm—and the beginning of a new life.

condom   A sheath used to cover the erect penis to prevent conception or infection.

contraceptive   Any device used to prevent fertilization and conception.

copula carnalis   Latin for sexual intercourse between man and wife.

copula fornicatoria   Latin for sexual intercourse between man and prostitute.

copulation   Sexual intercourse, or coitus.

corpora cavernosa   Two erectile areas within the penis.

corpus albicans   The scar tissue formed in the ovary after the egg is shed.

corpus luteum   The Graafian follicle after the egg has been shed.

corpus spongiosum   An erectile area of the penis which encloses the urethra.

Cowper's gland   A paired gland near the prostate gland which adds small amounts of secretions to the seminal fluid.

cryptorchism   A developmental defect in which the testes remain in the abdominal cavity.

cunnilingus   Oral contact with the vulval area.

diabetes   A serious metabolic disorder with many manifestations.

diaphragm   A rubber dome which fits over the cervix and is used as a contraceptive.

dilate   To enlarge an opening or canal.

dimorphic   Occurring in two distinct forms.

diplococcus   A group of bacteria which usually grow in pairs.

diploid   The normal number of chromosomes found in the cells of a particular species. In humans it is 46.

DNA   Deoxyribose nucleic acid; the hereditary substance found in the chromosomes of cells.

douche   The washing out of the vagina with the help of a syringe.

ego   A mental process of the mind which mediates between the id and the superego.

ejaculation   The sudden expulsion of semen via the urethra during the male's orgasm.

embryo   The early development stage of the human up to about eight weeks from fertilization.

endocrine   Internal secretion, applied particularly to glands which secrete directly into the blood stream.

endometrium   The internal lining of the uterus.

enzyme   Specific proteins which catalyze biological reactions.

epididymis   A coiled organ attached to the upper part of each testis. This is where sperm mature and are stored.

episiotomy   The surgical incision of the vaginal opening during birth.

epithelium   Any surface layer of cells.

erection   The process of engorgement with blood, by which any tissue becomes rigid or erect. This refers in particular to the male's penis during sexual excitement.

erotic   Pertaining to sexual love or sensation.

estradiol   The principal sex hormone of the female which is produced in the ovaries.

estrogens   A group of sex hormones produced in the female's ovaries.

estrus   The restricted period of sexual receptivity in many female mammals.

etiology   The study or theory of the causation of any disease.

excitement phase   The initial part of the sexual response cycle.

exhibitionism   The display of the body or genitals for the purpose of attracting sexual interest.

Fallopian tube   A paired tube which extends from the side of the uterus to the region of each ovary.

fellatio   Oral contact with the penis.

fertilize   The fusion of a sperm with an egg.

fetishism   Sexual behavior in which some article, such as clothing, has a sexual attraction for the individual.

fetus   The embryo from after eight weeks of development until it is born.

flaccid   The soft state of a tissue, particularly the male penis when unexcited.

follicle stimulating hormone (FSH)   A gonadotrophic hormone produced in the anterior pituitary gland of both male and female. It stimulates production of sperm in the male and development of the ovarian follicle in the female.

fructose   A sugar with a special structure called ketose.

genetic   Inherited.

genital elephantiasis   A disease of the genitals in which there is great inflammation and distension of the genitals.

glans clitoris   The head or tip of the clitoris.

glans penis   The head or tip of the penis.

glucose   A sugar with a special structure called aldose.

gonad   An ovary or testis.

gonadotrophin   A hormone having a stimulating effect on the gonads.

gonococcus   The organism that causes gonorrhea.

gonorrhea   A venereal disease.

Graafian follicle   A bundle of specialized cells in the ovary, and within which an egg develops.

granuloma inguinale   A venereal disease.

gumma   A soft gummy tumor of the skin occurring in tertiary syphilis.

gynecology   The branch of medicine that concerns itself with the diseases of women.

haploid   Having half the diploid number of chromosomes, as in the egg and sperm.

herpes   A venereal disease.

heterosexual   A person who is sexually attracted by the opposite sex.

homologue   An organ similar in origin to another organ.

homosexual   A person who is sexually attracted by the same sex.

hormone   A chemical substance secreted into the body fluids by an endocrine gland which has a specific effect on the activities of other organs.

hymen   A membrane that partially covers the opening of the vagina.

hypothalamus   A part of the brain that controls many bodily functions, including sexual ones.

id   A mental process of the mind composed of basic biological drives.

impotence   The inability of a male to achieve an erection.

infanticide   The killing of an infant.

inguinal canal   A canal in the groin.

interstitial cell stimulating hormone (ICSH)   A gonadotrophic hormone produced in the anterior pituitary gland of the male. It stimulates the production of testosterone in the testes. It is identical to the luteinizing hormone (LH) in the female.

interstitial cells   Cells between the seminiferous tubules of the testes which produce the male sex hormone testosterone.

intrauterine device (IUD)   A small coil, loop, etc., usually made of plastic, which is inserted into the uterus and acts as a contraceptive.

intromission   The insertion of the erect penis into the vagina.

labia majora   The large thick folds of skin on either side of the vulva.

labia minora   The thin folds of skin between the labia majora.

lactation   The secretion of milk.

lactogenic hormone   Same as luteotrophic hormone (LTH).

lesbian   A female homosexual.

lesion   Any pathological tissue or loss of function of a part.

libido   The sex drive as part of the id.

ligament   Any tough, fibrous band which connects bones or supports viscera.

Lippes loop   An intrauterine contraceptive device.

louse   A parasitic insect.

luteinizing hormone (LH)   A gonadotrophic hormone produced in the anterior pituitary gland of the female. It probably causes the rupture of the ovarian follicle and the release of the egg. It is identical to the interstitial cell stimulating hormone (ICSH) of the male.

luteotrophic hormone (LTH)   A gonadotrophic hormone produced in the anterior pituitary gland of both male and female. Its function is not all clear.

lymph gland   An organ in the lymph system that secretes various substances.

lymphatic duct   A tube of the lymphatic system.

lymphogranuloma venereum   A venereal disease.

mammae   The mammary glands.

mammal   An animal that suckles its young.

mammary gland   A gland that secretes milk.

masochism   The obtaining of sexual pleasure by being physically hurt or cruelly dominated.

masturbation   Sexual self-stimulation, usually by the hand, commonly to the point of orgasm.

maturation   The process by which a cell, an organ, or a whole individual becomes mature.

meiotic   The process in the development of eggs and sperm cells by which the chromosome number is reduced from diploid to haploid.

membrane   A thin layer that encloses a cell or a layer that covers a surface.

menarche   The first menstrual period in a girl's life.

menopause   The period in a woman's life when menstruation normally ceases, usually about age 45 to 50.

menses   The monthly flow of blood and tissue from the genital tract of women.

menstruation   The recurring menses.

mesentery   Folds of tissue that attach various abdominal organs to the body wall.

metabolism   The sum of all the physical and chemical processes taking place in the body.

micron   One millionth part of a meter, used as a unit of measurement in microscopy.

mitotic   The process of cell division in which the diploid number of chromosomes is maintained.

ml   Abbreviation for milliliter, one thousandth of a liter.

mons veneris   The rounded and hairy pad of fatty tissue above the vulva of the female.

morphological   Referring to form or structure.

motile   Having a spontaneous movement.

mucus   A viscid watery secretion that covers mucous membranes.

myometrium   The muscular substance of the uterus.

navel   The umbilicus.

nerve   A cordlike structure which conveys impulses from one part of the body to another.

neurohumoral   Pertaining to the nerve impulse and the response of the tissue to it.

neurosyphilis   A form of the venereal disease syphilis, in which the nervous system is damaged.

nipple   The conic organ on the breast that provides outlet for the milk.

nucleus   A spheroid body within a cell that plays a vital part in cell function.

nutrient   A substance that nourishes.

obstetrician   A physician that specializes in childbirth.

oedipal complex   Erotic attachment to the parent of the opposite sex.

oocyte   The original cell of the egg, before the formation of the polar bodies.

opaque   Will not transmit light rays.

optimal   The best or most favorable.

oral contraceptive   A substance taken by mouth which prevents conception.

orgasm   The climax of sexual excitement during which sexual tensions are released.

orgasmic phase   The stage in the sexual response cycle during which orgasm occurs.

orgasmic platform   The muscular tensions in the outer third of the vagina from which orgasm starts.

ovary   The female sexual gland in which eggs are formed.

ovulation   The process by which an egg is discharged from the Graafian follicle and ovary.

ovum   An egg; the female reproductive cell which, after fertilization, develops into a new human.

oxytocin   A hormone secreted by the posterior pituitary gland, and which is important during parturition.

parturition   The process of giving birth to a child.

patrilineal   Descended through the male line.

pedophilia   The condition of having a sexual interest in children.

pelvis   The basin-shaped ring of bone at the base of the trunk.

penicillin   A substance extracted from the mold Penicillium which has anti-bacterial properties; the first and still the most widely used antibiotic.

penis   The copulatory organ of the male.

perineal muscles   The muscles of the perineum, i.e., those at the lower end of the trunk between the thighs.

perineum   The area at the lower end of the trunk between the thighs.

peristalsis   The muscular movements by which various canals in the body propel their contents.

peritoneum   The membrane lining the abdominal walls and surrounding the viscera.

permeable   Capable of being penetrated (usually refers to a surface or tissue).

pH   The symbol used as the measure of alkalinity and acidity.

pharynx   The muscular sac between the mouth, nares, and esophagus.

physiology   The science of how an organism and its parts work.

pituitary gland   An endocrine gland situated at the base of the brain.

placenta   The organ within the uterus which establishes communication between mother and the developing embryo.

plateau phase   The second stage of the sexual response cycle, where sexual tensions reach a peak.

polar body   A small impotent cell formed from the egg after fertilization.

pornography   Writings or visual materials considered obscene, usually of a sexual nature.

posterior   Situated behind, or toward the rear.

posterior fornix   A recess behind the cervix and within the vagina.

pregnant   Having a child developing within the womb.

prepuce   The fold of skin covering the glans penis.

primordial follicle   A young undeveloped Graafian follicle.

procreation   The entire process by which a new individual is brought into the world.

progesterone   A hormone produced by the corpus luteum.

prolactin   A gonadotrophic hormone produced in the anterior pituitary, same as LTH.

promiscuous   Having sexual relations on a casual basis with a number of partners.

prophylactic   Something that tends to ward off a disease; a condom.

prostaglandins   Substances obtained from the prostate gland and seminal vesicles.

prostate gland   A gland in the male which surrounds the neck of the bladder and the urethra.

proteins   Complex organic compounds made up of chains of amino acids.

protozoans   A group of single-celled animals.

psychic   Pertaining to the mind, mental.

puberty   The age at which the reproductive organs become functional.

pubic symphysis   The line of junction of the pubic bones.

pus   A liquid product of inflammation made up of cells (leukocytes) and a thin fluid.

pustule   A small elevation filled with pus.

rape   Coitus without the consent of the woman or against her will.

rectal sphincter   A circular muscle at the anus, which is usually tightly closed.

refractory period   A period during which sexual arousal is not possible.

regenerate   To renew or repair.

resolution phase   The final stage of the sexual response cycle, when sexual tensions subside and the body returns to normal.

sadism   The obtaining of sexual pleasure by physically hurting someone, usually the sexual partner.

scrotum   The pouch that contains the testes.

sebaceous   Referring to a substance called sebum, which is secreted in the skin.

secretions   Substances produced by cells separate from the blood.

semen   Thick whitish secretions from the prostate gland and seminal vesicles, containing suspended sperm.

seminal fluid   The liquid part of semen.

seminal vesicle   A paired convoluted sac below the bladder which produces seminal fluid.

seminiferous tubules   Small ducts that make up most of the substance of the testes.

sensory nerve   A nerve that responds to a stimulus.

serologic   Pertaining to the serum of the blood.

sexual intercourse   Coitus, during which the erect penis of the male enters the vagina of the female.

sexual response cycle   The total process of sexual intercourse from beginning to end.

siblings   Offspring of the same parents.

sodomy   Usually refers to copulation between males by the anus, but sometimes also copulation between man and animal.

spastic   A situation in which the muscles become stiff and movement awkward.

sperm   A mature germ cell of the male.

spermatic cord   The structure by which each testis is suspended.

spermatogenesis   The process of the formation of sperm.

spermatogonia   Undifferentiated germ cells of the male.

spermatozoon   A mature germ cell of the male.

spermicide   A jelly, cream, or foam designed to kill sperm, used as a contraceptive in the female.

spirochaete   One of a group of bacteria. It is one of these that is the causative agent of syphilis.

sterilization   Ligation of the vasa deferentia in the male (i.e., vasectomy), or of the Fallopian tubes of the female. Its purpose is to make conception impossible.

steroid   A group of compounds that resemble cholesterol chemically, and includes the sex hormones.

striated   Striped.

subcutaneous   Situated beneath the skin.

superego   A mental process of the mind, mainly conscious, and composed of realities.

superincision   An operation on the male penis in which the skin is slit open on the upper surface.

suppository   An easily fusible mass to be introduced into the vagina or other orifice.

supraorbital process   A small bony projection found above the eye in the skeleton of males.

syphilis   A venereal disease.

tactile   Pertaining to the sense of touch.

tampon   A plug made of cotton, sponge, etc., usually used in the vagina.

testis   The male sexual gland in which sperm are formed.

testosterone   The principal sex hormone of the male which is produced in the testes.

thyroid stimulating hormone (TSH)   A hormone secreted by the anterior pituitary gland which has a stimulating effect on the thyroid gland.

tissue   A group of cells with a similar function.

transvestism   Behavior in which the individual derives sexual pleasure by dressing in the clothing of the opposite sex.

trophoblast   A layer of cells in the developing zygote.

tumescent   Swollen or tumid.

umbilical cord   The structure connecting the umbilicus with the placenta.

ureter   The tube that conveys the urine from the kidney to the bladder.

urethra   The canal which conveys urine from the bladder to the exterior. In the male it also conveys semen in ejaculation.

uterine tube   The Fallopian tube.

uterus   The hollow muscular organ in which an embryo is nourished and develops.

urine   The fluid secreted by the kidneys and stored in the bladder.

urogenital   Pertaining to the urinary and genital apparatus.

vagina   The canal in the female which extends from the cervix to the opening at the vulva.

vaginismus   Painful spasm of the vagina.

vas deferens   A paired duct which conveys sperm from each testis to the ejaculatory duct.

vasectomy   Ligation of the vasa deferentia in the male, designed to have a contraceptive effect.

vascular   Pertaining to blood vessels.

vasocongestion   The excessive filling of blood vessels with blood.

vein   A blood vessel that carries blood toward the heart.

venereal disease   A disease transmitted primarily by sexual intercourse.

vestibule   A space or cavity at an entrance; the space between the labia minora.

villi   Small vascular processes.

viscous   Sticky or gummy.

vitamin   A group of substances which are needed in small amounts for the normal metabolic functioning of the body.

voyeurism   Obtaining sexual satisfaction by observing others having sexual relations.

vulva   The external part of the sexual organs of the female.

vulval cleft   The line of junction of the labia majora.

wet dream   A dream experienced by the male during which ejaculation takes place.

zygote   A fertilized egg.

Index